# UNHINGED

# UNHINGED

## *A Memoir of Enduring, Surviving, and Overcoming Family Mental Illness*

**Anna Berry**

ROWMAN & LITTLEFIELD
Lanham • Boulder • New York • London

Published by Rowman & Littlefield
A wholly owned subsidiary of The Rowman & Littlefield Publishing Group,
Inc.
4501 Forbes Boulevard, Suite 200, Lanham, Maryland 20706
www.rowman.com

16 Carlisle Street, London W1D 3BT, United Kingdom

British Library Cataloguing in Publication Information Available

**Library of Congress Cataloging-in-Publication Data**

Berry, Anna, 1974–
Unhinged : a memoir of enduring, surviving, and overcoming family mental illness / Anna Berry.
pages cm
Includes bibliographical references.
ISBN 978-1-4422-3362-1 (cloth : alk. paper) — ISBN 978-1-4422-3363-8 (electronic)
1. Berry, Anna, 1974– 2. Mentally ill—United States—Biography. 3. Mentally ill—Family relationships—United States. I. Title.
RC464.B49 2014
616.890092—dc23
[B]
2014006838

∞™ The paper used in this publication meets the minimum requirements of
American National Standard for Information Sciences Permanence of Paper
for Printed Library Materials, ANSI/NISO Z39.48-1992.

Printed in the United States of America

# CONTENTS

# AUTHOR'S NOTE

Although this is chiefly a work of nonfiction, certain portions of this narrative have been altered from the actual events. Names and identifying characteristics of everyone depicted in this book as well as certain institutions and locations (including the city and state of my birth) have been changed in order to protect the privacy of the persons involved; certain details of actual incidents have been altered for the same reason.

I have also compressed the timeline of certain events for narrative purposes. Some conversations between me and other depicted persons have been reconstructed to the best of my ability from long-ago memories that may have altered over time. The two psychotherapists who figure prominently in this narrative—Dr. Chatterjee and Dr. X—are composites of several different psychotherapists I had over a period of many years, and the therapy sessions I describe with these characters are composites of the discoveries and insights I made over more than fifteen years worth of psychotherapy.

I hold no personal malice against anyone depicted in this memoir, even those who may feel they may have been portrayed negatively. I believe that in all cases I have been true to my own recollections and opinions of events, and I have also tried to be fair in my depictions of those events. My purpose for writing this book is solely to help educate the public about the crippling effect family mental illness has on society at large, as well as to help reduce the stigma associated with it by showing that while mental illness is a chronic condition, it is also a *treatable* condition—not to mention a condition that affects a majority of American families in some way, shape, or form.

It is my sincere belief that no one should be ashamed of mental illness, whether they have it themselves or whether it affects someone they love. I hope this book helps you, the reader, learn more about the challenges of living with mental illness, while offering hope and healing to the afflicted.

Anna Berry

# PROLOGUE: CHICAGO, APRIL 2002

**I** am sleeping in a flophouse. An *actual* flophouse.

Single.

Room.

Occupancy.

The kind of joint where heroin addicts and transient alcoholic men sleep. The kind of joint twenty-eight-year-old women with master's degrees from the University of Chicago should only encounter on the pages of a fifty-year-old pulp fiction paperback procured from the rare-book store on the corner of Belmont and Sheffield.

I am sleeping in a flophouse. Well, not sleeping, really. Crying, shaking, shuddering with disbelief at how this could possibly have happened to me, yes. Sleeping, no.

An old man is screaming obscenities at the stale air in the room next door. The bedspread smells like a mixture of urine and imported clove cigarettes. The dirty, cracked window has an old-fashioned roller blind stained brown with at least fifty years' worth of tobacco smoke and grime.

The bed sags so far in the middle that the mattress touches the floor, which is carpeted with an ancient horsehair rug that smells like a stable. The lamp has no shade, and the desiccated remains of a horsefly are stuck to the stark yellow bulb.

I am sleeping in a flophouse with a cheesy name—I'll call it "The Sunflower Arms," though the rundown joint isn't sunny, and no self-respecting flower would be caught dead in the place. It's a six-story pile of sooty bricks complete with the stereotypical flickering red-neon sign advertising "FREE COLOR TV" and "TRANSIENTS WELCOME." The Sunflower Arms is the only lasting remnant of the skid row that this posh North Side neighborhood once was, until the real estate developers and Yuppies took it over in the late 80s and early 90s. It's the only place where a poor girl down on her luck like me can flop for the night with no luggage, no change of underwear, no contact solution or deodorant—not to mention no dignity—all for the bargain price of $29.99, plus tax. Except I don't have the money for the tax. I have only thirty dollars and a nickel, and that's not enough to cover the room and the $4.97 in Chicago and Cook County hotel taxes.

I also have no credit card, only a debit card linked to a checking account that is at least a hundred dollars overdrawn. But that's okay with The Sunflower Arms. The emaciated, bearded man who gives me the room doesn't even ask for my ID, let alone a credit card. When I tell him I don't have the extra five bucks to cover room taxes, he shrugs, hands me my key, and says, "Just pay it next time, hon."

As if there will *be* a next time.

The emaciated clerk watches me climb the moldy stairs (the rusty cage elevator is Out of Order) and shakes his head. I hear him say to some unseen person in the back office that I am the first single white woman he's seen check into The Sunflower Arms in more than a year.

I guess I can understand why. The Sunflower Arms isn't exactly the kind of place that makes a single, white, graduate-educated female in her late twenties feel safe. I'm only up one flight of stairs by the time I see my first dead rat. The whole place smells of death, actually. Old cigarettes, dust, moldy 1940s-era upholstery, and death. I'm sure that most of the women who've stayed here over the years were prostitutes. I can almost feel their collective shame oozing from the peeling plaster walls.

My room is on the fourth floor, at the end of a dimly lit hallway. My key sticks in the lock; I have to jiggle it several times before I can open the door. That's heartening, at least—maybe that means it will be hard for anyone to break into the room during the night. Still, it isn't as if I have anything valuable left to steal. And I doubt any of the drugged-out, strung-out old men staying in this hotel would have the stamina to try raping me, anyway.

The room is awful, of course. But I suppose it could be worse. There isn't the corpse of a dead junkie in the closet, or a pile of shit in the bathroom sink, and the toilet and shower work fine. Most of the room is filthy and reeking, but the bedsheets are clean, cool, and pressed. And there aren't any dead rats or bedbugs behind the headboard. (I check.)

When you get to the end of your rope, like I have, you learn to appreciate the small things.

As I settle into the sagging, creaking bed, my mind settles on one thing. Why am I stuck sleeping in a flophouse, flat broke and with no toothbrush or change of underwear when my place of residence—a cozy bedroom in a decent-but-not-fancy Lakeview apartment with a marble bath and remodeled kitchen (the very same bedroom I share with my boyfriend, Dean)—is less than two blocks away? How can a sagging flophouse bed and one city block be the only things separating me from that decent-but-not-fancy Lakeview apartment and life on the street?

The answer to that one is easy.

I'm wacko.

Wacko. Looney-Tunes. Insane. Psycho. Disturbed. Distraught. Unstable.

A *nutjob.*

Or, as my boyfriend's best friend has so aptly put it, "The misbegotten spawn of Satan, a female succubus witch-bitch."

And a *crazy* Satanic female succubus witch-bitch at that.

It doesn't matter that I have a good education. It doesn't matter that I used to have a good job. It doesn't matter that my home (or it *had* been my home until an hour or so ago) is only a block or two away. It doesn't matter that I am young and single and attractive and alone.

None of it matters.

Because when you're *a nutjob*, sleeping in a flophouse with five cents to your name is all you might ever expect.

# I

# HEARING VOICES

I've had a lot of psychotherapists. More than I can remember, actually. When you spend as many years in psychotherapy as I have, the therapists—male, female, psychologist, guidance counselor, licensed social worker, psychiatrist, ordained minister, whatever—all start running together like a melting watercolor painting, until I can no longer visualize their individual faces in the overstuffed archives of my memory. The region of my brain dedicated to self-improvement and self-analysis is stuffed to the brim. I'd need another ten years of therapy just to recatalog the scores upon scores of therapy-session transcripts, the passive-aggressive defense mechanisms, and the battles with insurance plans and employers over co-payments and time off that are stored between the thousands of neural synapses in my frontal lobe.

The true nature of my various psychoses rests buried somewhere beneath a tangled demilitarized zone that built up slowly from the subtle manipulations and emotional games of chess between me and many different therapists. I was often an uncooperative patient too, which didn't help matters.

There's an old joke that circulates around and around—I heard it first when I was in college over twenty years ago, and I still hear someone tell it at least once or twice a year.

Q: "How many psychotherapists does it take to change a lightbulb?"

A: "Just one, but the lightbulb has to *want* to change."

Truer words were never told—and that's precisely why this tired old joke always gets a laugh from me, no matter how many times I hear it. I spent many years in psychotherapy running around and around on the same hamster's wheel, sprinting and sweating yet never getting anywhere, simply because I didn't want to recognize my own role in my ongoing mental misery. But there comes a point in almost every mentally ill person's life when she concludes she doesn't want to live like that anymore, and finally she decides to put her nose to the grindstone and get to work. Whether that means finally taking meds as prescribed, or keeping weekly therapy appointments, or dumping all the liquor down the drain, or switching therapists—or just doing the hard introspection required to recognize and change destructive behavior patterns—it's all hard work.

And truly hard work is seldom fun. Hence, we avoid it.

And sometimes, the most difficult task of all is just finding out what is really wrong with you in the first place. For example, even after seeing at least (that I can remember) twenty different counselors, shrinks, social workers, psychiatric residents, and therapists over a period of fifteen years, I never once got the same clinical diagnosis.

Not once. Ever. Had I received overlapping diagnoses, I may have been more accepting of one, but it's difficult to see where I fit in when so many professionals have had so many different diagnoses. And I can't say that I agreed with any of the suggested disorders in my case anyway. Not only that, but some of the diagnoses I got at various times are either no longer categorized as illnesses by the *Diagnostic and Statistical Manual of Mental Disorders, Fifth Edition* (DSM-V) at all, or else they've gotten merged with other, "new" disorders. Trying to keep up with all the recent changes in diagnostic criteria isn't just hard for psychotherapists and medical billers—it can wreak havoc on patients too.

It's a common problem: few if any people fit perfectly into the rigid boxes constructed by the DSM-V, the manual the American Psychiatric Association uses to categorize mental illness, which the health insurance industry in turn follows when it comes to paying for therapy—or far more often, psychiatric drugs. If my own experience is any example, this is one case where the one-size-fits-all approach of so-called cookbook medicine just doesn't work. And if you can't even get diagnosed with the right illness, it can be downright hard to receive the right treatment—let alone get better. Let me show you what I mean.

I've been diagnosed as having any and all of the following at one time or another.

*Clinical depression* (also known as *major depressive disorder*). I'd definitely say I've been depressed. So have millions upon millions of other people. But I don't fit the criteria for clinical depression as outlined in the DSM-V, which requires I have at least five of their nine possible listed symptoms every single day. I had maybe two or three symptoms at best, and not every day. True, I often had feelings of sadness, even to the point of being suicidal at times—but I was missing several other criteria as required by the DSM-V. Despite what the diagnostic criteria say about depression, I never lost interest in my favorite activities, nor did I have difficulty concentrating at work or at school—quite the opposite, in fact. My weight didn't fluctuate up and down, nor did I have significant problems with my sleep patterns. I did have the inappropriate fascination with death and the dark moods that went on for weeks at a time that the diagnostic criteria require, but the rest of the picture was missing. Which might be why I wasn't given prescription medication for my depression, but then again, who knows? Whatever the reason, I got crammed in a box that wasn't the right size for me. If anything, I believe my depression was actually a symptom of other disorders, which I'll elaborate on later.

*Manic depression.* Well, sure. Many creative artists like me have this to some extent, as our creative juices ebb and flow in cycles that can seem like a roller coaster at times. We might be super-productive for a day or two, then tired and blocked the next. I've sometimes gone for weeks having to force myself to write despite a profound lack of inspiration, which can be downright painful. But I still couldn't agree with this diagnosis because I did not experience bouts of clinical mania. No going around for days without sleep, no frantic attempts to start a bazillion projects that I never finished (indeed, I'm known for my discipline, attention to detail, and ability to meet deadlines even when I'm feeling at my worst). I did have the occasional shopping spree, and I was what some would call promiscuous, but I wouldn't call either one of these tendencies manic. "Manic depression" is also an antiquated definition of what is now known as *bipolar disorder*—which itself now has two types according to the DSM-V: *bipolar I* and *bipolar II*. (And I haven't been diagnosed with either one of those.)

*Severe bipolar disorder* (non-artistic personality). Never bought this one. At the time I received this diagnosis, the DSM-IIIr was in vogue, and it used different diagnostic criteria than those in use for bipolar disorder today. This diagnosis also suggests that I would not be able to function well on a daily basis. But I could, just perhaps not always well. This disorder is now known as *bipolar I disorder*. A different variation is *bipolar II*, which wasn't even identified as a distinct illness until 1994 and still remains a difficult diagnosis for most psychotherapists to make.[1] (If I had to choose between the two, I'd say I fit the criteria for bipolar II a lot better, but even then it doesn't seem to work because I don't really suffer from mania, and never have.)

*Borderline personality disorder* (BPD). I should point out that there is currently considerable dispute in the psychotherapy community whether this is a legitimate diagnosis at all—even to the point that some insurance companies refuse to reimburse for BPD treatment, and some psychotherapists will even refuse to treat BPD patients.[2] It's even referred to rather flippantly by some in the psychotherapy community as the "garbage bin diagnosis," according to *Psychology Today*.[3] But it's the label that has been applied to me the most often by far, so I'd say there's more than a grain of truth to it. But given the fact that none of my many therapists could ever agree on what was wrong with me, it seems fitting (and appropriately hilarious), then, that I'm chronically ill with BPD, a disease that many clinicians apparently don't consider a disease at all.

The current disease criteria for BPD in the DSM-V state that BPD patients have a history of unstable personal relationships and poor self-image, impulsive behavior (like overspending and sexual promiscuity), chronic feelings of emptiness, and difficulty controlling anger. But, frankly, most young people have all of these problems at one point or another—it's called *being young*. Indeed, the American College of Pediatricians says that young people's brain and emotional development, especially in the frontal lobe that regulates emotional impulses, are not fully complete until their mid-twenties—and therefore adolescents are especially prone to impulsive behavior and unstable relationships.[4] If the disease criteria for BPD in the current DSM-V are to be believed, it seems to me most young, single women in America have BPD to some extent, which would make having at least some of the criteria for BPD perfectly normal for women in their late teens and early twenties. Indeed, there is quite a range of behavior and severity chalked up to the disorder, covering the extremes of suicidal behavior on one end, mere serial monogamy on the other, and just about everything in between. Susanna Kaysen of *Girl, Interrupted* fame was locked up for almost two years for being "borderline" in the 1960s, while most contemporary psychologists say her condition at age eighteen would barely merit more than a few cognitive therapy sessions—or at worst, a very brief hospital stay followed by psychotherapy. Drugs tend to be ineffective against BPD, experts say, though they are still frequently prescribed.[5]

It is in fact extremely common for persons eventually diagnosed with BPD to have had numerous other disease labels applied to them first, not only because many clinicians are not trained in recognizing BPD symptoms, but also because BPD tends to coexist with other mental illnesses, such as depression and anxiety disorders.[6] Indeed, it is common for *all* mentally ill persons, regardless of their specific illness, to receive as many as a dozen different diagnoses from scores of different practitioners over the course of their lifetime. I think this helps explain why I've frequently been diagnosed with various types of depression—but whether that depression was actually a symptom of BPD or a coexisting condition is up for debate.

Psychologists who support the diagnosis of BPD state that the ability to "act" as if you are perfectly sane and stable to those around you while feeling suicidal and volatile inside is trademark "borderline" behavior. And my trademark "perfect storm" of near emotional collapse buried underneath a serene, happy exterior is indeed one of the classic symptoms of BPD.

The ability to act as if everything is all right when in fact nothing is leads many BPD sufferers to pursue careers in the arts, especially the performing arts. Indeed, "unusual artistic talent" has been identified as having a strong correlation with BPD.[7] The day-to-day torture of having to create inner and outer selves simultaneously, and maintain both convincingly, is perfect real-world training for a professional actor. It's just as effective for someone who wants to be a writer too. When your mind is split into two complete selves—one peaceful, self-lobotomized, and seemingly perfect; the other a raging, screaming, frightened, depressive monster—your entire existence revolves around fabricating scenarios for both of those characters (neither of which represents your true self) in which to dwell. Living with BPD is like living inside your very own custom-made, three-dimensional soap opera, with your split self playing all the roles and doing all the histrionic backstabbing on a TV series that runs only in your own mind.

What else have I been diagnosed with at some point or other? Let's see.

*Multiple personality disorder*. Again, I couldn't buy this one because I never had other personalities, so I'm not sure why this one was even offered.

*Episodic depression*. This means you only have depression at certain times, cycling with either normal behavior or mania. Your depression becomes a series of episodes, popping up at regular intervals like a running gag on a TV show. I suppose you could make the argument that I did have this because I had episodes of depression starting in my early teens through my late twenties; but that seems to me more "chronic" than "episodic."

*Seasonal affective disorder*. I suppose this diagnosis is common for people who live in the Upper Midwest like I do, given how dark, long, and cold our winters are. But I'm not sure it applies to me since some of my worst depressive and psychotic episodes occurred in sunny, warm weather. My moods never depended on the weather, per se—I just happened to get this applied to me when I saw a psychotherapist during a January cold snap.

*Cyclothymic disorder and/or dysthymic disorder*. These are both mood disorders related to depression. Cyclothymic disorder involves cycling between mild to moderate depression and mania and is considered a less severe version of bipolar disorder, while dysthymic disorder means you've had a constantly depressed mood for two years or more, feeling hopeless and unable to concentrate, without necessarily being suicidal. As with their more severe counterparts, I was missing several of the required criteria for these diseases, and since I considered suicide more than once, I don't think either was the right fit for me.

*Antisocial personality disorder*. I take particular offense to this one. I don't appreciate being placed in the same basket with murderers and rapists. Antisocial personalities possess a profound lack of empathy and act without conscience or regard to the well-being of others. That can mean anything from being a career criminal to the guy who steals his coworkers' lunches from the office refrigerator and then lies about it. Since I've frequently been plagued by guilt or fear of what and how others will think of me or do to me if I make this or that choice, it seems a profound lack of empathy isn't one of my problems. I'm also the first to cry at sad movies, I often beat myself up for not giving enough to charity, and I frequently do way too much volunteer work at the expense of my personal and professional obligations. In that regard, I'm really more of a codependent with a guilt complex.

*Histrionic personality disorder.* The DSM-V also calls this disorder the "theatrical" or "dramatic" personality disorder. Since I'm a trained actor and playwright, I suppose I can see why I got this diagnosis, given that my livelihood depends in part on a flair for the dramatic. But I don't think it fits me because when I'm not participating in theater (which isn't much these days, now that I'm raising two young children), I actually cannot stand being at the center of attention all the time, as the disease criteria require. Unlike when I'm on the stage, in reality I'm more of an introvert. I prefer a quiet evening at home catching up on reading or cleaning the bathroom to making a spectacle of myself at the discotheque or in the returns-and-exchanges line at the mall.

*Schizotypal personality disorder.* The DSM-V states that this disorder is one that elicits behavior of "extreme solitude." Sufferers tend to show deep anxiety in social situations, have odd or strange social behaviors, and be extremely uncomfortable maintaining close relationships with others. None of those criteria apply to me. While I am a bit of an introvert, I have a wide circle of friends and enjoy going to parties and gatherings, and I'm frequently complimented on my politeness and knowledge of social etiquette—hardly a symptom of being socially awkward. The only reason I can think of why I might have received this diagnosis is because at the time I was choosing to hang out with people who didn't share my values and often belittled me, but that had more to do with my own low self-esteem than social anxiety.

*Brief psychotic episode.* This isn't an illness so much as it's an acute symptom of a larger problem, which can have any number of causes ranging from several different psychiatric diagnoses to drug or alcohol intoxication and even dehydration.[8] But in the interest of being truthful, I'll admit to having more than a few of these. You'll read more about a couple of them in this book.

*Post-traumatic stress disorder* (PTSD). This one I wholeheartedly agree with, and you'll learn more about some of the childhood (and adult) trauma I endured that is likely behind it in this book. Some of the symptoms of PTSD can mimic other psychiatric disorders, and that might explain why I've gotten so many different diagnoses over the years.

Exhausted yet? Then just imagine what it must be like to be a patient swimming through this constantly changing alphabet soup of illnesses! Imagine a diabetic being told by his doctors that he isn't diabetic, but he actually has lung cancer, and he gets treated for that instead of diabetes. Then a couple of weeks into chemotherapy, he finds out he never had lung cancer in the first place, but in fact he actually had Crohn's disease, so his treatment protocol has to change. And his diabetes still hasn't been diagnosed at all, let alone treated. It seems absurd, but it's not all that different from what a lot of people with mental illness go through. Small wonder most people with mental illness don't seek help at all.[9]

The one thing I can conclude from all of this is that the DSM-V is a good starting point for identifying and treating mental disorders, but if my experiences are any example, it's far from perfect. Clinicians should always remember that people don't always fit into these neat little boxes. And being different or outside the established "norm" for one illness or another doesn't mean we're beyond help. Quite the opposite, in fact. We should also recognize that mental illness is a chronic disease that can change and evolve over the course of our lives. The diagnosis we got twenty or thirty years ago might no longer apply, but that doesn't necessarily mean we're "better," either.

"Chronic" means treatable, but *not* curable. If you're unfortunate enough to be born with *nutjob* DNA, or to grow up in a *nutjob* family environment that skews and scars you for life, *you will never be cured*. Not totally, anyway. The best you can hope for is merely to *manage* your chronic illness—that is, keep it from killing you—just as a diabetic must manage his sugar levels with painful insulin shots to keep from dying, just as a cancer patient must endure excruciating radiation and chemotherapy to get her life-threatening tumors to go—temporarily—into remission. So it is, too, with mental illness. There are no miracle cures, no final triumphs over this most sinister and misunderstood of afflictions. There is merely an ever-present series of small battles and skirmishes, fought one day at a time, in an endless war against the terrorist acts committed by an unstable mind.

Sounds depressing, doesn't it? And it is. But it doesn't have to be.

Mental illness—this most difficult and costly of all chronic diseases—*is* manageable. It's survivable. Better yet, it's even a disease under which you can thrive, improve, better yourself, and reach a higher human potential than you ever thought possible.

And despite what the American pharmaceutical industry wants you to believe, in many cases, you can accomplish all of these things without ever popping a single pill.

How do I know this?

I'm very proud to say that in more than fifteen years of psychotherapy, I've never once taken any psychiatric medication.

Not *once*. Now before you dismiss me as a crackpot for saying that and throw this book across the room, please know I realize that for some people this may not be an option and that psychiatric medication may be good and even necessary in some instances. But for me, I've managed to avoid going down that path.

That's not to say that I didn't *want* to be medicated. Often, I did. I even specifically asked psychiatrists for antidepressants on more than one occasion. But every time, I was denied the prescription—either because my health insurance wouldn't pay for it (90 percent of the time) or because whatever therapist I had at the time thought I'd respond better to cognitive therapy (10 percent of the time; and those were the therapists who had my best interests at heart. Thank you).

I'm also very proud to say I don't "hear voices." Not the demonic ones that tell me to hurt myself or others, anyway. The ones I hear are inspirational, like the character voices I hear when I'm writing a play, or the plot bunnies that pop into my head when I'm taking a shower and that I have to go instantly write down so they can become part of my latest novel. There can be good voices and bad voices inside our heads. The good ones can be truly beautiful, and it can be just as damaging to suppress those as it can be to listen to the demons who tell us to destroy ourselves.

And any playwright can tell you that "hearing voices" is absolutely necessary when writing a play. Playwrights "hear voices" in their heads in the same way that composers of symphonies hear entire string quartets or woodwind sections in their heads, in the same way that architects see unfinished buildings floating before their eyes or sculptors see a beautiful woman's body in an uncut block of marble. Whenever I sit down to write a play or a story, I stop to listen to the voices in my head and then strive to give them a home of their own.

I suppose in my own peculiar way, I've managed to channel one of the main afflictions of my family DNA into a creative art form. I also suppose that if I couldn't write plays, I would be heavily medicated, unemployed, and on permanent mental health disability—just like my older brother Mark[10] is now. Just like my mother is too—even after more than thirty years under the care of psychologists and psychiatrists.

The "crazy artist" stereotype is ubiquitous for a reason. Many of us artistic types walk a very thin line between sanity and madness, a very thin line painted at varying thicknesses according to our ability to express ourselves. If ever that ability gets trampled upon, if it ever melts or is simply erased, then the mad-bad voices start creeping in to start telling us that we must destroy ourselves in order to survive. It's a strange dichotomy, but I know from experience that self-destruction—whether through alcoholism, drug use, abusive relationships, casual sex, or whatever—is what keeps someone whom the mad-bad voices have imprisoned alive. For a time, anyway. Some, like Brian Wilson,[11] Carrie Fisher,[12] and Dick Cavett,[13] manage not only to stay alive but to triumph over the mad-bad voices and even to harness them as tools that make their art that much more successful and beautiful. But others—Vincent Van Gogh, Spalding Grey, Marilyn Monroe, and scores more—take the bargain but lose the battle, finally succumbing to the demons that help murder artists by their own hands. The mad-bad voices suck all the doomed artist's lifeblood dry in order to feed the great Beast that dwells above all of us, the Manic Muse that we both love and hate, that we both rely upon and fear.

My mother, my brother, and several of my ancestors have all "heard voices" at one time or another. My mother and brother still hear voices whenever they forget to take their antipsychotic medication—and sometimes they still hear them through the drug-induced haze they live in while medicated.

Years ago, my mother heard the voices of tired old women telling her that "company was coming to visit soon"—special, fancy company that required an immaculate house and exceedingly well-dressed children. I remember days when I would come home from school to our house in Indiana and find my mother in a frenzy—dusting furniture that had no dust, straightening pictures and throw pillows that weren't crooked, mopping floors already so clean they could be used as polished platters for baked Alaska. As soon as my brother and I set foot in the house, Mom would order us to change out of our school clothes and into the "best of our best"—me, a crisp, white-lace, ankle-length dress I wore for my first communion at St. Mary of the Lake Catholic Church; my brother, a three-piece suit of light blue polyester and a clip-on maroon tie he'd gotten as a present from our grandmother, Memaw Jones. Then Mom would make us take up prim positions on the striped-blue velvet couch in our living room to wait for the mysterious, name-less "company" that never arrived.

The only person ever to show up at our front door on those long, itchy afternoons when I sat motionless, trying hard not to scratch at the First Communion lace around my neck, was my father when he got home from work demanding his dinner and wanting to know why the hell everybody was dressed like it was the goddamn Academy Awards.

Each time this happened, I asked Mom where she'd heard that company was coming. Did someone call? Did she get a letter? Did the Jehovah's Witnesses that came by our house once a week maybe want to stay for coffee and cake? What? She avoided the question the first couple of times. Then the third or fourth time, she said simply, "I thought, maybe. I thought *maybe*." Every time thereafter, whenever the voices told her something was going to happen that didn't, her standard response to those of us outraged at the inconvenience of First Communion lace and rearranged furniture was "I thought *maybe*."

It wasn't until years later, when I was in college and Mom was in one of her rare periods of unmedicated lucidity, that she told me the truth about the dry old women she heard in her head, the ones who insisted she clean and dress us for the phantom company that she thought for sure would come, the company that *had* to come so she wouldn't die.

My maternal great-grandfather Papaw Scott—whom my mother says my older brother Mark resembles in many ways—heard the voices too. I only met Great-Papaw Scott once before he died when I was barely a toddler, but the stories of the voices in his head are legendary in my family. Great-Papaw Scott grew up desperately poor in the mountains of western Virginia and got a job working on the railroad when he was in his teens. He married young and had children before he was twenty. He "retired" young too—in his late forties, by bribing a doctor to write a letter to the railroad company saying he had a heart condition that

rendered him unable to work. (He was in perfect health. Physically, at
least.) He then moved from rural Virginia to Evansville, Indiana, to be
closer to his children (including his daughter, my Memaw Jones,[14]
whom he constantly begged for money) and spent the rest of his life
tinkering in his tiny bungalow, building beautiful folk-art model houses
out of scrap wood and trash and listening to the voices in his head.

Great-Papaw Scott's voices started out in the mid-1950s as the FBI.
By the 1960s, they had become the CIA (and occasionally, Interpol).
The FBI, Interpol, and the CIA told Great-Papaw Scott, via all-points
bulletins only he could hear, that he could not work outside the home
because they were spying on him, monitoring his every move, and if
they didn't like what he did or where he went, they would kill him. My
mother believes that the voices told him to quit his job with the railroad
and told him to bribe a doctor to write the fake disability letter for him
too. The voices wanted Great-Papaw Scott under their complete and
utter control. They used him as a tool for their own ends—just as they
use everyone who falls under their spell.

At first, Great-Papaw Scott's voices only affected him. But near the
end of his life, his voices so controlled him that he refused to leave the
house—even to go out into the yard or collect the mail—and forbade
everyone who came to visit him from speaking aloud in his presence.
He would only communicate through notes written in a simple letter-
replacement cipher code because he didn't want the CIA and the FBI
to overhear him and track him down. Relatives and friends avoided him
because they didn't want to write coded notes back and forth to Great-
Papaw Scott just so they could have a conversation.

Great-Papaw Scott never saw a psychiatrist for an official diagnosis,
but he was probably a classic paranoid schizophrenic. And like many
paranoid schizophrenics, he died relatively young, in his early sixties.
My Memaw Jones inherited several of his beautiful folk-art houses and
now keeps them in her basement, where they sit and collect dust. I've
told Memaw several times that the only things I want from her after she
passes away are those beautiful folk-art houses, the only things that
remain from my great-grandfather, who was crazy as a loon but also
quite possibly an artistic genius.

My older brother Mark—my only full-blood sibling—is like a younger version of Great-Papaw Scott. He *heard voices* from an early age.
Mark's first breakdown happened as a teenager, officially starting when

he walked out onto the top of an ancient Indian burial mound across the street from the top-secret nuclear facility where my father worked, pulled his long, dirty gray trenchcoat over his head, and shouted, "The Russians are coming! The Russians are coming!" over and over again until security personnel came to restrain him. The voices in Mark's head apparently ordered him to sound a warning to the soldiers guarding the nuclear reactors across the street that World War III was imminent.

Mark was hospitalized for the first time not long after that. He was never exactly what anyone would consider "normal," even as a child. Diagnosed as a paranoid schizophrenic in his teens, Mark flunked out of several different colleges (including a large Midwestern university, where before dropping out he accused one of his male professors of sexually harassing him) until ultimately deciding to join the U.S. Army. His past mental illness kept him from enlisting until he found a psychiatrist willing to draft a letter saying that his paranoid schizophrenia (for which he'd been heavily medicated since the age of sixteen) didn't exist. Mark stopped taking his meds, went to the recruiting center with his phony bill of good mental health in hand, and was promptly admitted to the Army infantry division.

Mark stayed in the Army for less than eight months. Shortly after completing basic training and being stationed in Korea as a medic, he wrecked the ambulance he drove in the South Korean demilitarized zone and got a medical discharge from the Army that entitled him to a monthly disability payment for life of $800. He went back on antipsychotics as soon as he got home from Korea, and he hasn't held down a real job of any kind for more than two or three weeks since. I've often suspected he wrecked that ambulance deliberately, though I have no proof.

There is a long tradition of suicidal paranoia and hallucinations in my family, lending credence to the theory that mental illness, especially schizophrenia, is in part a genetic condition that runs in families. For example, two of my great-great-grandfathers on my mother's side committed suicide in the late 1800s. Details are sketchy now, but after interviewing several of my older relatives, I discovered that one of my great-great-grandfathers holed himself up in one of rural Virginia's many mountain caves one winter night and killed himself by drinking a Mason jar full of carbolic acid. He left a note saying he committed suicide because he had witnessed a murder in the backwoods and the perpetrators had promised to come and kill him if he told anyone what he'd seen. My mother and grandparents insist that he only killed himself because "that's what people did in the olden days when they saw something bad."

My mother goes as far as to say that our ancestor had no choice but to kill himself before the "murderers" he saw came and killed him themselves. But I believe that the "murder" he saw was merely a hallucination, and the people supposedly coming to kill him were simply the schizophrenic voices in his head, the same voices that demanded he steal the bottle of carbolic acid from a neighbor's barn and drink it.

Another of my great-great-grandfathers killed himself by putting the barrel of a shotgun in his mouth and pulling the trigger. Nobody knows why he did it—just that he did. I'm sure the family voices told him to do it too.

The dark, demonic voices caught between the double-helix strands of my family's DNA run very, very deep. I don't hear those voices anymore, but I used to. They were there for me as an odd, wayward child who talked to herself; they were there for me as a morbid, disturbed, and distraught teenager who shaved the back of her head and drew skeletons and death-metal symbols on her frosted blue jeans with a Sharpie. They were there for me all through my twenties, which I spent wasting away in one destructive relationship after another, polluting my body with alcohol, drugs, and compulsive sex. Even after all the personal insight and behavioral changes I've worked so hard to instill in myself after more than fifteen years of psychotherapy, those voices are *still* there for me, whether I like it or not. They're *always* there. They're just dormant, is all. I managed to beat them back into submission. But they could rise again.

This book is the story of how I finally learned not to listen to the mad-bad voices that have crippled my family for at least seven generations. This book will show you that no matter how bad it seems, no matter how hopeless your illness or a loved one's illness is, *recovery is not impossible*. This book will show you how you can stop listening to the mad-bad voices too.

Buckle up, folks. You're in for the worst—and best—ride of your life.

# 2

# VIENNA, AUSTRIA, OCTOBER 1999

I am sitting in St. Stephen's Cathedral, the stunning Gothic medieval church in the center of Vienna and just a short walk from Dieter's apartment. It's six a.m. The church's grand stone ceiling soars above my head; the patterns made by the dewy Austrian morning light pouring through the stained-glass windows paint themselves onto my face and arms in fields of blue-green lace. The only sound is the soft footfalls of the Eastern European cleaning woman who mops the ancient, pock-marked stone floor. She guides her huge gray mop around the feet and legs of the few early-morning faithful who have come to kneel and pray.

The drab-faced woman, her face sunken inward from a lack of teeth, looks at me with surprise when she finds me just sitting in a pew, wearing my faded Levis and battered Doc Martens instead of the pressed, crisp, and formal European clothing all the other faithful wear. I hold no rosary, make no move to even pretend that I am here to pray or ask forgiveness.

Although I have the same long, lean build and fair blonde features as many Austrians, I'm dressed in my cheap American clothes, sporting my gaudy American hairstyle and making no effort whatsoever to blend in. The cleaning woman mutters something in Polish, probably a complaint about how even this ancient, holy place has been overrun by ugly American tourists. She doesn't seem to notice that the padded kneeler just in front of me is damp, and not from the dewy condensation that has formed on the ancient stone walls as a result of the early-morning Alpine drizzle and fog.

The kneeler is damp with my tears.

I meet Dieter Franzl[1] in the early spring of 1999, in Chicago. He's an Austrian graduate student from Vienna working on a doctorate in business administration. Dieter is tall, blonde, blue-eyed, and dreamily handsome, and he lives in a studio apartment a few el stops away from me. His accent is somewhere between Dr. Freud and Arnold Schwarzenegger, and it turns me on like nothing I've ever heard, before or since.

In the early spring of 1999, I am two years out of graduate school and have gone back to work for my old boss at a large university library, where I once had a part-time graduate assistantship. I work for a pittance as a full-time department manager in the library's acquisitions department.

I am back on campus working a low-wage job with a ninety-minute bus-and-train commute each way from the North Side because my brain and I both have had too much trouble adjusting to the real world. My former high-stress job as a financial editor at a brokerage firm burned me out to the point of a near-nervous breakdown a year ago. I accepted the deep pay cut offered by my old grad-school boss and embraced the comfortable, familiar territory of my former graduate-school campus like an old friend. I had also gone through an extremely bad breakup with a medical student (the latest in a long string of bad breakups dating back to high school) just before I quit that brokerage job, and I took the job on campus, just blocks from my ex-boyfriend's condo, almost as an act of personal revenge. I even stalked that medical student for a little while because doing so helped assuage the low-self-esteem demons that dominated my brain. But my ex-boyfriend was smarter than I was, and a doctor-in-training to boot, which made him a less-than-ideal target for stalking. So in 1999, I gave up on stalking my ex and set out to find my next self-destructive relationship.

When I start searching for that relationship, I am poor, anxious, and more than a little battle-scarred. Still, other than the occasional rainy blue Saturday when I spend the whole day in bed, crying and hyperventilating, I am content with my life in general.

Sort of. But I want—*need*—something more. And that something more has to be in the form of a man, preferably a loving one who will share my bed each night, worship me by day, and become an essential extension of my body, my mind, my very existence. I am sure that if I can find that man in question, I will be totally happy and won't have to spend any more rainy blue Saturdays in bed crying and hyperventilating all day long. In other words, I need a man to fill the gaping black hole in my brain.

That gaping black hole is slashed into my brain while I am still in the womb, a zygote absorbing my mother's hormones while my genes replicate, two by two. The gaping black hole gets bigger and bigger as I grow up, deeper and deeper as I watch my mother and my brother succumb to the illnesses that run inevitably through our veins like toxic waste. It gets deeper and deeper, wider and wider in college and then in graduate school, until I can't function normally without a man—*any* man, real or imagined—filling it up. I fear being alone the way some people fear God. For me, intimate companionship is like a drug. Latching onto another person who can fill up the parts of me that are missing therefore becomes my primary objective in life, and like any addict seeking a fix, I'll take less-than-perfect options given no other alternative. A man who ignores me, insults me, or uses me for sex is better than no man at all, just as a junkie knows that shooting up with a dirty hypodermic needle is better than going into heroin withdrawal in a dark alley, at least in the short term. And no addict seeking a fix is ever thinking about the long term.

Whenever I can't find a man to fill the gaping, black hole in my brain for me, I find myself trapped at the bottom of an even deeper black hole, bound and gagged by hopelessness, fear, and despair, my own personal version of drug withdrawal or the DTs.

For some, finding love is a matter of life and death. And so it is for me.

By the spring of 1999, I've grown tired of the regular dating scene, but I still need a man to fill up the gaping black hole in my brain before I drown. So on a desperate whim, I place a personal ad in the local alternative weekly paper.

TALL, SMART, EDUCATED BLONDE, FIT, CUTE AND 25, seeks intellectual and sophisticated male 22–30 for dating, conversation, and love. Must adore the arts, liberal politics, culture and the all-around Bohemian life. Knowledge of Kant and Hegel a plus. No Republicans, please.

I get only a few responses, none of which seem promising, until the day before the ad is set to expire. For the last time I log into the private e-mail account I got with the ad and find a titillating response.

> Hi this is Dieter franzl I am from Austria. I am working on doctorate degree at norwestrn, also work very good job for a top consulting firm, good money and travel income. I adore american wmen, you sound so lovly, pls do call me and we will talk/have nice fun. (Oh and BTW Hegel rocks.)

Even if the e-mail is plain-text and badly typed, I can almost hear Dieter's lilting Austrian accent in my mind's ear, like electric telepathy. He attaches his picture in a GIF file. I open it, take one look, and nearly faint.

It's good enough for me. I call Dieter that afternoon.

That first telephone conversation, Dieter and I talk for hours, well into the night. We talk as if we've known each other our entire lives. We talk in a way that has my body and mind buzzing with a sexual high that is better than heroin, better than speed or crack. And it isn't just me that's buzzing and high with raw sexuality that speeds its way down and across telephone wires and nerve synapses. Dieter is buzzing with it too.

"I needt to zee you right avay," he says. His thick Austrian accent is so powerful, so penetrating. I picture myself lying underneath him while he speaks to me, his deep Germanic voice like the incessant pounding of rough sex. I can't get enough of it.

We agree to meet for breakfast the next morning. I am working second shift at the library that day, and I don't have to show up for work until two. That gives us the whole morning and early afternoon to talk, bond, maybe even make love.

When Dieter and I sit down for apple pancakes and Danish together, a powerful connection forms immediately. Within seconds, we are clutching hands across the table and cooing and making eyes at one another in a manner so childish and absurd that everyone else in the restaurant turns to stare. Within minutes, we are professing love for one another. Until this moment, I've always believed "love at first sight" is the stuff of silly fairy tales. But there it is, love at first sight with blonde hair, blue eyes, and a sexy Austrian accent, sitting across from me over a plate of syrupy apple pancakes.

"Can you skipt verk today?" Dieter asks, sensuously stroking the back of my hand with his thumb and forefinger.

"No, I can't afford to," I sigh.

"Vhy nodt?"

"I'm kind of poor."

Dieter kisses my hand. "Vell, zen vee vill have to do somethingk aboudt dat."

He walks me to the el station, kisses me passionately, and makes a show of cupping my breast in the middle of the busy street. People walk by and tell us to get a room.

"Don't vorry, vee vill get a room very soon," he tells them, laughing.

He asks me for my phone number at work, and I give it. The whole long el ride down to the South Side, I think about Dieter Franzl, his accent, his penetrating, deep-set blue eyes, his long, lean hands upon my body. I keep on thinking about him at work, distracting myself to the point that I drop an entire shipment of new books on my foot.

Dave, my co-manager on second shift, rushes over. "You okay?"

"Fine," I say, dreamily rubbing my foot. I have my steel-toed Doc Martens on, thankfully—otherwise those heavy hardcovers on British literature and German philosophy would have smashed all the bones in my instep. But I couldn't care less. My whole body is floating on a pink cloud thirty feet above the earth. Someone could douse me with gasoline and set me on fire, and I wouldn't even care.

Dave looks at me funny, then shakes his head. "You on something, Anna?"

I don't answer him. I bend over and open another box of books. Dave shakes his head again and walks off.

An hour or so later, the Acquisitions Department phone rings. Dave answers it, frowns, and motions me to come over.

"Hey, Berry, get over here. There's some German-sounding guy on the phone for you. Won't say from where."

I set down my box-cutter and dust off my hands. "I'll take it in the copy-cataloging room."

"It's not the new sales guy from Stern-Verlag, is it? The department head said not to take any more calls from him."

"No, Dave, it's a personal call. Excuse me." I duck into the glass-enclosed room where we download Library of Congress data onto the mainframe and shut the door. Dave hangs by and watches. He's always had a bit of a crush on me, though I find his weak chin and the tufts of thick, dark back hair that stick out of his T-shirt collar repulsive.

"Hello, this is Anna." My voice is throaty with desire. It's all I can do to keep from fainting.

"Anna, my darlingk, I needt to zee you." Dieter doesn't identify himself, but he doesn't have to. "Vhen are you home from verk?"

"Not 'til after eleven."

"Mudst you go to verk tomorrow?"

I bite my lip. It's a Thursday. The next day is Friday, when I work first shift because there are no student workers to supervise in the evening. I have no vacation days coming for a while, but I am a model employee at the library who rarely calls in sick. I suppose I can play hooky for one day, with Dieter. It will be worth it.

"I guess I can call in sick."

"*Gut*," Dieter says. "For I have judst boughdt us two tickedtz to New York."

Dieter meets me at the train station that night at eleven-thirty. When I step outside the station, Dieter sweeps me into his arms and kisses me so passionately my knees buckle underneath me. "I missdt you zo much," he breathes into my left ear. His accent comes through even in whispers. It drives me over the edge.

We walk back to my apartment together. A light mist of early spring rain falls; an ambulance speeds past, its lights casting red shadows like blood on the rain-slick pavement.

"I was supposdt to meet width my ditzzertation adtvizor today," he says as we walk along, hand in sweaty hand. "Budt I cudt not. You vere too muchdt on my mindt. All I cudt do vas to think up vayz for usdt to be alone together. I searchdt and I foundt us a way to be alone together andt yet in the midst of so much. I vandt to take you somewhere and show you the thingkz that express my love for you. Andt zo, vee are going to New York."

We stop at a corner. Dieter picks me up in his arms and spins me around and around. "Vee are goingk to New York tomorrow! Can you believe dat?"

"No!" I shout, giggling and dizzy. "I can't believe it at all. This is crazy."

"*Ja*, it is crazy," Dieter says. "Because I am crazy in love width *you*."

We go back to my apartment, make love well into the night, until we are both sweaty and spent. After so many rounds of pounding, biting, and orgasms, after our bodies collapse into each another, I cross over to another plane and sleep the sleep of the dead.

It's a strange foreshadowing. I don't know it yet, but when my affair with Dieter ends months later, I very nearly take it one step further—almost choosing full, real, waking death instead of just sleeping it.

Dieter wakes me the next morning at seven.

"Anna, we mudst go. Our plane leaves at eleven-thirty. I mudst get thingks from my apartmendt and zen vee will go to airport."

"Okay," I agree. I walk to the bathroom in a daze, see my glassy-eyed reflection in the smudged, dirty mirror. In my innocence I think that vague, glassy-eyed stare is the look of a passionate young woman in love, not the look of an addict in the throes of her latest fix. But that's exactly what it is. I am an emotion junkie with a gaping black hole in my brain, and Dieter Franzl is my heroin.

I call in sick at eight-fifteen. Dave is the only one in the office that early, and he can tell that I'm playing hooky. "You're faking it, aren't you?" he says when I feign a sore throat and cough into the phone.

"No," I lie, and cough into the phone again.

"Whatever. I'll tell the boss you aren't coming in. Have fun." Dave hangs up.

We fly to New York. We stay at a posh midtown hotel just off Times Square. Dieter buys me an expensive cocktail dress and I wear it to a Broadway show then to a late-night dinner at one of the most expensive and exclusive restaurants in town, where we have a private booth behind a set of swinging Dutch doors in a private dining room, with a charming wine steward who wears a silver tasting spoon on a chain around his neck and offers us the best vintages. We drink wine from 1965 served by three different white-gloved waiters. I order risotto primavera and seventeen-layer chocolate tiramisu from a menu that has no prices.

We go back to the hotel and have the most mind-blowing sex of our lives. And the next day, Dieter rows me around Central Park Lake in a wooden dinghy with rusty oars. When we make it to the middle of the lake, he says he wants to marry me.

And I am naive (and sick) enough to believe him.

"You make me vandt to abandon everythingk I have in Vienna and live here width you," he says, and kisses me so hard he almost drops the oars into the murky green water and strands us.

We fly back to Chicago that afternoon, cooing to each other for the entire flight. Dieter asks if I will accompany him to San Francisco two weeks later when he goes there with other members of his graduate program to give a presentation to business-school alumni in the area. Not knowing how I'll manage to get the time off, I agree. He promises we'll finalize our plans for the future once the San Francisco trip is complete. In the meantime, he'll need to spend the next two weeks working on the San Francisco "presentation" and his doctoral dissertation project without distraction.

He bids me a long, fond goodbye at my apartment building. "I vill call you," he promises.

He doesn't.

Five days pass, and no word from Dieter. I shrug it off and request two unpaid days off from my boss for the San Francisco trip. Dave overhears me ask for them, and his eyebrows raise.

"Going on another trip with that German guy, huh?" he mocks later when our boss has gone to lunch. It's obvious he's figured out the real reason for my hooky day the week before. "Where to this time?"

"San Francisco," I chirp, not looking up from a pile of invoices.

"What for?"

"Just a trip with my boyfriend. He's Austrian, not German."

Dave grunts. "What the hell are you, some kind of kept woman?"

I don't answer. I keep staring at my pile of invoices and pretend to ignore the feeling in the pit of my stomach that tells me Dave might be right.

The day of our San Francisco trip approaches, and I've still heard nothing from Dieter. I leave messages, send emails. All are ignored until the following Sunday, three days before we are supposed to leave.

"Vhy do you call me zo much?" he demands in an angry late-night call to my apartment, the first time we've spoken in nearly a week. "Do nodt call me zo much. I am very busy."

"I just need to know what is going on," I plead.

Dieter doesn't try to hide his irritation. "Width vhat?"

"You know, with the trip, and everything. With *us*."

"You needt to schtopp beingk so fuckingk needy," he hisses, and hangs up.

I feel my stomach drop out, my mouth turn to cotton. What's happened to the man who proposed to me in Central Park and bought me a designer evening dress and a fancy dinner that probably cost more than my monthly rent? What's happened to the feeling of warmth and euphoria that fills my belly and head whenever Dieter speaks, the dazzling, spinning sensation that his touch evokes in my body like a drug? In an instant, they are gone, all gone.

An hour or so later, the phone rings again. It's Dieter, apologizing profusely.

"I am zo zorry about judst now," he says, his Deutsch Don Juan persona back in full swing. "I am judst zo stressdt oudt. I have this San Francisco pretzendtatzion andt my ditzzertation andt my consulting job is givingk me projectz from Vienna even though I am on leave. Whadt I needt now more than anythingk ist to be width you. Can I see you now?"

I swallow, sigh, and say yes.

Dieter appears on my doorstep fifteen minutes later. I think he's come to make up, then frolic in bed with me. But he hasn't. He's come to talk business.

Dieter opens his briefcase and takes out several floppy disks. "You are a profetzzional edidtor, no?"

"I was," I say. "I'm not anymore. I work at a library now."

"Budt you know how to edidt words in English, no?"

"Yeah."

"I am vonderingk if maybe you cudt edidt my ditzzertation for me."

I glance from the stack of floppies to Dieter's expression—emotionless—and back again. I search in vain for clues about how he feels—if he still feels anything at all—about me. He is a brick wall, blank and drab and mortared tight.

"Why are you asking me to do this?" I finally ask.

"As a favor," he says. "Andt I vould pay you."

My scalp skin crawls the slightest bit. "If you pay me, it's not a favor."

"As you wish," he says, and smiles. "I am only askingk because I don't know anyone who wouldt be better at it zan you."

I can't help but be flattered, but at no time in our whirlwind courtship have Dieter and I ever discussed anything about my business writing experience or editorial skills, other than the fact I once worked for a high-priced brokerage as a stock reports editor and want to be a successful playwright someday. It all seems a little out of left field.

Dieter grows impatient. "Vill you do it or nodt?"

"Sure, yeah, I guess."

"*Gut*." He hands me the floppies and a stack of handwritten notes. "I mudst go now," he says abruptly. "I have an important pretzendtatzion tomorrow morningk for my ditzzertation adtvizor. I vill send a taxi for you on Thursday morningk to take you to ze airpordt." He's up and out the door before I can say another word.

Watching him go, I don't move, I don't speak. I don't do anything—I can't. I feel as if I've been rammed through the stomach with a telephone pole.

Instantly, I start to rationalize. Surely Dieter's sudden cold shoulder is just due to some kind of Austro–Central European cultural difference. Europeans are reserved and careful, aren't they? Perhaps Dieter is just pulling back a bit, finding steady ground to stand upon after rushing into such a wildly passionate, instantly committed relationship. Or perhaps he's just saving all his warmth and love and opiate-like romantic maneuvering for San Francisco. He's saving it up for that special occasion, like a nest egg or a rare vintage of wine.

That *has* to be it. It can't possibly have anything to do with *me*. Of *course* not.

He wouldn't be asking me to do such an important job as editing his monumental PhD dissertation if there really were something *wrong* with me. Would he?

Of course not. *Of course not.*

Everything is fine. *Everything is fine.* I tell myself this lie over and over, even though I know it isn't true. Denial is a powerful tool, and it's a tool I've trained myself to use well. You can't go through life making the choices that I do unless denial is the sharpest, deadliest weapon in your arsenal.

Everything. Will. Be. Fine.

I tell myself this over and over again as I pour myself glass after glass of Skyy vodka from my freezer, as I shred three of my favorite silk dresses with a pair of scissors, as I soak in a long, hot bath scrubbing a strange, unnamable sensation of cheapness and filth off my body.

The San Francisco trip is a disaster.

Dieter does send me a taxi on Thursday morning (why he can't share one with me I'll never know), but it's an hour late. I barely make it to the airport on time, and security is slow to boot. By the time I make it to the gate, the air hostess is preparing to shut the gangway door when I rush up and beg to be allowed to board.

"Vhat took you zo longk?" Dieter demands when I make it to my seat.

"The taxi you sent me was an hour late."

Dieter ignores this and reads the in-flight safety card aloud to himself in German.

We barely speak for the whole flight out to the California coast. Thanks to his business connections, Dieter and I have bulkhead seats in business class in one of the airline's fanciest new planes, and he spends almost half the trip on the Airfone bragging to some of his work buddies in offices scattered around the world about our fully reclining seat-beds, personal televisions preloaded with dozens of films and TV shows, and Internet connection. The time Dieter isn't on the Airfone, he sleeps.

Things only get worse when we land. When we get to the baggage carousel, Dieter retrieves an electric guitar case and amplifier with his baggage.

"What's that for?" I ask.

"Ze pretzendtatzion," he snaps in the thickest Austrian accent I've ever heard, and heads straight for the taxi line.

"Why do you need an electric guitar for a business presentation?"

Dieter rolls his eyes, flags a taxi, and doesn't answer my question until we're less than a mile from Fisherman's Wharf. After twenty minutes seething on his side of the cab, he speaks. "I thoughdt dat you knew vhat a pretzendtatzion vas, you beingk a theater person and all."

"I'm sorry, I'm not following."

Dieter goes on to tell me that we're here so he can perform in "The Money Show,"[2] an annual talent show the business school he attends runs. Current graduate students perform onstage for alumni living in the Bay Area, many of whom work in Silicon Valley and help pay for the show's venue and scenery as part of a career-development and professional networking program.

"The Money Show," Dieter says, as if I should have already known. "You know, like 'Show me the money!' Ist funny, no?" He's clearly amused with himself as we pull up to a shabby hotel near the Presidio. I bite my tongue to keep from telling Dieter that he really doesn't understand American humor at all, and to keep from telling myself I was an idiot to ever agree to go on this trip to begin with. Instead, I fake a laugh. It's the best I can do.

We arrive in the peeling faux-marble lobby to find a gaggle of Dieter's fellow graduate students milling around the hotel bar. "Dieter!" they all call.

A cocky, twenty-twoish blonde with impressive breasts shakes Dieter's hand and hugs him. "We thought you'd never make it in!"

Dieter cuts his eyes at me. "I hadt some difficuldty gettingk *hier*, ist all."

"Oh! Well, most of us have been here since yesterday, rehearsing. The venue's great, but it's way out in the middle of nowhere." Cocky Blonde and Dieter walk off arm-in-arm to the far side of the bar, talking and whispering to one another, and the gaggle of grad students follows them. Dieter doesn't even introduce me to anybody. I stand tongue-tied in the middle of the peeling lobby with our luggage and Dieter's three-foot-tall Fender Stratocaster amplifier next to me until an annoyed bellman nudges me toward the front desk.

I figure I might as well check myself and Dieter's giant amplifier into our room. When I give our names to the desk clerk, though, he informs me that Dieter and I are booked under *separate* rooms.

Separate rooms. Great. Lovely.

*Wünderbar.*

I guess that means I won't be needing my diaphragm.

I spend the next hour pacing my cramped hotel room, wondering whether it makes sense for me to ditch the trip altogether and get a standby seat on the next available flight back to Chicago.

Just when I'm about to call the airline's reservations hotline, there's a knock at the door.

It's Dieter, alone, with a peace offering. "Wouldt you like to go to Chinatown for dinner? Judst you and me." He pecks me on the cheek, a drug dealer offering one last free hit before jacking up his prices.

"Sure," I stammer. "Sounds fun."

We walk all the way from the Presidio to Chinatown and stop at a restaurant seemingly at random. The host says he already has a table waiting for us. And there's already someone sitting at it. Victor, one of

Dieter's college friends from Austria, who now works in international finance here in San Francisco.

So much for a private, romantic dinner. I spend the entire evening shoving cold eggrolls around on a plate with disposable chopsticks while Victor and Dieter discuss Austrian politics, switching back and forth from English to German and mostly pretending I'm not there.

Dieter apologizes on the walk back to the hotel. "Zo sorry. Victor calledt at the lasdt minute. I hadt to see him. Ve vill have time alone together tomorrow, after the pretzendtatzion, I promise."

When I wake up the next morning, Dieter's already gone. He's left me a message at the front desk that he'll be at rehearsal all day, but in the evening I can take a prepaid cab he's arranged out to San Jose, where the concert is. He promises to reserve me a seat.

I spend the entire day wandering the streets of San Francisco alone, walking to all the tourist sights—Haight/Ashbury, Union Square, the cable cars, and Chinatown, again—until my feet bleed and my head aches from dehydration. I have little money budgeted for food and entertainment, so I buy myself a vegetarian hotdog and bottled water at a stand as my only real nourishment for the day. I get lost for an hour or two near the Tenderloin and weep in the middle of the street when I think for sure I'll be mugged and raped at any minute.

When I finally find my way to Golden Gate Park, I stare out into the bay, contemplating whether it might just be easiest and best for all concerned for me to walk out to the center of the Golden Gate Bridge and jump off. At the insistence of architecture purists, there are no suicide barricades on the bridge. Nobody even knows I'm in San Francisco except for Dieter and my boss, and I doubt either one of them will miss me very much if I jump. It's tempting—I can almost feel the cold orange steel of the bridge underneath the pads of my fingertips as I clutch the railing, can almost savor the cold waters of the bay envelope me like a velvet blanket. It would be so easy, so dramatic.

But I can't do it. I just don't have the balls.

It's not the first time or way I've contemplated suicide, but it's certainly the most romantic. There's something strangely beautiful about jumping off the Golden Gate Bridge, which is why I suppose so many people do it. About one suicide every three days, or so they say.[3] It certainly beats some other methods I've toyed with, like slashing my wrists or taking pills or jumping on the third rail of the subway. I know that all of these thoughts are bad, and that I shouldn't be having them at all, but I can't stop. Or rather, I *won't* stop. I just keep torturing myself because it's all that I think I deserve.

By midafternoon I'm exhausted. I walk back to the hotel and ask the concierge if he knows anything about a prearranged taxi to take me to San Jose. He does. I ask if the concierge can arrange for it to take me to San Jose three hours early. He can.

I've had enough of Dieter's rigid routines, his backhanded manipulations. I'm sick of being pulled and danced about by invisible marionette strings. I want to do one thing, just one thing on this fiasco trip *my* way.

If only I had the willpower to stick with that strategy for longer than that forty-minute cab ride. If only.

If only. But I don't, because I can't. I simply don't have the fortitude to take care of myself, especially when I think what I need most is what's really the worst possible thing for me. Never try to reason with a *nutjob*—we'll choose to sit on a rusty sawblade over a chintz sofa every time, because in our world, *the rusty sawblade is better.* We dwell in a distorted universe that's full of contradictions and makes sense only to us.

I arrive at the San Jose performance venue—a large, snow-white, Spanish Colonial–style auditorium with an art-nouveau, gold-leaf proscenium stage—at 4:45. I can hear the sounds of an out-of-tune concert band and marginally talented singers doing vocal warm-up exercises. Even outside, I understand why all of these people have chosen MBAs over careers in the arts. They're hopeless. I'm embarrassed for them. And for myself, for being there in the first place. But I still don't leave.

I walk into the auditorium and take a seat right in front of the band. Dieter looks up from his amplifier's knobs and turns pale. He won't meet my eyes.

A man carrying a cymbal in each hand comes up to me. "Who the hell are you?"

"I'm Anna. I'm here with Dieter Franzl."

The cymbal man looks me up and down. "Oh. Right." He chuckles, looks me up and down again. "I'm sorry about that. Boy. Boy, I'm sorry for *you.*"

"Why? What do you mean?" But I know why.

Sort of.

Cymbal Man chuckles again, shakes his head, and goes to mess with his drum set.

I stay in my seat for the rest of the rehearsal, then the performance. I don't go to the box office for a ticket and no one makes me. In fact, everyone at The Money Show—a combination talent show and sketch-comedy spoof of business school and corporate life—seems to know who I am already, and to pity me. Everyone in the audience—and the cast and crew at the after-party at some wealthy alumni graduate's house in Pacific Heights—seems preprogrammed to give me a wide berth, to avoid touching me or talking to me lest they catch bubonic plague or leprosy. They treat me the way wealthy people treat a home-less, stinking junkie on the street—because in many ways, that's exactly what I am. Why else would I be willingly choosing to do things that make me miserable? Why did I ever decide to date Dieter in the first place, a man who is using me for sex and free editorial services, when I could have seen the warning signs a mile away? It's a compulsion. A dirty, destructive compulsion. The first hit of this love-drug is bliss, but it quickly turns into pain—and you just take more and more of it in a vain effort to get that fleeting, blissful feeling back, even if just for a second or two.

I stand alone in the corner of that anonymous Internet millionaire's Pacific Heights living room, clutching a highball filled with a blue drink I don't know the name of, staring helplessly across the room at the tall, blonde Austrian who brought me there and hoping that he'll give me another hit of his wonder love-drug for free and snap me out of my raging DTs. But he doesn't, and won't, because I don't have anything left that he wants in trade. I can't even suck him off for it because we have separate rooms at the hotel and he won't tell me which floor I can go to so I can blow him in exchange for a nickel bag of self-worth. And in the meantime, the gaping black hole in my brain keeps getting bigger and bigger and bigger, until I think it will swallow me up and make me disappear. I know that the black hole is bad, and wrong, and dangerous, but I don't yet know why, or even how it got there—let alone what to do about it. When you're sick in the head, that kind of deep, ordered thinking isn't exactly within your reach.

Another prepaid cab appears and takes me back to the Presidio. I sleep alone, again. Dieter meets me in the peeling marble lobby the next morning. He's already checked out of his room.

"Sorry aboudt lasdt night. Parties. You know. I needt to netverk. You know. *Schtuff.*"

"Sure." I play with lint in my pockets. "I had a nice time here. It's very pretty here."

I lie. I lie and smile. I lie and smile because it makes the gaping black hole in my brain shrink.

Just a little.

Dieter calls me two days after we get back to Chicago and says we need to take a break. As if we aren't already on one.

"I am sorry. I judst need some time," he says over tallboy Warsteiners at a downtown hotel bar. "My feelingks for you—they are, they *were* genuine. Budt now I judst dond't know. I need time. I am goingk back to Vienna for now. I leave in two weekzt."

"What? But I thought you were going to stay *here*! I thought you were going to transfer to your company's Chicago office and stay here. I thought we were going to get married." I stare at the lemon slice floating in my Warsteiner. There's a tiny black speck on it, stuck to the cool lemon flesh. I don't know if it's dirt or just part of the lemon, and I don't want to find out.

"*I dond't know.* I needt time. I am going back to Vienna. Dat ist all I know righdt now. In meantime, you can help me edit my ditzzertation by e-mail. I vill pay for you to come to Vienna in the fall. It vill be zo nice for you. You can meedt my mother then. We will make plantz then. Vienna, it is beautiful in the fall. I vill pay for everythingk. This is vhat you will do, no?"

"Yeah. Sure. I get two weeks' paid vacation a year. Okay."

"*Gut.*" Dieter stands up too fast, bumps the table with his knee, and knocks both tallboy Warsteiners into my lap. The lemon slices land on my chest. Beer soaks through my cheap polyester skirt and runs into my underwear. He doesn't apologize. He doesn't even offer to get me a towel.

I just smile. Nod, and smile. It makes the hole in my brain smaller. It feels good, just to nod and smile sometimes. But that feeling doesn't last. The gaping black hole in my brain is too big and too strong, and it's growing fast. I can't keep fighting it alone, even if I think that I have everything under control. I simply don't have the tools. Not the right ones, anyway. Denial is about as useful in this battle as a cotton swab would be on D-Day.

Even if I don't yet understand how or why, I'm hell-bent on a path to self-destruction. And that path leads straight to the land of waltzes and Mozart.

The spring and summer of 1999 fly by. I work at the library. I ride the el. I go home each night. I rarely go out. I sleep a lot. I charge a new travel wardrobe on my credit cards in anticipation of the Vienna trip, buy frivolous facials and beauty treatments too, until all my cards are maxed out and I have no idea how I'll pay them back. I wait for Dieter's correspondence and phone calls, which rarely come and always have something to do with his dissertation. He has promised me a draft by May. May stretches into June, then into August, and there is no dissertation. The floppy disks and notes he's given to me so far are merely "background information." I've read through them a dozen times and they still make no sense. I don't know if they make no sense because they really are nonsensical, or because my *nutjob* brain has trouble making sense of anything anymore. It's probably a little of both.

Dieter dangles the editing project just out of my reach, like beef jerky ten feet over the head of a hungry puppy. He hasn't paid me anything yet, but it's not the promise of money that keeps me interested. It's the promise of a continued connection to him—*any* connection, even a crappy, dysfunctional one. We speak on the phone every two weeks or so, and only at Dieter's leisure and pleasure. And every brief conversation we have is the same.

"What's going on? Why don't you ever call me anymore?" I wail. I can't call Dieter myself. He won't give me his number in Austria, and even if he would I can't afford that kind of long distance anyway. He holds me out at arm's length, at absolute mercy to his whim and will.

"I have been too busy."

"I'm all ready to edit your stuff. I'm looking forward to it. I hope you still want me to do it, because *I* want to do it." I say it just like the scrappy, hyperactive little Chihuahua jumping around the giant bulldog did in the old Warner Bros. cartoons. Every pedantic phrase I offer up to him on a jittery plate is methadone, a mere substitute for the love-drug the black hole in my brain needs filled so desperately.

"Yeah, yeah, sure sure, I'll do it for you," I jigger. I'm pathetic. But I'll do anything, *anything* for another hit. Anything at all.

"The ditzzertation ist not done yet. I needt more time."

"Am I still coming to Vienna? Am I? Am I?"

Dieter sighs. "Yes, yes. I'll ship you some plane tickedtz."

"When? When?"

Another sigh. "Soon. *Gut*-bye."

And that's the end of it, until Dieter sees fit to dangle the beef jerky and call me again. He's master of my domain, and his. He rules two hemispheres.

Plane tickets arrive unannounced at my doorstep in early September, for a departure three weeks hence. I'll fly to Vienna on Dieter's dime by way of Heathrow Airport. By then it's too late for me to ask my boss for a sixteen-day vacation, but I beg and plead and cajole and threaten to quit, and finally get it, though five days of it will have to be without pay. So I skip a student loan payment and sell half my CD collection to a used record store to help meet my bills for the month and still have spending money for the trip.

When I arrive at the small Vienna airport, I see a man in a dark suit standing between Customs and the baggage carousel. The man in the dark suit holds a cardboard sign with my name written on it in stilted black marker. I walk up to him, tell him I'm the name on the sign, but when it's clear he doesn't speak English, I have to show him my passport and fumble through a sentence I find in my German phrasebook. He grunts something back in German, waves for me to follow him outside, and leads me to a shiny black BMW with deep-tinted windows and walnut interior paneling. I expected—hoped—that Dieter would meet me at the airport himself. But he's sent a high-priced car service to fetch me instead, as if I'm a powerful international diplomat. Or a call girl.

The hired BMW wanders twisting Alpine roads and highways until it arrives in central Vienna. It drives past the Hotel Imperial, the opera house, St. Stephen's Cathedral, and dozens of gold-leaf art-nouveau streetlamps, and it stops in front of a drab, postwar, five-story apartment building a block or two inside the Ringstrasse. The uniformed driver ushers me out of the car, drops my baggage at my feet, and drives away.

I stare at the apartment building, an ugly hulking structure coated with dirty white ceramic tile. I have no idea if this is the right place, if Dieter lives here, or if this is merely some kind of cheap hostel where he intends to warehouse me for two weeks at his expense. I walk up to the gray metal door to scan the panel of buzzers and am relieved to find Dieter's name at the very bottom. I press the buzzer. No answer. I press it again. No answer, again.

I've flown halfway around the world to stay with a man who isn't home.

Dieter waltzes up to the building an hour or so later and finds me in his building's doorway, lying half-asleep from jet lag on top of my battered suitcase. At the sound of his trademark sigh of irritation, I open my eyes.

Imposing in an immaculate steel-blue suit, Dieter looks me up and down, rolls his eyes, shakes his head. He doesn't hug me or greet me. "Vhy are you *hier* now?"

"You sent me a car. It dropped me off an hour ago."

Dieter frowns. "The car was supposed to take you to Schoenbrunn Palace first."

"Why?"

"For sighdtseeingk. A mistake to bringk you *hier* so early. Never mind. *Komme* upstairtz."

He ushers me inside and up three flights of a corrugated metal staircase. He unlocks a wide maple door, and leads me into an ultramodern, luxurious apartment.

"*Wilkommen*," he said. "This ist your home for nedxt two weeks. Your room is *hier*. I vill sleep in the livingkroom on sofa. You are guest, you get ze bedt." He indicates a large, low Scandinavian-style bed with a thick eiderdown coverlet.

So we won't be sleeping together. Fine. I can live with that. He's just being a gentleman, surely. A gentleman. Of course.

"*Hier*, I had a key made." He hands it to me; it dangles from a sleek chrome ring that matches his apartment's luxe décor. "I am verking almost all ze time now, come andt go as you please. *Hier* are maptz of ze city. Walk aroundt. See ze sights. All ist close by."

"But—"

"But vhat?"

I sigh, bite my lip, swallow hard. This is it. The moment of truth. The moment when I can figure out why I have flown all the way to Vienna at Dieter's expense when he won't even let me sleep with him. The rules of sexual engagement have been thrown out the window. I need to know why, and I know if I wait another second to ask I won't have the courage to do it. "Dieter, why am I here?"

"Because you vandted to come."

"Why did you ask me? Why did you pay all this money out? Why am I here?"

"You are *hier* because I vandt to give you ze gifdt of beautiful Vienna. It is a gifdt. A gifdt, width no expectations. Zat ist all."

"But—"

Dieter holds up his hand. *"Zat ist all.* I do not vandt to talk aboudt anythingk more righdt now."

On the third night of my Vienna trip, Dieter takes me to a gritty Eurogoth bar around the corner from St. Stephen's Cathedral called *Steinzeit* (German for "stone age"). Situated in a former cheese cellar in a crumbling eighteenth-century building, *Steinzeit's* walls are plastered with peeling German metal-band posters and ancient newsprint. The floor is sticky with dried beer, and the bathrooms reek of vomit. Thrashing German death-metal vibrates from two giant speakers, and most of the patrons have shaved heads and at least one metal spike running through their faces. Hardly the right setting for a romantic conversation. I'm sure Dieter chooses the place on purpose.

He orders two bottles of beer from the dirty bar and sits down. "Vee needt to have a conversation," he shouts over the throbbing bass. The very idea of having a conversation in such a place is a joke.

I stare into my beer. I know what's coming. Dieter has been ignoring me as much as possible for three days. He's spent almost the entire time at his office in an ornate Second Empire–style building directly across from the Hapsburg Palace while I wander the beautiful city alone. The only real interaction we've had so far was a brief argument over which one of us broke a tiny, razor-thin, totally impractical glass soapdish that juts from the corner of his shower stall. (Neither of us, it turned out; his twice-weekly maid did it while cleaning.)

"Zis ist not goingk to verk out," he shouts over the din, indicating himself and me. "Vee are too differendt. Plus I no longer wish to verk in the United States. And you vould nodt fit in *hier*. And you could nodt have you theater writing career *hier* anyway. I vould nodt take zat avay from you. Vee are nodt goingk to verk out. I hope you understandt zat."

I go numb. I can't move. I just stare at the grey-green beer label and try to concentrate on how pretty the gold lettering in the center is.

"Do you have anythingk to say?" he asks.

I shake my head once. Slightly.

"All righdt. Finish your beer andt let's go."

I guzzle it and hiccup in time to the death-metal's thrashing bass. Dieter is already out the door and doesn't notice.

I think we'll be going directly back to Dieter's apartment, but he hails us a taxi instead. *"Komme,"* he says. "I know you mudst be upset. Let me take you out for a *gut* time."

I'm not exactly sure what happens next. I know there's at least one flashing discotheque, location and name unknown. There's beer, then wine, then some kind of semifermented local drink called *strumm*. A lot of it. The evening comes back to me only in flashes that now seem absurd and hardly possible—especially an indelible image of more than two hundred Austrian teenagers, all dressed in black, jumping up and down in unison and singing "A RAMMA-LAMMA-LAMMA, RAMMA-LAMMA DING DONG" in heavy Germanic accents at the top of their lungs on a sparkling dance floor. (The sound just doesn't go with the picture, like one of those old *Sesame Street* cartoon-puzzles that ask toddlers to pick out what doesn't belong.) It triggers something in me, something that comes to a head once we're back at Dieter's central Vienna apartment around three a.m.

I am on my way over the borderline into a full-fledged, rage-filled psychotic episode. Dieter Franzl has sent me over that borderline on an all-expenses-paid first-class ticket to hell.

Everything from that point on is hazy and distorted, like the wavy, stretched images in a funhouse mirror. I'm drunk enough for the room to spin. Dieter carries me from his bedroom to the sofa-bed in a forcible demotion. I scream and thrash and throw pillows from his leather couch around. I roll around on the floor and bang into the furniture. I hurl obscenities and wake the neighbors. He slaps me across the face repeatedly in a vain attempt to stop my hysterical, shrieking, keening, wailing sobs. At some point he packs a suitcase, tells me I'm a stupid, ridiculous bitch, and stomps out of the apartment while I thrash and writhe on the sofa bed. I don't remember exactly when or how I start crying and wailing and keening to the point that I think my insides are coming out through my mouth. I don't remember how or when I feel myself leave my body for a time and watch the whole thing transpire from somewhere on the ceiling. It happens almost in another dimension and in slow motion.

I sob until my whole body hurts. I sob until I think I'm going to die—wish for it, even. Dieter is a dangerous drug to me, I'm hopelessly addicted, and now he's finally cut me off. Dying is the only way I know to escape.

But I'm so far gone by this point, I don't even know how to go about dying. I've broken with reality completely. Sure, I'd been flirting with insanity for a while now. Plenty of young women my age would think a free, no-strings-attached trip to Vienna is great and wonderful, even if the guy who paid for it is a jerk. I'd thought so too, at first.

But the reality is, there were always *plenty* of strings attached. My sanity among them. When you can't separate yourself from the sleazy guy you're dating, when you honestly believe that your entire world and existence rises and sets on his head—and when he dumps you and you're a nonentity—well, no amount of beautiful Alpine scenery or Strauss waltzes will fix what ails you.

At this point, I envy the people who have the nerve to commit suicide. The black hole in my brain I've ignored for months now has finally swallowed me up, and there is nothing left of me to kill.

I stop sobbing when I hear the first birds of morning begin to chirp in the dark. Dieter's unattended alarm clock goes off in the hallway, blaring obnoxious Europop with English nonsense lyrics. Suddenly hungry, I get up and shuffle into his luxe Eurokitchen in search of breakfast. But the cupboards are bare save for some German oatmeal muesli that requires heating—useless, since Dieter's kitchen is loaded with shiny chrome Siemens appliances so complex and advanced that I can't figure out how to turn them on.

I abandon breakfast and decide that what I really need to do is pray.

I walk the Ringstrasse for a bit and then cross over toward the center of the city. The steep, checkered roof of St. Stephen's beckons. I've been inside its high gray walls once already, during one of my solo walks around the city center. I'd read the English-language pamphlet on its history and admired the stained glass windows and side chapels and sepulchers yesterday, and I'd gazed at the Holocaust memorial sculptures across the street when I came from its darkened cavernous interior back outside, blinking and squinting into the light. But today I will not go to St. Stephen's as a tourist. Today I will go to be saved.

I reach the church doors. One of them is open a crack. I open it a little too fast and almost knock over a middle-aged nun standing just behind it in her brown orthotic shoes while she fills a holy water font. I remember a snippet of my lapsed childhood Catholicism and dip my fingers into the cool water, cross myself with it. I smile at the nun and she smiles too. "*Guten morgen*," she says. I don't answer back.

It is not yet six. There is only one other person in the cathedral this early—an elderly woman kneels in the front-most pew on the left side of the nave, just beside one of the side chapels where a single penny-candle burns. I make a point to take a seat at the extreme rear right corner, as far away from her as possible. I know there will be more early-morning faithful coming in soon, but I want my own little ring of solitude for as long as possible. I don't want anyone to figure out that I've mostly forgotten what little I learned in Catholic catechism class. I've long since left the religion of my birth behind. It's been almost fifteen years since I set foot in a Catholic church, unless you count the time I spent in Notre-Dame and Saint-Denis Cathedrals in Paris as an atheist college student studying French medieval architecture one summer break on scholarship. I wonder for a moment if perhaps I'll burst into flames when I go down onto the kneeler.

I finally decide just to sit quietly in my pew (not even a pew really, just a row of joined wooden chairs) and wait for my body and mind to remember how to behave properly in a Catholic church. My eyes scan the massive stone walls, come to rest on this artifact or that—Emperor Frederick's tomb, Mozart's memorial chapel—but they finally come to rest on the worn leather kneeler at my feet. I stare at the kneeler for a long time. After a while, it goes blurry. I hear the sound of water dripping. It's a loud dripping, full of echoes, like the constant drip-drop water sounds one hears inside a cave. *Drip-drop-BOOM, drip-drop-BOOM*, the sound goes, amplified ten thousand times by St. Stephen's steep-pitched stone roof. The stir of echoes links with the sound of my beating heart, and the combination is deafening, yet somehow soothing. Other than the booming echoes my tears make when they hit the kneeler in huge, widening splotches, booming and booming until they puddle up and start to spill down onto the pockmarked stone floor, my weeping makes no sound. I don't keen, whimper, or even hiccup. My weeping becomes one with the pulse of the ancient building, and slowly builds itself up and out through the bell towers in a steady, even thrum. I am cleansed, in a way, though I don't think God or the wandering nuns or the church building is necessarily responsible. If anything is responsible for this small moment of healing—which by no means cures the gaping black hole in my brain, it merely shrinks it just enough for me to survive the rest of my time in Vienna—it is the collective spirits of all the hundreds, thousands of people buried underneath the church or within its heavy stone walls. The knowledge that they are there, and have endured far more than I ever have or will, sustains me.

At this point, I still think that I love Dieter, as ridiculous as it might sound. I cannot separate love from hate or lust or any of the other emotions raging through me. For me, love *is* pain. I don't yet know that something else is possible, but in that quiet moment there in the church, I get my first hint of it.

The church seems well-accustomed to receiving thick tear puddles on its kneelers and floor. The ancient cathedral accepts them with grace, and absorbs them into its stone heart in silence. The floor never seems to get saturated and just soaks up more and more of my spilling grief. This place, witness to plagues and fires and bombs and Nazis, this place knows sadness, knows it well.

"How long have you been involved with this man?" Dr. Chatterjee[4] asks. "This man from Austria. The one you call Dieter?"

"I don't *call* him Dieter. That's his name."

Dr. Chatterjee blinks and looks down his long aquiline nose at me. "Of course it is."

Dr. Chatterjee is my new psychiatrist. He's a third-year psychiatry resident at the university hospital. I'm seeing him three times a week for free so he can have a case to write about for his board exams. I got referred to him by an intake nurse at the only clinic my crummy HMO would pay for because my insurance would only cover five sessions at the clinic.

"You're going to need a lot more than five sessions, hon," the nurse said, and handed me a pamphlet about a free psychiatrist-in-training therapy program. "Between your condition and your income, you're the perfect candidate." At first I took it as an insult, and then I realized that the nurse was right. I knew I was sick, I just didn't understand why or what to do about it. Had I known the answer to either of those questions, I wouldn't have sought help to begin with. And you could hardly argue with free. I went to the free program's office that same day and they matched me with Dr. Chatterjee, who had a particular interest in depressed young women with relationship problems. It seemed like a perfect fit, since I was depressed and I had a relationship problem. Only Dr. Chatterjee and I didn't exactly agree on what the problem was.

Dr. Chatterjee is from London. East London, to be exact. He's a dark-skinned Indian who looks like Martin Bashir, talks like Michael Caine, and reeks of coriander curry. He wears custom-made Nehru suits and doesn't seem to like me very much.

"Whatever you wish to call Dieter in session is fine," Dr. Chatterjee says. "But to get back to my question—how long have you been involved with this man?"

"What exactly do you mean by *involved*?"

"How long have you known him? How long have you been in contact with one another?"

"I dunno—a year and a half, I guess."

"You said in our last session that you haven't *seen* Dieter in almost a year."

"That's right."

Dr. Chatterjee chews the end of his pen. "So, how exactly can you be *involved* with Dieter if you haven't seen each other in a year?"

"Well, we like, *talk* and stuff. On the phone. Sometimes. And I've been doing some writing work for him."

Dr. Chatterjee clears his throat. "Sounds more like a business arrangement than a relationship."

I shrug. "Maybe. But I really think we're going to get back together someday soon."

Dr. Chatterjee clears his throat again. "What makes you think that?"

"Well, sometimes Dieter tells me that we will. That we *might*."

"I see. Tell me something, Anna. Does Dieter ever talk about getting back together with you around the same time he sends you a writing project to work on?" Dr. Chatterjee leans forward, smiles. He seems pleased with himself.

I pause to think, realize that Dr. Chatterjee has discovered something that I know is true but don't want to acknowledge. So I just shrug.

"I see I've touched a nerve," he says. "Tell me something else, Anna. How long has it been since you had sexual intercourse with Dieter? You don't have to answer the question if you don't want to."

"It's been almost a year and a half," I say.

Dr. Chatterjee sighs. "Anna, has it ever once occurred to you that your relationship with Dieter might be very, very bad for your mental health?"

"No."

"I think it's high bloody time it did," Dr. Chatterjee snaps.

(Dr. Chatterjee says mean things like this to me all the time. He's not a very nice psychiatrist. I'm only seeing him because his sessions are free. I'd never *pay* to get talked to like this. Never.)

Dr. Chatterjee temples his long brown fingers under his chin. "Have you *ever* had a successful romantic relationship, Anna?"

"I dunno."

"What do you mean, *you don't know*? Surely you know whether you've had any *good* relationships or not." Dr. Chatterjee's bushy black eyebrows raise triumphantly, as if he knows he's pinned me under a bus with this question.

I blink. "I guess maybe that depends."

"On what, exactly?"

I blink again. "On what you think *successful* means, I guess."

"What do *you* think it means?"

"I dunno. Happy, I guess. Stable, maybe too."

Dr. Chatterjee leans forward again, grins. "Have you ever had a happy, stable relationship, Anna? With *anyone*—romantic or otherwise?"

I don't answer him. I just stare at the floor.

After almost five minutes of total silence, Dr. Chatterjee clears his throat. "We haven't spent a lot of time talking about your family or childhood, Anna. I wonder if perhaps we should."

"Why?"

Dr. Chatterjee's hardline expression softens, just for the tiniest of moments. "Anna, young women with the kind of personality disorder I think you have very typically come from volatile family backgrounds, dysfunctional backgrounds that cripple young women's emotional development to the point that they are incapable of having healthy, happy, stable relationships with anyone. Does that sound like you?"

*What*? I have a *personality disorder*? How could that be? I refuse to even consider the possibility. Dieter was the problem, not me. Didn't Dr. Chatterjee know that? But instead of saying any of this aloud, I just stare at the floor.

After a few more moments of silence, Dr. Chatterjee grows impatient. "Anna, you're getting very expensive psychiatric treatment for free. Do you really want to sit here not saying anything, acting like a spoilt child, wasting my and your time, when I could be offering these free sessions to someone else who could actually be helped by them? Or do you want to start participating like a grownup?"

"All right, fine. I'll tell you all about my crummy childhood and crazy family. That's what you want to hear about, right? I could go on forever. Where should I start?"

Dr. Chatterjee sighs. "Why don't we start out with the basics. Tell me a little about your mother. Go back as far as you can. What's the earliest memory you have of your mother?"

I chew on my thumbnail—it's already bitten down to the quick—as I walk backward through my mind's eye. "My earliest memory of Mom? I guess that would be when I'm about five years old."

"Mom, why are we going around the block again? We've been around this same block ten times already."

"*Quiet*," Mom hisses at me from the front seat. "*Quiet*." She sounds like the devil-possessed Linda Blair in *The Exorcist*. I just watched *The Exorcist* on *ABC Thursday Night at the Movies* the week before last, and I still can't get over how much the devil-possessed Linda Blair sounds just like my mom does when she's driving her rattling, rusted-out '74 Chevy Vega around and around and around the block—around and around and *around*.

Around and around and *around* the block—for *hours*.

"Mom, we were supposed to pick Mark up at three o'clock. It's after four now. We're late."

"Shut *up*."

"Mom, it's getting dark—"

*"Shuuuutttttt upppppppppp."* Mom's voice has gone from devil-possessed Linda Blair to something out of *Poltergeist*—maybe even the man-eating dead tree from *Poltergeist*, the one that ate the little suburban boy like an Italian hoagie sandwich.

Carpooling to my older brother's school with Mom every afternoon is like living inside my very own horror movie. Some kids my age would probably think that's cool. But I don't.

Mom is in her frayed aqua-green quilted polyester bathrobe, the same one she's been wearing around the house almost every day since I was a toddler. It's frayed and stained and old, and it stinks.

My mom stinks.

Mom hasn't bathed in a while. Her greasy, stringy hair hangs half-in, half-out of pink plastic curlers that haven't left her head in at least a week. The back of the quilted aqua robe has big red-brown stains from her unchecked menstrual blood. She's muttering to herself in a language that only she understands. She's muttering and laughing and crying all at the same time. And she's shaking like a cement mixer.

"Mom, can we *stop* going around the block, please?"

"*Quiet,*" she hisses, devil-possessed. "*I have to find them.*"

"Who?"

"I have to find the people I ran over. Have to, have to, *have to.*"

"You didn't run over anybody, Mom."

I'm only five-going-on-six, but I know that no matter how many times I tell Mom she hasn't killed anyone with her rusted-out Chevy Vega, she will never believe me. She will go around and around and around the same city block searching in vain for the dead bodies she absolutely, positively believes that she and the Vega have left in their wake. Mom believes there are dead bodies everywhere. Mom believes in finding dead bodies by the side of the road the same way that some people believe in God.

I settle in for the long haul. I figure it will be at least another hour before Mom is satisfied that all the random pedestrians and dog-walkers and little-old-ladies-hosing-down-their-driveways that she believes she has killed with her Vega have all safely gone up to heaven. If Mom decides that the bodies have gone up to heaven, then we are safe. If she decides the bodies have been raptured up to heaven without a trace, it means Mom won't be captured and prosecuted for their deaths. But I know that Mom is nowhere near the *dead-bodies-gone-up-to-heaven* stage yet. She's still stuck in the *where-the-hell-are-all-the-dead-rotting-bodies-I-murdered-with-the-car* stage, and she likely will be for hours to come.

I also know that by the time we get to my brother's school, he will have already found a ride home with someone else. The dirty asphalt playground will be empty, and we'll just go back home in the rattling, rusty Vega so my father can scream at my mother when we get there for being filthy and crazy and not cooking him his goddamned dinner.

Just another *nutjob* day in the *nutjob* neighborhood.

I unhook my seat belt and climb into the Vega's bumpy, peeling-upholstery hatchback. There's a fifty-pound bag of rock salt back there, the thick, chunky kind meant for dumping in water softeners. Mom and I went to the hardware store together a couple months ago to pick it up, back when she was still lucid enough to run errands during the few hours between me getting out of morning kindergarten at eleven-thirty and my brother getting out of first grade at three. The rock salt never made it into our water softener, though. Mom's latest meltdown stopped it mid-errand.

I reach inside the fifty-pound bag, grab a handful of the Morton White Crystal and put it into my mouth. It tastes good, like a pretzel. I lie down on the fifty-pound bag and close my eyes, relish the knobby feeling of the rock salt rubbing into my back through its torn plastic packaging. Olivia Newton-John comes on the radio, singing "I Honestly Love You." Olivia almost lulls me to sleep.

Almost.

Mom's shaking like a cement mixer on cocaine now, and she's taking the Vega along for the ride. The Vega bumps and zigzags along the suburban Evansville, Indiana, side streets—jumping curbs, stopping short when Mom stalls out the engine, nearly getting into a head-on collision with a Gremlin when Mom turns the wrong way down a one-way street. I get thrown against the side panel of the hatchback and almost choke on my mouthful of rock salt. Mom's entire body is vibrating like a lawnmower in the driver's seat, her trembling hands barely able to hang onto the cracked plastic steering wheel.

"I just ran over someone, Anna. I *killed* someone. I'm a *murderer*."

"No you didn't," I say, and climb back down to the back seat. I buckle myself in. "You didn't kill anybody, Mom. That was just the curb. You ran over the *curb*. Can we go home now?"

"Okay," Mom says, wild-eyed. But we don't. We drive around and around and around the block for another hour until Mom finally decides all the dead bodies have been raptured up to Jesus.

And then we go home.

"Well?" I ask an unusually subdued Dr. Chatterjee. "What do you think?"

Dr. Chatterjee takes his glasses off and polishes them on the hem of his Nehru jacket. "What do I think about what?"

"The earliest memory I have of my mom is all about how she was a total nutjob. That's what you wanted to hear, right?"

"Are you telling me the truth, Anna, or are you just telling me what you think I want to hear?"

I suck on my thumb, which has started bleeding. "I thought you wanted to hear the truth."

Dr. Chatterjee looks bored. "So your earliest memory of your mother is of her mental illness."

"Yeah."

"Are you ashamed of your mother?"

I shrug.

"Was your mother ill for most of your childhood?"

"Yeah. She's still sick now."

"I see. How do you feel about that?"

I wipe the blood from my thumb on my jeans. "I dunno."

"Surely you must have some opinion of your mother's illness, Anna."

"Not really."

Dr. Chatterjee is surprised. "Why not?"

"My mom has been sick for basically my entire life," I say. "It gets to a point where you don't have an opinion about things like that anymore."

"Is that so? Why?"

I roll my eyes. I don't understand why, with all his advanced degrees and training, Dr. Chatterjee just doesn't get it. "Because it's pointless to think about something that's never going to change."

"Why do you think your mother will never change?"

I roll my eyes again. This guy is really dense—no wonder his sessions are free. "Because she won't. She's always been this way, and she always will be. There's not really anything I can do about it."

"Why not?"

I stamp my foot. "Because! Because she's hopeless. My mom is hopeless. And so am I. Honestly, I don't know why you think you can help me."

Dr. Chatterjee frowns. "I see. What makes you say that *you're* hopeless?"

Now I'm furious. This is really too much. "Look buddy. Everybody in my family is a fucking nutjob. My mom is a nutjob. My brother is a nutjob. My dad is a nutjob. So it goes without saying that *I'm* a nutjob. You of all people should know that by now. But my mom and my dad and my brother aren't the ones who are in here talking to you. *I* am. What do you think I'm doing spending three afternoons a week in your office? You're supposed to be *helping* me get back together with Dieter, and all you're doing is asking me how I feel about having nutjobs for a family. What a crock of shit."

Dr. Chatterjee is noticeably irritated. "Why do you think talking about your family mental illness issues won't help you deal with your abusive relationship with this Dieter person?"

My palm slaps my forehead with a sweaty *whack*. I can't believe what I'm hearing. "My relationship with Dieter is *not* abusive. We're just having some problems, is all—"

Dr. Chatterjee shakes his head. "Look Anna, I'm going to level with you. You have a personality disorder. You're what we call *borderline*. You actively seek out destructive relationships with people, and then don't understand why you feel miserable all the time. You're so scared of being alone and abandoned that you trap yourself in one bad relationship after another. Then you act out in rage whenever someone reaches out to you or tries to help. All classic symptoms of the borderline personality."

I scoff. "Okay. So I'm a nutjob, just like my mom—"

Dr. Chatterjee holds up his hands. "No, *not* just like your mum. It seems to me your mother had advanced obsessive-compulsive disorder, among other things. This is quite different."

I grab my purse and get up to leave. "All right. So now that we both know what's wrong with me, can I go now? And by the way, fuck you."

Dr. Chatterjee finally loses his patience. "Anna, sit down."

"No."

"*Sit down*. We still have fifteen minutes left in today's session. If you choose to leave now, you will not be permitted back into the free-therapy program."

"Fine." I sit, but leave my jacket on and clutch my purse tightly in my lap, just in case I need to make a quick getaway.

"Now Anna, you told me a bit about your mother's illness at the beginning of session. But it seems to me there's a lot more you haven't told me. And you haven't talked much about how your mother's illness affected you. Why don't you spend the rest of today's session talking about that?"

"Okay, sure, whatever." And even though I think it's pointless, I start to talk.

By the time I'm in the third grade and my brother Mark is in the fourth, we are both known throughout the local public school system as "the kids with the crazy mom."

My mother is insane. Very, very publicly insane. She comes to pick my brother and me up at school wearing dirty, stinking clothes that are on backward and upside down. She has psychotic episodes at the neighborhood pool and uncontrolled raging-screaming-crying fits at PTA meetings. She hears voices talking to her when she's at the mall—sometimes she even answers back. She cries all the time. She stays in bed for days, sometimes weeks at a time without even getting up to take a bath. She drives around the block looking for dead bodies. She screams in the supermarket. She hasn't washed a dish in almost a year, and the house smells of curdling milk glasses and rotting kitchen-sink food that never seems to make it down the garbage disposal.

Mom takes pills. Lots and lots of pills. She has a psychiatrist who gives her as many pills as she wants, and the pills just make her crazier. Mom's favorite book is the *Physicians' Desk Reference*. She pages through it almost every day, looking for attractive bargains. Mom lusts over the pages of her *Physicians' Desk Reference* the same way other suburban moms daydream over the polyester suits and designer bedroom sets in the JC Penney Big Book Catalog. The bathroom counter is littered with dozens of amber prescription bottles. Her purse rattles with them too. She's a walking pharmacy.

My mother is insane. Everyone knows it. Even my brother and I know it. But nobody seems to know what to do about it. Least of all my father.

My father is a chemical engineer who works for a government defense contractor. He has a Level Four federal security clearance and is not allowed to talk to anyone about what he does for a living. I think his job has something to do with making nuclear warheads. I've overheard him use the words "plutonium" and "tritium" in late-night telephone conversations. U.S. Marines with M-16 machine guns guard the entrance to the chemical plant where he works.

My father likes everything in his life to be precise—neat, clean, sterile, and perfect, like weapons-grade plutonium. And if her high-school yearbook pictures are to be believed, Mom *used* to be neat, clean, precise, and perfect. My mother's high-school yearbook, which I find in her room and read when I know she's too drugged to care, is bookmarked to a shot of her standing next to my father—he in a white tuxedo, she in a yellow prom dress and matching long evening gloves, her makeup 1968-gaudy-perfect with electric-blue eyeshadow and fake lashes, her hair a shellacked beehive that glistens like the sun. The glossy photograph in the dog-eared, mothball-smelling yearbook shows what my parents were like before insanity killed them both and turned them into the walking, talking corpses my brother and I have learned to hate. At eighteen, my mother was neat, clean, precise perfection. At thirty-three, my mother is anything but. And my father hates her for it too.

Mom is a contradiction in terms. She pathologically fears germs, but she lives in filth. She shakes uncontrollably even when she's fast asleep. She fawns and fusses over the cat for hours, then forgets to feed her own children. She laughs hysterically at *Sophie's Choice* when it plays on HBO but sobs through Carol Burnett reruns. She seems to have problems remembering how to stay alive.

Dad is pissed off most of the time now. The only words he speaks to Mark and me nowadays are *shut up, goddamn it*; *stop it, shitforbrains*; and *settle down, both of youse before I talk a strap to the both of youse*. He's stopped talking to my mother entirely. These days, Dad mostly has conversations with the blue-and-teal-striped pattern on the dining-room wallpaper. Every night, when he's sitting alone in the dark dining room eating a dinner of Welch's grape jelly on Wonder Bread, he asks the wallpaper questions. He asks the wallpaper what he ever did to deserve a lunatic wife who hasn't cooked him a goddamned decent dinner in at least two years. He asks the wallpaper why the hell is it he can't just have a normal wife who doesn't drive around the block looking for dead bodies like a military ambulance driver in a world war, who doesn't spend entire days scrubbing her hands raw with Brillo pads and Lysol. He asks the wallpaper why he's the father of two spoiled selfish brats who are both bound to grow up as crazy as their mother.

The wallpaper doesn't answer.

One night, I decide to answer on behalf of the wallpaper. When Dad asks the blue-and-teal vertical stripes where his goddamned dinner is for the fifth time this week, I answer, "It's on your plate, Dad." Dad stares down at his plate of soggy jelly bread for a minute, then picks up his copy of *Perry's Chemical Engineering Manual*, which weighs at least eight pounds, and whacks it upside my head.

"Shut up, goddamn it Anna." Dad whacks me again—this time on the other temple, so I'll have a matching set of bruises. I'll wear my hair feathered over them tomorrow so my teacher won't call Child Protective Services.

Dad's starting to lose it too, and no wonder. Insanity is contagious, after all. It spreads like kudzu, then consumes flesh and bone like the Ebola virus. Dad's already half wasted away. He's grasping at straws. When Dad's not at work or yelling at the wallpaper, he spends a lot of time on the phone with Mom's psychiatrist, Dr. Nickelback.[5]

Dr. Nickelback's guiding psychiatric philosophy is drugs, drugs, and yet more drugs. He passes out pills like cotton candy at the carnival, and my mother inhales the treats he offers her like a four-year-old on a sugar binge. Whenever Mom gets too weird, too sad, too loud, or too dirty for Dad to handle, he calls Dr. Nickelback and asks him to give Mom some more drugs. And Dr. Nickelback is always happy to oblige.

I've never actually *seen* Dr. Nickelback. But even at age eight, I feel like I've known him my whole life. He's as much of a fixture in our house as our burned-out console television. He's an invisible force that's always there, projecting grainy, full-color images of what kind of happy, healthy, well-balanced family we are really supposed to be. But like the families on television that are just a little too perfect to be real, we never quite match the family image Dr. Nickelback and his drugs tell us is possible. No matter how hard we try, the best we can do at our house is a snowy picture that flips every few seconds, and even that's only with a lot of extra aluminum foil on our antennas.

Dr. Nickelback is so good at pushing all manner of controlled substances on suburban Indiana housewives, he makes the worst Dr. Feelgoods of Beverly Hills look like 1950s soda jerks. He can effectively blow out the brains of a thirty-something woman without the blood or mess of a .38. He's elevated the act of prescribing tranquilizers and sleeping pills to a tactical arms sale, and my father—top-secret designer of nuclear warhead components that he is—has latched onto the deal with as much gusto as a Libyan terrorist in a Soviet bargain basement. Dad signs the three-carbon insurance forms that pay Dr. Nickelback's bills as if they are seven-figure Hollywood movie contracts and a one-way ticket to a better life, not to mention a better wife with a notarized certificate of permanent sanity.

Mom gets refills on her dozen or so psychotropic drug prescriptions at least once a week. We visit the pharmacy more often than we buy groceries or fill up on gas. I've got a huge supply of cheap plastic toys that I've convinced my mother to buy for me in the small convenience store near Dr. Nickelback's office. She's always easy to convince when she's waiting around for her pills—strung-out pill addicts are the easiest overpriced-toy sell ever created. Dr. Nickelback's preferred pharmacy even has a home delivery service for when Mom is too out of it to move, let alone drive the fifteen minutes to his office. She's been using the delivery service a lot this week. But this week, it seems that no matter how many drugs Dr. Nickelback has delivered to our house in their little stapled white paper bags, Mom just isn't going to "snap out of it" this time.

Dr. Nickelback calls Dad tonight, interrupting his jelly-and-bread dinner to inform him that Mom has to go to the hospital.

Mom will be locked up and pumped full of more drugs, lots of them, especially the heavy, intravenous kind that are only available behind the locked, heavy steel-reinforced doors of the booby hatch. All the drugs will be administered with huge hypodermic needles before, during, and after electroshock treatments, just like I've seen in the movies.

Mom is going to the booby hatch. I'm jealous of Mom for getting to spend time in the hospital pumped full of drugs and wrapped in a nice, comfortable straightjacket. To me, going to the hospital to be pumped full of drugs—preferably with a slim plastic tube slipped elegantly just under the nose for extra oxygen—is glamorous and exciting. I wish it was me going and not Mom. I guess I've watched too many episodes of *General Hospital* with her after school. All the patients on *General Hospital* are crazy *and* beautiful, after all, and the longer they stay in the hospital, the more beautiful they get. By all logic, this means that by the time Mom comes home from the psych ward, she'll be Miss America.

In my jealousy of Mom's soap-opera-glamorous predicament, I secretly hope Dr. Nickelback gives my mother a lobotomy as soon as she arrives at the hospital. That way, she'll forever have those two little ugly red scars on her forehead, just like Jack Nicholson does at the end of *One Flew Over the Cuckoo's Nest*. That would suit me just fine.

Dr. Chatterjee stops me mid-sentence. "Pardon me, Anna. Say that again."

"Say what again?"

"What you just said. *What* would suit you just fine?"

I chuckle. "Are you hard of hearing?"

Dr. Chatterjee clicks his pen a few times. "No. I just want to make sure I heard you correctly."

"I said, I wish my mom would have had a lobotomy, like Jack Nicholson did in *One Flew Over the Cuckoo's Nest*."

Dr. Chatterjee tosses his pen and paper aside, disgusted. "Why would you say such a horrible thing about your mother?"

"I thought you psychiatrist types *liked* giving people lobotomies."

Dr. Chatterjee looks ready to puke. "Anna, frontal lobotomies were a barbaric, inhuman practice that destroyed people's brains and turned them into vegetables. They haven't been used to treat people for more than thirty years."

"Yeah, well, I would have been a helluva lot better off if my mom had just been a vegetable instead of a drugged-up nutjob."

"What makes you say that?"

"You tell me. You're the shrink." I glance at the wall clock and notice with glee that we're out of time.

I'm back in the cramped, dusty waiting room of Dr. Chatterjee's office at the university medical school for my next session two days later. He's keeping me waiting today, probably in revenge for what an obstinate bitch I was in our last session. Fifteen minutes go by, then thirty. I count the leaves on the office philodendron over and over until my eyes cross. I glance at my watch and see that my lunch hour is more than half-over; my boss over at the library will surely start asking questions if I'm gone much longer. The scheduled hour of our session is nearly over when Dr. Chatterjee's square brown head finally appears around the flimsy office partition.

"So sorry to keep you waiting, Anna. I'm so glad you're still here." (Dr. Chatterjee's Cockney lilt does nothing to hide the fact that he's lying.) "We had a bit of a tricky situation with one of my test patients on the locked ward today, and it held me up a bit."

"Whatever. I have to go now anyway, or I'll get into trouble with my boss." I get up to leave.

Dr. Chatterjee stops me. "You work for the university, right? I can call your boss and explain that you'll be a little late. I've done that for many of my other patients who are university employees."

"No way. I don't want him knowing I'm a nutjob in a crummy free-therapy program."

"I have no intention of breaching your confidentiality, Anna. I have a ready-made canned rubbish story I use for my patients at times like this."

I wave my hand at him. "Whatever."

I have to work hard to keep from laughing when Dr. Chatterjee calls my boss over at the library and tells him that I passed out at the campus free clinic after I got a flu shot on my lunch break and will need at least an hour to recover before returning to work.

"You're a good liar," I say.

"I've had a lot of practice." Dr. Chatterjee picks up his notebook and pen, flips back a few pages until he finds the sheet of notes he took at our last session. "As I recall, at the end of our last session, you and I had a little disagreement about lobotomies."

"Yeah. So?"

"I seem to recall you saying that your mother would have been better off if she'd been lobotomized. Why would you say rubbish like that?"

"Because it's true."

Dr. Chatterjee flips his notebook shut. "Really? Because I don't believe you."

"Whatever." I silently wish that I really were in the free clinic recovering from a fainting spell. My session with this annoying British quack is going nowhere.

"You know Anna, I might believe you if you persuade me otherwise. Why don't you spend some time trying to convince me?"

That appeals to me a little. I chew my lip for a minute or two, mulling it over. "All right. Here goes."

I am ten years old. My parents are divorced now. I live with my mother and brother in a roach- and rat-infested welfare apartment on the bad side of town. My mother is strung out on drugs.

Not crack, or cocaine, or heroin, or LSD, or even pot. Mom is strung out on various tranquilizers and benzodiazepenes, very legal, but also very potent, psychiatric drugs. Her doctors give them to her. They write the prescriptions. They hand her "free samples" under the table when the Medicaid drug benefits for the month have run out. The Medicaid shrinks have picked up right where Dr. Nickelback left off. The Medicaid shrinks are Mom's dealers, and they charge by the pill.

My mother—a white, formerly middle-class, formerly competent suburban housewife, a formerly prim, proper, and precise *non-crazy* spouse of a successful engineer with a Level Four federal security clearance—is a pill-popping nutjob. But Mom's not a *drug addict*. No way. Mom has a prescription for every pill she takes, so that makes it okay, they say. It's okay that she hasn't gotten out of bed in four weeks. It's okay that her bedroom floor is littered with dozens of pill bottles, food-encrusted dirty plates, and filthy underwear. It's okay that she speaks in unintelligible, slurred gibberish and forgets her own children's names. It's okay that there aren't any groceries in the house, it's okay that my brother and I run wild while our mother rots under a prescription drug haze. It's all okay because my mother is only doing what the good doctors tell her to do. *Take the pills, and rest. Rest, and take the pills. Draw the blinds, stay in bed, ignore your children, don't bathe, and take twenty or thirty different pills a day, and you will feel better*, say the psychiatrists from three separate free clinics that don't communicate with each other. *Rest and heavy meds are the way to beat severe depression with psychotic features*, they all say. They are doctors—they are MDs. They know what they're talking about. They're following clinical guidelines. They don't know that Mom is seeing three different doctors at once, all of whom have her on conflicting medication regimens simultaneously. She fills little plastic trays with seven compartments each—one for each day of the week—with all the pills she's been prescribed and in the correct amounts. This pill with water, that one with milk, this one with bread, that one with a small meal that I cook for her from our ever-dwindling supply of nonperishables.

But Mom doesn't feel better, so she figures she must need more drugs. She asks the doctors for more drugs, and they give them to her, they tell her how much more to take, they promise that the increased dosage will work wonders for her illness, will lift all the dark clouds and hallucinations and obsessions until she feels fresh and happy as a daisy. The psychiatrists make promises, promises.

But Mom never, ever gets better. She just gets worse.

I am ten years old. My brother is eleven. Our father is gone, and our mother is basically comatose. We are out of control, both of us. We are "problem children," we are "at-risk," we are "delinquent." And nobody cares. Teachers send concerned letters home that Mom never reads. My brother and I do all manner of "cry for help" behaviors—getting into fights, staying out all night, compulsively lying, running away from home for a day or two just to see if anyone will notice—and nobody cares. We are the unwanted, ignored children of a drug addict, lost in space because we don't have another hit of pills on us.

My brother Mark is failing all his subjects in school. He gets into fights. Thanks to his long, lanky figure, his Coke-bottle glasses, his dirty, thrift-store clothes, and his tendency to hallucinate and mutter unintelligible nonsense in class, the playground bullies eat him alive. So do the teachers, who can't seem to handle an eleven-year-old boy who sees green men coming out of the coat closet and spiders covering the blackboard and who hears little devil voices in his ears. My brother freaks out in class like a hippie on a bad acid trip, but the only drug tripping him out is the excess of serotonin in his brain. The playground bullies hit Mark at recess, and sometimes he even hits back—but when he does, the people he hits aren't the ones who beat him up in the first place. They're shy, fragile girls, or hefty lunch ladies, sometimes even teachers. He hits, pulls hair, bites, kicks. Mark is full of something the principal calls "misplaced aggression."

Our elementary school doesn't employ a school psychologist, and the underpaid, half-time school nurse doesn't know what to make of a mentally ill eleven-year-old boy, other than to call him a "troublemaker." The principal requires he be sent back a grade, so now he's in the same class as me, hallucinating so many spiders that my English lesson on *My Side of the Mountain* turns into something out of Stephen King. Our fed-up teacher wants Mark placed in an institution, but of course there's no money for that—and Mom's too strung out to sign off on the consent forms, anyway. So he comes home from school each day covered in bruises, then goes to his room, where he mostly spends his time punching holes in the plaster and then eating the resulting chunks. When he's not eating plaster, Mark subsists on a diet of Frito-Lay Canned Cheese Dip, Domino's pizza, New Coke, and Tostitos. He's as hyperactive as a Rhesus monkey in glucose shock. He doesn't sleep, and he doesn't bathe much either. His room smells like a zoo cage. His bedsheets are encrusted with dried semen. He's starting to hang around some weird teenage boys from down the street who are into Dungeons & Dragons, petty theft, and dogfighting.

Mark needs a Strong Male Role Model. But the closest thing in our vermin-infested welfare apartment to a Strong Male Role Model is the picture of Chef Boyardee on our nightly cans of Ravioli-Os.

On the very few days that Mom isn't lying comatose in her bedroom, she runs about the house in a mad frenzy, as if powered by invisible jet engines. She talks at light speed, she can't sit still, she stays up all night for three or four days at a time, sometimes even forces Mark and me to stay up with her. These manic episodes happen every couple of months and are always followed by yet another increase in Mom's massive medication dosage.

Whenever Mom has a manic episode, she engages in mad bouts of "cleaning." But what Mom calls "cleaning" is more along the lines of industrial-grade waste disposal.

I come home from school one day to find our toothless neighbor and her two kids collecting my belongings from the Dumpster behind our apartment building and carrying them up the fire escape.

"What are you *doing*?" I scream at the girl, Angie, who carries my lilac Formica kiddie-nightstand in one hand and my stamp collection in the other. "That stuff's *mine*!"

"Your mama done throwed all this out," Angie's mom calls down to me from the fire escape. She in turn has my battered Sony boom box in one hand and a stack of my favorite cassette tapes in the other. "So we're a-takin' it."

"Yeah!" Angie's little brother Rodney shouts at me as he plucks my prized Care Bear and my pink electronic keyboard from the Dumpster and dashes up the fire escape. "We're a-takin' it!"

I glance inside the Dumpster and find it full of stuff from our apartment—dishes, clothes, books, most of my toys and games, even a good chunk of our furniture. By the looks of it, there can't be much left upstairs besides our kitchen table, beds, couch, and television.

I stomp up the stairs to our apartment. I find Mom in the hallway standing beside a mountain of overstuffed garbage bags. "What the hell is going on, Mom?" I yell. "Why are you throwing out all our stuff?"

Mom folds her arms and looks down her nose at me. "We *had* to throw it out, honey. It was *dirty*. It was all *dirty*, and we can't have anything *dirty* in the house, or we might get sick and *die*."

I gasp. If Mom thinks our entire house is contaminated and poisonous today, at the rate she's going, sooner or later Mark and I are going to find ourselves inside a Dumpster because she thinks *we* are contaminated and poisonous.

"Mom, that stuff isn't *dirty*," I hiss. "It's just *stuff*. And most of it is *my* stuff! You gave away everything! The neighbors are *stealing* it from the Dumpster! How *could* you?"

Now I'm screaming, and my mother is crying hard enough for her tears to land on the pile of garbage bags with audible plastic *tinks*. "Why do you have to embarrass me all the time?" I shriek. "Why do you have to *ruin* everything?"

I stomp off to my room, which by now is devoid of almost all my belongings save for my bed, an ancient record player dating from the 1960s, and a few meager outfits of clothing. My toys, stuffed animals, records, tapes, boom box, and most of my books are pretty much gone except for a badly scratched Madonna album and a couple of overdue library books. The unkindest cut of all was watching Angie carry my prized stamp collection—which had taken me years to compile—up the fire escape to her own room. The knowledge that she'll get to enjoy the exotic stamps I've collected via mail-order from around the world since I was in first grade is the final straw.

I decide to go across the hall and demand my things back. Then I'll go down to the Dumpster and take back whatever hasn't already been ruined by sticky garbage residue. I'm not sure how I'll carry the furniture up by myself, but I figure I can call my Memaw and Papaw Jones across town for help if I need it.

I trudge past my mother, who is still bawling over the garbage bags in the hallway. I know that those bags are probably full of my stuff too, but I can deal with that later. Getting my stamp collection and boom box and Care Bear back from the neighbors is my first priority.

Mom will have none of it, however.

That is, *the voices* will have none of it. *The voices* have taken over my mother's mind and body, making her fearful and irrational and strange—and they've also given her tiny five-foot frame superhuman strength. Just as I reach the back door so I can cross the hallway to the other apartment, Mom tackles me before I can get a hand on the doorknob. At ten years old I'm already almost as big as she is, but that doesn't stop her. Mom drags me to my room by the wrists and throws me like a boomerang onto my stripped bed. Her eyes take on the yellowish tinge of a predatory animal. Her voice drops from its usual timid soprano to a rough, masculine growl.

"YOU. WILL. NOT. TAKE. THOSE. THINGS. BAAAAAAAACK!" the green-eyed monster who moments ago was my thirty-five-year-old mother howls as she stands over me, her hands bent into raptor-claws and her pointy canines dripping saliva. "THOSE. THINGS. ARE. DIRRRTYYYY. *They will kill you.*" The primal rage in my mother's eyes is terrifying. At that moment, I know that if I dare disobey her and retrieve our discarded belongings now, the voices in my mother's head will take hold of her hands and use them to kill me.

Mom lets out a bloodcurdling shriek, then slams my bedroom door shut and locks it from the outside. I hear her drag a heavy piece of furniture—my brother's bunk bed—in front of the door, lest I somehow manage to jiggle the rusty old lock. I am trapped inside my bare room until well past midnight.

"There," I say. "Do you believe me now?"

Dr. Chatterjee blinks, then rubs his eyes. I notice dried sleep crust in the corners. He must have been up all night with one of his psych-ward patients. "What do you mean?"

I wonder if he's been listening to me at all. "If you'd grown up with a mom like mine, wouldn't *you* have wanted her lobotomized? Hell, you could have probably even done the job yourself. I'm sure they still teach how to do that in med school, even if nobody does them anymore."

Dr. Chatterjee rubs his chin carefully, and frowns. He seems to be having a lot of trouble with this. "Anna, I can certainly believe that growing up with a mother as severely ill as yours was as awful as you say. But no matter how sick your mum might have been, it still wouldn't justify ripping out her frontal lobe with an ice pick. The scary thing is, if you'd been born just fifteen years earlier than you were, your mum might indeed have been lobotomized. And if you think you were bad off under your mum's care while she was ill, it would have been twenty times worse for you had she been lobotomized. She'd have been institutionalized for life, and then you would have had no one to care for you at all."

"I would have been even better off if I'd just never been born."

Dr. Chatterjee winces. "Now Anna, that kind of talk isn't going to help you."

"These sessions aren't helping me anyway. I'll never get back together with Dieter at this rate. What's the point?"

"You keep coming back to this Dieter issue again and again, Anna. And frankly, I don't understand why you'd want to rekindle a romantic relationship with a man who treats you like you're less than nothing."

I immediately go on the defensive. "He *doesn't* treat me like less than nothing! Until we started having problems, Dieter treated me like a queen."

Dr. Chatterjee sighs. "Perhaps. But he hasn't treated you like a queen for a very long time. Surely you can acknowledge that much."

I don't say anything. I just study the blue-gray pattern in the carpet until it runs together and melts under my tear-filled gaze.

"Anna, this friend you call Dieter is just a typical sexual predator. A narcissist too. He swept you off your feet with expensive trips, lavish romance, and so on. He fed you a bunch of grandiose lies about being madly in love with you on the very day you met him, promised to marry you within a week. You had a week or two of wild sex, and when Dieter got bored with that, he discarded you. And now he's using you for free proofreading services. I say, the man certainly has a talent for using people. And I'm sure you're not the first woman he's done this way, nor will you be the last. But that doesn't mean you have to keep allowing this man to toy with you sight-unseen from the other side of the Atlantic. Does it?"

I don't answer. I chew my lip until it bleeds.

"Anna, I think you and I need to agree that you are not really here to learn how to mend your relationship with Dieter. You're here to learn how to mend yourself, and the first step in doing that is for you to cut off all ties with this man immediately."

"No way." I get up to leave. "I won't do that. You can't make me."

"You're in a bloody rut, do you not realize that, Anna?"

"No."

Our time is up.

On a whim, I decide after that day's session to try taking Dr. Chatterjee's advice, just to see what happens. I go to read my e-mail and find a message from Dieter.

> Hi Anna—attached is document with latest version of my thesis. I have been wrking like an idiot and I fnly have draft done now. Hope you can edit this for me. I need it edited/back to me by Friday, that gives you three days. Thx.

I feel my stomach churn as I read Dieter's latest attempt to get me to do his bidding. Maybe Dr. Chatterjee is right. Maybe I *should* cut off all ties with this man. It's worth a try, I suppose. On the one hand, I'm terrified of what Dieter might do to me if I do try it. But on the other hand, what could really happen? He's almost five thousand miles away and too busy with his high-paying consulting job and his doctoral thesis to fly back to Chicago just to hurt me, right? Of course.

I dash off the following e-mail, hold my breath, and hit SEND.

> Dieter, I have decided that I will not edit this stuff for you any more. Please DO NOT contact me any more. It's over. Good bye.

I shut down my computer and go to bed, where I toss and turn all night, scared to death of what might await me the next time I check my e-mail. I finally get to sleep around three, but I'm awakened an hour or so later by the phone. I answer it, groggy and fearful.

"H-Hello?"

Dieter's heavy-accented Austrian growl is on the line. "You fuckingk bitch."

"Wh-wha?"

"You fuckingk bitch. How *dare* you cudt me off afdter all zat I have done for you? You agreedt to edidt my thesis as repaymendt for ze Vienna trip, the San Francisco trip, all ze expensive dinners and thingks zat I boughdt for you—"

I gasp. "I did no such thing! You told me it was just a favor! You said *you* would pay *me*!"

Dieter sputters a string of unintelligible German that I assume are swear words. "You LIE! You vill finish ze edidt, or you vill pay." He hangs up.

I try to go back to sleep, with no luck. I finally drag myself out of bed around five a.m. and log onto my computer, only to find about fifty raging e-mails in my inbox, all from Dieter. I read the first one only, and delete the rest.

> You fucking childish bitch . . . you will complete the tasks I gave you or I will come to US and sue you little bitch . . . I will sue you for many thousands dollars US, and you will lose. Do the job, or PAY.

I don't know what to do. The logical side of me knows that legally, Dieter has no leg to stand on.

On the other hand, I'm afraid of him. I know he is smart; I know he is a powerful, highly paid international businessman with lots of connections all over the world, connections he could use to extort money from me, even to physically harm me if he really wanted to. I know that even though doing so would be crazy and wrong and totally illegal, Dieter could indeed use his whim and will to force me to repay him every cent he spent wooing and manipulating me into his beaten-down mind slave. But even considering all that, there's something I'm even more afraid of.

I'm most afraid of losing Dieter forever.

I skip my next several sessions with Dr. Chatterjee. As far as I'm concerned, this whole situation is his fault. After all, it was Dr. Chatterjee who told me to cut all ties with Dieter Franzl, the supplier-in-absentia of the love-drug that I need to fill the gaping black hole in my brain. And as far as I can tell, it's Dr. Chatterjee's fault that Dieter Franzl is leaving me twenty raging voicemails and fifty obscenity-laden e-mails a day, all demanding thousands of dollars in "restitution" if I fail to edit his doctoral thesis as I promised to do. It's Dr. Chatterjee's fault that I'm getting intimidating FedExs sent postage-due from Austria, all demanding that I send immediate payment in cash or a certified international money order or face an immediate international lawsuit filed by a former lover I'm having a harder and harder time admitting was never really a lover at all.

After a week of constant phone and e-mail harassment from Dieter, I give in. I empty out my savings account—all three hundred pathetic dollars of it—and turn it into a certified international money order. I send it registered airmail to Dieter's apartment in Vienna, along with a five-page, rambling note telling him that although it's three hundred dollars more than he deserves, and thousands of dollars less than he actually spent on me during our whirlwind relationship, it's all he's ever going to get. I tell him he is an asshole and a creep. I tell him I never, ever want to hear from him again—which, of course, is a lie. Even after all he's done to me, if Dieter were to call me up tomorrow morning and tell me he's sorry for everything, that he's changed his mind and wants me to move to Vienna right away so we can get married, I'd still do it in a heartbeat.

I'm a masochist, sure. That goes without saying. But Dieter Franzl has the only ready supply of the love-drug I need to fill up my brain just so I can survive.

I'm a love-junkie, and junkies will do anything they have to do to get their next hit. We often don't know why we torture ourselves, just that we need to numb some deep, nameless pain that comes from inside a part of ourselves we don't want to acknowledge exists. Whatever our drug of choice is—booze, heroin, sex, or psycho rich ex-boyfriends who toy with us and give us a sick and twisted thrill—it helps keep our nasty, painful parts at bay. We fear that if we ever let those polluted, scary, deformed parts of our psyches out into the open, they'll destroy us. So we just let our addictions destroy us instead. It's less messy that way. Or so we think.

It makes no sense, of course. But nothing in my mind does at the time.

I suppose that if I can't get any more love-drug on mail-order from Vienna, I can always go looking for it somewhere else.

So I do.

I'm back in Dr. Chatterjee's office three weeks later. After skipping eight sessions with no explanation, I have to literally beg him to take me back into therapy. He finally gives in, but only at a price.

"Anna, you need to be forthright with me about what you've been up to the past couple of weeks," he says, his voice harsh with disapproval. "Although I can probably well imagine."

I'm too mortified to answer him. I just rub my sweaty palms up and down on my jeans, up and down, up and down, until I leave a dark trail on each thigh.

"Anna, remember our agreement. Either you show up to these sessions as scheduled and participate, or we terminate therapy. Those are the rules. Are you going to abide by them or not? If not, I'll have to ask you to leave."

I take a deep breath in and out. "I umm—well, I followed your advice, Dr. Chatterjee, and tried to cut off all contact with Dieter."

Dr. Chatterjee smiles and rubs his palms together. "Good! That's excellent! Excellent progress! When did this happen?"

"The day after our last session," I mumble, blinking back tears.

"Ah. I take it things did not go well?"

"Uh, nope," I scoff. "No thanks to you."

Dr. Chatterjee doesn't seem surprised. "I see. Dieter did not take well to you cutting him off, did he?"

"No. He went ballistic. He harassed me. He made me pay him *money* to leave me alone. I sent him three hundred bucks. He wanted more, but that's all I had."

Dr. Chatterjee strokes his chin. "He extorted money from you, eh?"

"Yeah."

Dr. Chatterjee pulls my file from his desk and flips through it. "I expected he'd try something like that. Dieter's reaction is typical narcissistic behavior. But based on what your intake form says that you earn working at the university, it doesn't seem to me you can much afford to pay extortion to anyone. Why would you agree to do such a thing?"

I don't answer.

"Did you think paying Dieter all the money you had in the world might get him to love you again? Or at the very least, keep him from abandoning you?"

I shrug.

"Anna, you're a borderline. Which means you are naturally attracted to narcissists, and they to you. But just because you're naturally attracted to narcissists doesn't mean they're good for you, as I'm sure you've seen with how Dieter treated you. Not to mention all the other old boyfriends you've told me about in therapy. You need to recognize these patterns of behavior in yourself so you can begin to change them."

"Okay, sure, whatever." I study the pattern in the carpet again.

Dr. Chatterjee sighs heavily. "Why don't you spend some time telling me what else you've been up to for the past three weeks? Why have you been avoiding therapy?"

I bite my lip. "I've been, umm, busy."

"Busy doing what?"

"Well, you know," I stammer. "Just general stuff."

Dr. Chatterjee frowns. "I highly doubt that. I suspect you've probably been acting out in any number of self-destructive ways. Am I right?"

I shrug, again.

"Anna, if you don't start being honest with me right now, I'm terminating therapy with you. I'm preparing for my board exams and I don't have time to waste with difficult patients."

I fix my eyes on the now-familiar carpet pattern. "I ummm, I've been getting drunk and—umm, picking up a lot of guys in bars."

Dr. Chatterjee smiles slightly. Now I'm giving him something juicy to work with. "I see. How many men have you picked up?"

I think back for a moment or two, then count on my fingers. "I dunno. Eight, that I remember. Maybe nine or ten. I was really drunk for a few of them and don't remember everything."

For the first time ever, Dr. Chatterjee seems shocked. "Nine or *ten*? In three weeks?"

"Yeah. I think that's about right."

"I see. You've been having intercourse with all these men?"

"Duh!" I say, as if it should be obvious. "Sometimes I just give them blowjobs, though. It depends."

"On what?"

"I dunno. On how I feel at the time, I guess. Sometimes I'm too drunk to have sex, or I'm just not in the mood, so I give the guy a blowjob so he'll leave me alone and let me get some sleep."

Dr. Chatterjee is scribbling like mad in his notebook now. I've finally gotten his attention, and I'm enjoying the hell out of it. "So now that Dieter has abandoned you, you spend your evenings and weekends getting drunk and picking up strange men. Do you enjoy these sexual encounters?"

"Sometimes they're okay."

More scribbling. "What about when they're not okay, Anna? Tell me about those."

"You mean like, what happens with the bad ones?"

"Precisely."

I take a deep breath. "Well, sometimes they get mad at me if I won't do certain things with them."

Dr. Chatterjee leans forward, his pen stuck in midair. "What kinds of things?"

"Well, this one guy last week, he was kind of into bondage-type stuff. He had one of those S&M chambers in his condo. A whole room of whips and chains and harnesses and shit. I'm really not into that kind of thing, so I wanted to leave as soon as he started showing the stuff to me. But he wouldn't let me leave."

"Why not?"

I sigh. "Well, he said that after he'd spent all that time and money at the bar sweet-talking me and buying me drinks, he needed to get his return on investment, or something like that. So when I tried to get out of there, he grabbed me before I could get to the door, and—" My mouth feels like it's full of thorns.

"And what, Anna?"

"He umm, he tied me up in one of his S&M harness things, and, well, we ended up having sex like that."

"You mean he raped you."

I bite down on the inside of my cheeks until I taste blood. "I wouldn't call it *rape*, exactly. I wanted to have sex with him, just not that *kind* of sex."

"Then what would you call it?"

"I dunno. Rough sex, I guess. And me being stupid enough to go home with the guy. I should have known better than to do that. He was kind of funny-looking, with an eyebrow piercing and a bunch of weird tattoos—"

Dr. Chatterjee holds up his hand to stop me. "So you think it's *your* fault he raped you?"

This catches me off-guard. "Yes. I mean, no. I mean—"

"Anna, do you have *any* idea what a healthy sexual relationship is like?"

"Sure I do."

Dr. Chatterjee raises an eyebrow. "You and I both know that's not true."

I don't say anything for a long time. I just kick my sneakered feet back and forth underneath my chair and watch the second hand on Dr. Chatterjee's wall clock swoop around and around.

After several minutes, Dr. Chatterjee speaks. "Anna, perhaps I'm reaching a bit here, but I get the feeling that perhaps you grew up with very distorted notions of what healthy sexual relationships should be like. Am I right?"

I don't answer. I just keep swinging my feet and staring at the clock.

"Were you ever sexually abused, Anna?"

"What? No!"

Dr. Chatterjee sets down his pad and pen. "All right, fair enough. Maybe you weren't sexually abused yourself, but there are plenty of other things that can happen to a child sexually that while they don't involve intercourse, can be just as damaging to a child's psyche. Did anything happen in your home, or at school—did you *see* anything, or hear anything in your environment growing up that might have confused you sexually? A late-night cable movie? A porn magazine? Walking in on your parents having sex? Seeing someone masturbate in the bathroom? Anything out of the ordinary that you can remember at all? Take your time."

I relax a bit. If that's the kind of thing Dr. Chatterjee's looking for, there are at least a hundred different examples I could give. "If you put it that way, yeah."

"Go on."

"Well, for one thing, my dad's always been a sex maniac."

Dr. Chatterjee blinks at this. "I see. Why don't you tell me about that?"

Everything I ever need to know about sex I learn from watching my father.

When I am ten years old, I walk in on my father having sex with his new girlfriend Martha[6] at his new bachelor pad. I walk in on my father having sex with his new girlfriend at four o'clock in the afternoon, with their bedroom door wide open and a lot of screaming and thrusting and banging going on.

I walk into Dad's wide-open sex chamber at four in the afternoon on a Saturday because it's visitation weekend with Dad, and Mark and I haven't had anything to eat since yesterday afternoon.

Dad's been too busy having loud, sweaty sex with the door wide open for eighteen hours straight to bother with feeding his kids.

Dad and Martha don't notice I'm there for several minutes. I stand beside Dad's waterbed and watch them go at it. I can't quite get a good look at their actual equipment or how it works, because they're both too tangled up in Dad's polyester velour bedspread. As far as I can tell, sex just seems to involve a lot of rubbing and banging and screaming and "yes, yes, yes." I don't understand what the big deal is.

Martha is fat. Her breasts are huge and pendulous. Whenever Dad pounds down on her, her dimpled thighs vibrate and her breasts jiggle. I find this fascinating. Whenever Dad's hips thrust, he grunts in the same way I've heard him grunt in the bathroom when he's taking a shit. I find this disgusting.

When they're finished, I tap Dad on the shoulder. He looks up, startled. His mouth hangs open and he seems to be caught somewhere between panting and screaming.

"Yikes!" Martha screams, then wraps her jiggly, dimpled body in Dad's velour bedspread. She slaps Dad's bare behind hard enough to leave a mark. "I told you not to let your damn kids come over here!" She hurls a look at me that could fry an egg. "Little brat!"

Martha starts to cry and dashes off for the bathroom. I don't know whether to laugh or throw up.

Dad finally finds his voice. "Anna, what the hell are you doing coming in here like that?"

"You left the door open, Dad. It's not like we didn't know what you're doing. Besides, it's four o'clock and Mark and I, we're sort of hungry. There's nothing to eat in the house. Don't you ever go to the store?"

Dad and Martha never make any effort to hide what they're doing during those weekend visits, when our total actual "quality time" with

Dad often adds up to less than twenty-five minutes. It never once registers with Dad that his wild sex antics with his soon-to-be-new-wife Martha might bother Mark and me, might even have serious psychological consequences for both of us down the road.

Dad never gives these matters any thought. He never asks Mark and me if we can hear what he and Martha are doing to each other, if we know what it is, how we feel about it, whether it bothers or scares us.

Dad doesn't ask us any of these things. Dad doesn't do anything to hide what goes on in his bedroom (and on his bathroom floor, and in his den, and sometimes even on his kitchen counter) from his kids. And why would he? He doesn't care.

I'm not sure what motivates Dad to put his sex life in a wide-open fishbowl right under his kids' noses for years. And I also know for a fact that Dad knows it's wrong. But Dad feels entitled to do it anyway. After all, he married Mom early, pretty much right out of high school. He missed the whole 60s sexual revolution, and when he was at his sexual peak to boot. He never had a chance to have the kind of variety- and experimentation-filled sex life most young men enjoy until he was well into his thirties. And with Mom heavily sedated, delusional, and searching for dead bodies for almost half of their marriage, I doubt Mom and Dad had a very healthy sex life. Dad probably figures he's making up for lost time.

Mom is not the only addict in our family. Dad uses sex as a drug to survive just as much as Mom uses prescription drugs to keep from throwing herself off tall buildings.

When Mom is in lockdown on the psych ward, intubated with a half-dozen heavy meds, Dad hides behind a curtain of rampant womanizing. Never happy with just one woman, he cheats on my mother throughout their thirteen-year marriage with a series of younger women, the last of whom is Martha, who becomes his second wife. With her appetite for wild, in-the-open sex, Martha thinks she'll be the one who makes him monogamous, but she is wrong. After he and Martha have been married less than a year, Dad is on the prowl again—this time, with Martha's best friend. (The latter later becomes Dad's third wife, and she agrees to have an open marriage.) Dad makes tasteless sex jokes in public, wears a "University for the Sexually Gifted" gag T-shirt on weekends, and leaves his copies of *Jugs* out in the garage for me to find. During his second and third marriages, after Mark and I move in with him because

Mom can no longer care for us, he keeps a stash of hundreds of bootleg porno tapes in the basement, and teenaged Mark and I watch them out of curiosity. Sometimes we invite the neighborhood kids over to watch them with us, and even though they are more than willing to do so, we end up paying dearly for it in the cutthroat social game that is high school, like when a bunch of older boys ambush me in the hallway after gym class, demanding I flash them my breasts since they heard I live in the "house of porn."

Dad is a sex addict. And like a dope-fiend junkie who will die when his stash runs out, Dad will die if he doesn't have something to fuck.

Dr. Chatterjee doesn't say anything for a long time. He seems antsy, in fact.

"Well?" I ask. "What do you think?"

Dr. Chatterjee rubs his earlobe and fidgets. "That's—that's—I don't even know what to say."

I roll my eyes. "Well, that's just *great*," I seethe. "I thought you were supposed to be my therapist here."

Dr. Chatterjee sighs heavily, and fidgets some more. Finally, he speaks. "Anna, what you have told me is very, very tragic. Very sad and tragic indeed. Being exposed to graphic sex prematurely is very traumatic for any child, but even more so when the child's father has abandoned the mother and is engaging in that sex with someone else. With the childhood you had, it was probably inevitable that you would develop some kind of personality disorder. It doesn't make you crazy, per se—it's just that all the defense mechanisms your brain had to concoct in order to survive your childhood have made you sick as an adult. You'd probably be sick even without being exposed to your father's sex antics, but that certainly didn't help."

"Well, duh. Are you going to tell me anything I don't already know?"

Dr. Chatterjee raises his hand. "Hear me out. Emotionally, Anna, you're still a child. With as horrific a childhood as you had, not only did you never have the opportunity to mature into an emotionally balanced adult, you also have no idea what healthy, intimate sexual relationships should be like. You act out in sexually self-destructive ways to try to run away from all the years and years' worth of pain you have pent up inside, but all that does is make you feel worse. You are stuck in a very destructive pattern of behavior, Anna, and unless you change it, you are never, ever going to get better. And the fact is, Anna, I don't think you are ready to change. In fact, based on what I've seen from you in therapy, I highly doubt you ever *will* change. You're what we psychiatrists call a hopeless case.[7] As far as I'm concerned, you'll be sick like this for the rest of your life. And that's really too bad."

I'm stunned. Here I am, sitting in intensive, three-times-a-week therapy sessions with a psychiatrist-in-training, making what I think is my best effort to get well and lead a normal life, and this British quack is telling me I'm doomed to failure before I even start. What's the point of trying? What's the point of living? What's the point of doing anything?

I should just get the hell out of here while I still can.

As I gather my things to leave, Dr. Chatterjee offers one last tidbit of advice. "Anna, I'm only telling you this because I believe that you don't want to change. You're in a bloody rut, Anna. And I can't help you unless you help yourself. Nobody can."

I stop seeing Dr. Chatterjee. Not necessarily because I *want* to stop seeing him, but because two weeks later, when I show up for my regularly scheduled session, the receptionist tells me that Dr. Chatterjee unexpectedly moved back to London, and the free program won't take any more patients, so I'll either need to start paying someone else to talk to me or stop going. So I stop going. And even though Dr. Chatterjee has abandoned me just like all the other men in my life have, I decide to take his advice and get out of my bloody rut in my own bloody way.

For the next year or so, my life goes roughly like this: I max out seven different credit cards in rash spending sprees on clothes, shoes, expensive dinners out, makeup, cable TV, two trips to Amsterdam for pot and hashish, and lots and lots of booze. I spend the money because I'm depressed; I feel guilty about spending the money and subsequently get more depressed; and I then spend even more money just trying to keep up with the bills that pile up from all the money I spent before, which makes me even more depressed than I ever thought possible, which makes me apply for more charge cards that I max out too, and then—

Then I file for bankruptcy.

I quit my library job and go to work for a dot-com firm downtown for a higher salary and stock options. I blow the extra salary on booze and partying, the stock options are worthless, and I get laid off a year or so later, so financially speaking, it's kind of a wash.

But in that year or so, I also manage to get laid. A lot.

I have so many one-night stands during those eighteen months or so that years later, when my husband-to-be asks me how many men I've slept with, I say I can only give him a ballpark estimate. Every single weekend, I have at least one one-night stand, sometimes even two or three when I stretch the weekends out from Thursday to Tuesday. I dress in skimpy halters and tight miniskirts (with nothing underneath either) in the dead of a Chicago winter, strut in stilettos to clubs and bars even through a foot of Chicago snow. At the end of a booze and popper-filled evening, I make out in taxicabs with the unknown men I pick up at the clubs; they plunge their hands down my blouse and up my skirt and I don't stop them, even when the cabbie threatens to throw us out onto the curb. Some of those men end up back at my apartment (or theirs), and we have sex on hallway rugs and bathroom counters. I sleep with these men in a vain effort to feel loved—or even just to feel *something*—but I end up feeling nothing at all. With each one, I grow more and more icy, more and more numb.

I don't remember all of those one-night stands, but I do remember at least a couple of them involve me waking up drunk or stoned in the middle of the night in a strange apartment to find an equally strange man I don't remember meeting before on top of me, grunting and sweaty as a lame horse in July. And what is strangest of all, I don't think that there is anything wrong with this—even when I'm standing in line for a free HIV test at a charity clinic in a bad neighborhood because I don't want to risk claiming an HIV test on my health insurance.

At a certain point I decide that I'm still in a bloody rut, and I make up my mind to get out of it—and life itself—for good. I contemplate suicide, but don't bother to actually try to off myself—not out of fear or laziness so much as because I just don't know how to go about it, at least not in a way that isn't too messy or expensive. I just can't quite bring myself to buy a gun to shoot myself, or to mix up just the right cocktail of booze and pills to send me off the planet on a permanent vacation. Besides, I have plenty to keep me occupied here on earth. There's always another man to seduce, always another expensive dress to charge on Visa, always another throbbing club to visit on Saturday night. I'm starring in my own personal version of *Looking for Mr. Goodbar*, and it's literally the only thing keeping me alive.

So I keep right on shopping, and boozing, and screwing random people until 9/11 happens and puts a freeze on the gaping black hole in my brain and everything sort of just grinds to a standstill when in a final, fabulous finale, the gaping black hole in my brain collapses and then turns inside out.

# 3

# CHICAGO: OCTOBER 2001–APRIL 2002

I am walking up and down Ashland Avenue, cell phone in hand, carrying a backpack with two bottles of Alberto VO5 Shampoo (on special at Walgreens, two for 99 cents), a toothbrush, a change of underwear, and a one-liter bottle of Diet Coke.

I am twenty-eight years old, and I am in the early stages of a *brief psychotic episode*.

I am calling Jacey Wills,[1] one of my theater friends. She's a costume and set designer originally from Missouri. She lives in an apartment filled with costumes and bags of retail overstock and sewing machines and stage flats and moldy old props. Jacey works on indie films for peanuts, on theater productions mostly for free, and she doesn't have a day job. Drawing upon survival skills she learned growing up extremely poor in a large rural-Missouri family, Jacey finds clothes and props for her design gigs in Dumpsters and alleys, buys expired groceries at bodegas and flea markets for pennies on the dollar. She's always somehow dressed at the height of fashion in clothes she's either found in the garbage or made herself. I've never known how she pays her bills, but she always manages it, and she also manages to help out her struggling theater-artist friends with cash and food whenever they need it. She's kind of like a junkyard saint that way.

Jacey is my last resort. She's not my best or my only friend in Chicago, but she's the only one I trust to get me out of the situation I'm in, the only person I know who won't judge me, or think that I'm acting crazy. Even when I am. Because Jacey is just a little bit crazy herself.

I have only about ten minutes left on my pay-as-you-go Verizon calling plan (my credit's too bad to get a regular calling plan), so I'm praying as hard as I can to a God I no longer believe in for Jacey to please, please pick up her cell.

"Hello?"

"Jacey, it's Anna. I need a place to stay."

"Anna, I can't talk to you right now, I'm right in the middle of a shoot—"

"Jacey, this is an emergency. *I need a place to stay.*" My voice is breaking. I'm pacing up and down in front of a shopping center on the corner of Ashland and Barry streets, in the midst of a neighborhood that is fast becoming too expensive for me to afford. My hands are shaking, my heart is racing, and my mind has an electric buzz that I know only means a panic attack is coming. I'm dancing up and down on the sidewalk, trying in vain to keep warm against the bitter, cutting Chicago wind. Yuppie women on elliptical trainers inside the shopping center's Gym-n-Tan are staring at me through the frosty window. They probably think I'm one of the strung-out, teenage-junkie runaways who inhabit the corner of Clark and Belmont day and night, that perhaps I've gotten lost and wandered too far west into their sacred territory.

It's cold. Too cold for April, even in Chicago. And I'm not wearing a coat. I left it back in my apartment. I forget why. I'm having trouble thinking straight. All I know right now is, I'm scared, I'm nervous, I had to leave my apartment in a hurry, and I need a place to stay. Now.

Now. *Right* now.

I forget why.

"Anna, you sound really weird. What's goin' on, hon?" Jacey's Missouri twang thickens as she lowers her voice. "I'm on a shoot downstate right now. I won't be back in the city for three more days. And Tim's not home right now either—he's back home visiting his mom, otherwise I'd just tell you to take the el up to Evanston and wait for him on the doorstep. Can you wait three days?"

"No. No, that won't work. I need somewhere I can go right *now.*"

I hear Jacey sigh. She and I are a lot alike—poor theater artists with Southern-Midwestern roots living in a big city and struggling to get by between jobs, poor theater artists with Southern-Midwestern roots who always help each other out. I helped her get her last three paying stage-design gigs, so she owes me. Big time. "Anna, where are you right now?"

"I'm on Ashland Avenue just north of Belmont, right across from that big shopping center."

"Hang on a sec." I hear Jacey tell someone on the set of the low-budget indie film she's costuming that she's taking a break. "There's nowhere else you can go?"

"No."

Jacey sighs again. "Is something weird going on with you and Dean? He's not—beating you up or anything?"

"No! No, it's nothing like that. It's—complicated."

Jacey clucks. "But it *is* something with you and Dean, isn't it? You need to move out of his place?"

"I dunno. Maybe."

Although Jacey doesn't say so, I know what she's thinking. She's thinking I shouldn't have moved in with Dean after only knowing him for two months. Hell, *everybody* thinks that. Even me, sometimes.

But Jacey doesn't judge me. She doesn't judge anybody. "Look, if you're in some kind of immediate danger, Anna, go to a shelter."

"I'm not *in danger*, Jacey I promise." But I'm not entirely sure about that. I don't need other people doing things to me to be *in danger*. I can be a pretty big danger to myself sometimes.

"Okay then. If you're not in danger, just sit tight until I get back in town. I should be back on Thursday. You can come stay with me if you haven't figured something else out by then. Tim and I will get you taken care of. Is that OK?"

"Yeah," I sigh. It's obvious I'll have to go back to Dean. For a while. It could be worse, I suppose. At least Jacey didn't ask *why* I need a place to stay, or why I need to leave Dean's apartment, which I share with him and another couple, although the situation there is fast becoming untenable. The fact is, I don't know exactly *why* it's becoming untenable. It's just a feeling I have. An intuition, something that borders on ESP.

I've always had a keen ability to sense doom in a relationship just before it happens. Either that, or I hallucinate relationship doom to cause relationship doom to befall me. I constantly second-guess the relationship, wondering why anyone would willingly choose to be with someone like me. I'm too skinny, I'm too fat, I come from the wrong side of the tracks, I don't have a good enough job, my hair is wrong, my eyes are wrong, he's probably dating somebody else, surely he must be embarrassed to be seen with me, and so on. These kinds of self-defeating thoughts boil and bubble in my brain, and even if I never speak them aloud to anyone, their effect on my outer behavior is still unmistakable. I'm distant, irritable, and foggy. I blow up or snap at the slightest provocation, or I puff myself up and try to act "bigger" than I am— giving terse orders to my subordinates at work or during theater productions, making petty complaints at restaurants, or holing myself up in my room all weekend, not talking to anyone. With such bitterness and self-loathing eating me up inside, I alienate boyfriends without even trying. And then, once the damage is done, I freak out, get whiny and clingy, cook fancy meals, desperately beg them to take me back. I write lovey-dovey cards and e-mails, I send gifts and flowers, I agree to do kinky things in bed. Sometimes these gestures work and the boyfriends come back, and the cycle repeats for a while. But mostly it just hastens the inevitable.

One of my many psychotherapists (I forget which one) once called it my unique "self-fulfilling sexual prophecy" neurosis. It makes me needy. So needy that I just end up driving away the people I need the most. And now, with Dean, it's happening once again. I still don't have the insight to recognize my destructive relationship patterns, but I can feel the impending doom approaching deep in the pit of my stomach the same way a seasoned sailor can feel approaching storms in his very bones. The "why" doesn't matter to me yet, just the "how."

"Jacey, I know you're out of town and all, but can you help me? Now? Please?"

Jacey sighs again. "Give me a couple days, Anna, I gotta go. We're doing a big group shot tonight and I have thirty extras to costume. I'll call you Thursday on your cell. Bye."

Jacey hangs up. Of course, I know that I'll be out of prepaid cell phone minutes by the time she gets back to Chicago. There will be no way for her to reach me. The whole conversation has been a waste of time.

I shrug my shoulders and head back to the apartment.

I meet Dean Takahashi[2] in the fall of 2001. I've been laid off from my job as a proposal copywriter at the dot-com consulting firm since September 13, 2001, and haven't been able to find another job since. The Chicago job market is in the toilet, flooded with thousands of layoff victims with skill sets just like my own. Writers and editors can't even get jobs breathing. The temp agencies are turning applicants away, and all the waitressing jobs are already taken by all the other struggling writers and actors who've been out of work since the first recession hit in 2000. I can't afford to move to another city to look for work either.

I accept long-term unemployment as a fact of life and decide to live on my meager savings and unemployment checks until something better comes along. The small women's theater company I founded and have run on the side for the past couple of years provides me with no income and takes up a lot of time, but it has provided me with the benefit of a strong network of other poor, struggling theater artists, all of them trying to manage day jobs and expensive city rent and the performing arts all at the same time. I try my network of fellow actors and writers, some of whom have day jobs at employment agencies, but none of them have leads on where I might find a steady paycheck in the dreadful post–9/11 Chicago economy, which was already devastated a year earlier when Enron's Chicago-based accounting firm Arthur Andersen imploded, saturating the job market with its thousands of sacked employees.

Someone in my circle of friends suggests I audition for a role in a community theater production just to get myself out of the apartment. An acting job, even a low-paying one, would give me the opportunity for creative expression and socializing without the stress of fundraising, ticket sales, and the liability insurance I've always had with the shows I've produced with my own small theater company. And who knows—it might just lead to a good-paying gig too.

I get the most recent issue of *Performink*, Chicago's theater- and film-industry trade paper, and check out the audition notices. I gave up acting in favor of playwriting, directing, and producing theater years ago; with my size-twelve build, freckles, and wiry hair, I'm a character actress. And there just aren't many roles in Chicago theater for non-Equity character actresses in their twenties. I'm thirty years too young for all the character parts that are available, and without my Equity card can't get cast in them anyway. And as might be expected, all the week's audition notices are calling for young, size-two ingénues, men of any age or type, or sixty-something women with Equity cards. I'm about to toss the paper aside in frustration when I notice a small ad at the bottom of the page.

> JUNKYARD HEART[3] Uptown Performance Ensemble seeks actors of all ages and types. Non-Equity. Perform in an ensemble-created show at various venues in Chicago. Critically acclaimed; *Chicago Tribune* and *Chicago Reader* Recommended! No pay. Call 773-555-xxxx for audition.

The name of the theater company sounds vaguely familiar. I know I must have read a review of one of their shows somewhere, but I can't quite place where. A paying gig would be preferable, but this appears to be the only option if I want to get onstage and out of my apartment in the next couple of weeks. I call the number and a pleasant-voiced woman answers.

"Hello, thank you for calling Junkyard HEART! Can I help you?"

"Umm, yeah, I'm calling about the audition?" I flip on CNN with the volume muted; there's a feature story running about mail-order anthrax.

"Yes! The first rehearsal is tonight starting at six p.m., at the Park District building on the corner of Marine Drive and Lawrence."

Rehearsal? This doesn't add up. "Umm, don't I need to *audition* first?"

There's a pause, followed by an easy laugh. "Well, you can audition if you like, but it's not required."

I turn up the volume on CNN. I can't decide what's more unbelievable—video footage of an anthrax-infected hand or a Chicago theater company that doesn't require auditions for actors. "An audition isn't *required*?"

"Oh no, dear. We give everyone a part who wants one. It's very collaborative. But again, if you prefer to do an audition, you can still do one. Just show up at six and tell the director you'd prefer to do an audition. We're very flexible that way."

"Okay, but—"

The pleasant, calm-voiced woman laughs again. It's a very musical laugh. "You're a professional actress, then, I take it?"

"Well, yes. That is, I used to be. I'm more of a freelance theater producer and writer now, but I've kind of hit a dry spell, so—"

"Oh, wonderful! We especially enjoy having professional actors in our shows. You'll be so inspirational to the patients and special-needs performers. Please, do make sure to come promptly at six. Would it be all right if some of the special-needs performers watch your audition?"

Patients? *Special-needs* performers? "Umm, I don't know—usually only the director is supposed to watch auditions, right?"

That same musical laugh again. "Well, as I said before dear, we're very collaborative. But if you don't want anyone to watch your audition, that's all right too. Can you bring headshots? We *love* headshots."

I walk with the cordless phone to the tiny nook that holds my bedroom office, and pull out one of my old actor headshots from a drawer. I'll need to update my resume. "So, okay, well, I'll just bring headshots and do a monologue, then. Do you want classical or contemporary? I can do both." At least, I think I can do both. It's been more than a year since I've auditioned for anything, and I'm not sure I can remember the stock monologues I've used on auditions since my sophomore year of college. I'll need to work on that too. It's not as if there's anything else for me to do with my time.

"Oh, hon, like I said, just do whatever you want. We're very flexible that way. Now if you'll excuse me, dear, I have another call coming in. See you at six."

The pleasant-voiced woman hangs up without even asking my name.

My first impression of Junkyard HEART isn't exactly a good one. Whoever I've just finished talking to has broken every cardinal rule about what it means to take audition calls from professional actors. Still, I'm curious. The woman on the phone sounded so cool and soothing, so calm and laid back. And I need something calm and laid back rather badly.

Between the anthrax on the television, the still-looping nonstop video images of the crashing Twin Towers, and the long, idle hours sitting alone in my apartment—in which my restless, tense mind cooks up all kinds of twisted things to torture me with—perhaps a strange theater group that doesn't require auditions is exactly what I need.

I don't have a car, and cash is too tight for me to justify taking the bus the mile or so up Marine Drive from my apartment to the Junkyard HEART rehearsal. So I walk. In late 2001 I live in a mid-rise apartment building on the northern border of Chicago's Lakeview neighborhood, about a half-mile north and east of Wrigley Field. I have a large two-bedroom apartment with baseboard heat and ultra-cheap rent that I've shared with a series of roommates over a period of about five years. The ultra-cheap rent will come to an end soon; my North Lakeview neighborhood, which was still the denizen of mostly young artists, gay hustlers, junkies, and hookers who worked the corner of Broadway and Sheridan just five years earlier, is now in the midst of full-swing gentrification. (It's ironic now that I'm in my forties and married with a comfortable six-figure income I can no longer afford the hip neighborhood I lived in when I was twenty-something and broke.)

During my last year in this big, cheap apartment, my roommate is a non-practicing Muslim immigrant from Malaysia named Aziz Muhammed. Aziz works as a computer programmer downtown and is rarely home. But he takes off for Malaysia about two months after 9/11 in justifiable fear of anti-Muslim sentiment, stiffs me for three months' rent, and becomes, indirectly, one of the chief reasons I move in with the man I will meet and fall in love with at my first Junkyard HEART rehearsal.

My neighborhood might be rapidly gentrifying right now, but the neighborhood that lies directly between my apartment and the Junkyard HEART rehearsal—Uptown—is still one of the most dangerous and decrepit in the city of Chicago in 2001. Drug-dealers, gang-bangers, and violent criminals galore stand on every street corner in Uptown. The Uptown streets are filthy, half the buildings are condemned, and the only thriving businesses are greasy jerk-chicken shacks and African hair-braiding emporiums. And scattered among the Uptown homeless, the junkies, and the poor, single mothers who huddle in the slumlord-owned, burned-out apartment buildings are the incurably mentally ill—those forgotten, desperately poor, and overmedicated people who would still be in Illinois state mental hospitals if it weren't for the Reagan administration's relentless budget cuts in the 1980s that sent them permanently out onto the streets.

Uptown has the largest selection of single-room occupancy apartment buildings in the city, and many of them are owned and operated by either the U.S. Department of Veterans Affairs (VA) or private charities for the purposes of housing recovering addicts, troubled Vietnam veterans, and the chronically mentally ill,[4] who live on a combination of disability checks and panhandling. I occasionally come to Uptown for theater rehearsals and performances in the Preston Bradley Center, or for a night of jazz at the world-famous Green Mill nightclub—the only islands of culture and civilization in the desolate neighborhood until forward-looking real estate developers start moving in years later—but otherwise I avoid it like the plague. In 2001, Uptown just isn't a place for a young, single woman to walk alone, even a young woman as citified and street-smart as I am. You never know when a junkie or crazed lunatic who's forgotten to take his medication will jump out of an alley brandishing a switchblade or a gun.

But the sense I've possessed since childhood that borders on psychic intuition tells me that whatever misgivings I might have, there is something waiting for me at Junkyard HEART. Something that will satisfy me, something that will help me find sanity in those insane months just after 9/11, when I am jobless and witless and nervous and paranoid.

I finally make it to the weathered brick Margate Park fieldhouse, a 1950s-era Chicago Park District building on the northernmost edge of lakefront Lincoln Park. The old community building contains a gymnasium frequented by poor kids from the surrounding neighborhood, a makeshift workout facility used by students and senior citizens who can't afford to join a gym, and three large classrooms used by city-sponsored daycare on weekdays and rented by local community groups for meetings on evenings and weekends. At just before six in the evening, the building lobby is filled with a mixture of unruly children leaving daycare, middle-aged women toting yoga mats for a class, and several oddly dressed, fidgety people whom I immediately recognize as Uptown's ubiquitous psychiatric patients. There's a hand-lettered paper sign reading JUNKYARD HEART THIS WAY with an arrow pointing to the end of the hall.

I stride down the hall to a cluttered, dusty classroom. There's a squat, middle-aged woman with short hair and Coke-bottle glasses standing behind a folding table, along with a scrawny teenage boy and an elderly woman in dirty, secondhand clothes. They're all filling dozens of paper Dixie cups with red Kool-Aid and talking to each other in low voices. Some of the psychiatric patients I noticed in the lobby come in and sit down in the folding metal chairs someone has set out. Two nervous-looking women, both very overweight, poorly dressed, and about my age, sit in a corner checking and rechecking their watches. A thirtyish woman with long hair and glasses sorts a box of castoff clothes. Another small group of poor local women comes in and sits down, and at least three of them are quite obviously street people—I can smell their unmistakable stench of urine, dirt, and stale sweat from across the room.

It doesn't look like much of a theater rehearsal to me—it seems more like a combination soup kitchen and church rummage sale. I figure I have the wrong room and turn to leave. But the squat, middle-aged woman stops pouring Kool-Aid for a moment and looks up.

"Hello, miss. Are you here to audition?" She points at the glossy headshot I carry in one hand. "I believe you and I spoke on the phone this afternoon."

I feel my face go red. "Yes. Umm. No. That is—I don't think I belong here."

The squat woman comes from behind the folding table, takes my hand, and shakes it. "Yes, you *do* belong here. I'm Carol. Please stay. You'll have a wonderful time with us, I promise. What's your name?"

"Anna," I say, not trying to hide my embarrassment. I suppose Carol is right, in a way. After all, I'm unemployed, nearly broke, and I have a long personal and family history of mental problems. I shudder as I realize that I'm probably only a few strokes of good luck shy of being one of the motley crew of homeless people and mental cases waiting patiently in their metal folding chairs for the rehearsal to begin.

"Welcome, Anna. Welcome to Junkyard HEART. We're so glad you're here. Have some Kool-Aid." Carol thrusts a soggy paper cup into my hand. Almost against my will, I take a sip. It tastes like a red crayon.

"It's all right to be a little nervous your first time with us," Carol goes on. "I know you're probably used to something a little more profession-al than this, but I guarantee you'll grow as a performer if you work with us." She gives me a broad, crooked-toothed smile; Carol's sincerity is palpable. I can't walk out of here and hurt this woman's feelings, I just can't.

I decide I can stay for an hour or so. I figure the story of how I attended a theater rehearsal full of mental patients and smelly homeless people will make for fun cocktail-party conversation.

That is, if I ever actually get invited to a cocktail party again. The isolation and desolation of the past few weeks makes that seem unlikely. That, and my increasingly precarious financial and mental state. I'm more like the people sitting in that shabby room than I want to admit.

"Sit down, make yourself comfortable!" Carol beams once she figures out I'm staying. I get the feeling she's convinced many others like me to stay in the past—and understandably so. Her voice is even more calming and soothing in person than it is on the phone, and her big brown eyes have the adorable-puppy-dog quality that most people lose after the age of six or seven. "The director's just down the hall, finishing a meeting with the board of directors. I'm sure he'll be happy to do a private audition with you before we start the rehearsal, if you still want to do that. But I promise you, it's not necessary at all."

As if on cue, the director appears. He's a tall, handsome middle-aged man in khakis and a sweater. He holds out a hand, I shake it. "Welcome, nice to see you. I'm David Wiley,[5] artistic director of Junkyard HEART. You're a pro, by the way. I can tell just by looking at you. Let me see that headshot you've got there."

Stunned, I hand it to him. He glances at my headshot and reads over my resume. "Ah, a seasoned performer. Good. We need you. I'll be calling on you to lead some rehearsals and warm-ups. How about you go outside, just behind the fieldhouse? There are some other pros back there, just like you, preparing a warm-up for the community performers. Sound okay with you?"

It doesn't seem like I have a choice. I blindly gather up my things and walk out through the rear door of the building.

That's when I see him.

*Him.*

Dean.

He's standing in the middle of a small circle of other young, fit, attractive twenty-somethings like myself. He looks about twenty-eight, my age. He's short, but with an elegant, compact, athletic body, and his skin is a beautiful, creamy gold, his eyes almond-shaped and the color of ripe chestnuts. I've never been attracted to Asian men before, but my attraction to Dean is almost immediate. He stands there in a circle of his peers, standing on grass that is warm and wet with October dew. He wears—I will never forget this, not as long as I live—creased and pressed khakis with a lilac polo shirt that hugs every rippled curve of his chest and shoulders. He bends to the side and down over one leg, slowly moving his arms along in front of him in a single, fluid movement that reminds me of a slow, sensual waterfall. Tai Chi, by the looks of it.

The other people in the circle—at least two of whom have the long, lithe, ripped bodies of professional dancers—follow Dean's lead.

Godamighty.

He has me even before he's said hello.

I timidly shuffle up to the circle, clear my throat by way of introduction. Dean (only I don't know his name yet) and the others look my way.

"Hi," he says in a smooth tenor voice. "And you are?"

"Umm, Anna. Anna Berry. I'm, umm, new around here. That director guy told me to come back here with the rest of the . . . professionals."

Dean and a few of the others laugh. "Professionals? Professional whats?"

Everyone in the small circle stares. Now I'm embarrassed. Again. I need to make a quick recovery, so I flash my headshot at them. "You know. Professional *performers*."

Dean laughs again. "None of us here are professional anything. This is a *community* theater group. We're just some of the veterans, is all. We've all done at least three Junkyard HEART shows." He crosses to me, offers me his hand. It's cool and smooth as talc. "I'm Dean. I'll be leading the physical warm-up tonight, and I need some folks to help me teach the moves to the others. Wanna help?"

Dean's sweet, smooth voice and almond-chestnut eyes have my panties in such a pretzel that I can't speak, so I just nod and follow along as he demonstrates some warm-up calisthenics that are a mixture of Tai-Chi and modern dance. Within minutes, I've mastered the whole sequence—all without once taking my eyes off Dean's baby browns. They're like deep sienna whirlpools that have me whirling in an inescapable abyss.

Oh boy, I have it bad.

And it will only get worse.


Dean walks me home from rehearsal that first night. And on the third night, we go on a date that ends back at my apartment, where we have some of the oddest sex of my life. I remember my shock (and strangely, delight) when I see that Dean's penis, even when fully erect, is about the same size, shape, and thickness as a French string bean. Since I'm accustomed to well-endowed men, the resulting sex is little more than a tickle. But Dean makes up for his shortcomings in other ways.

Within days, Dean and I are inseparable. He picks me up for Junk-yard HEART rehearsal each evening in his mint-green Honda Accord. We rehearse and perform alongside poor city teenagers and homeless mental patients, and we fall in love. We sleep together each night— mostly at my apartment. For reasons that become clear later, Dean is reluctant to take me to his apartment or introduce me to his roommate and childhood best friend, "Raj." But after the Junkyard HEART show finally opens and Dean has already made the rounds of introductions with my circle of friends, he finally relents and invites me to attend his roommate's twenty-ninth birthday party with him.

Dean and his roommate, Raj, are both graduates of prestigious Oak Park–River Forest High School (OPRF), an elite public high school in Chicago's affluent western suburbs. OPRF has countless celebrities, politicians, and successful businessmen among its graduates—Ernest Hemingway, Dan Castellaneta, and McDonald's founder Ray Kroc, to name just a few. And the lucky students who attend OPRF now include the sons and daughters of Chicagoland's wealthiest professionals—doc-tors, lawyers, judges, corporate executives. The tiny twin suburbs of Oak Park and extremely wealthy River Forest are dotted with large, beautiful Arts-and-Crafts and Prairie Style homes that ooze power, wealth, and success—as well as, purportedly, open-minded liberalism.

But as Hemingway once so eloquently put it, "Oak Park is full of wide lawns and narrow minds." I run full-throttle into some of the youngest of those narrow minds whenever I date any of Oak Park's favorite sons. It's a very different echelon than my own hardscrabble background, with my mentally ill mother who couldn't care for me properly and a dad who spent most of his time, money, and energy on womanizing. It's a revolving parade of nice young men from happy, stable families, with their beautiful homes and fat bank accounts, who never seem to stay attached to me for long, and yet I keep dating them over and over again. I think they're attracted to me at first because I'm earthy, simple, outspoken, a pull-herself-up-by-her-bootstraps type, a breath of fresh air compared to all the polished, cookie-cutter, prep-school girls they've grown up with. And I'm attracted to them because they come from the happy, stable families I wish I could have had growing up. But like those trendy, fizzy dance-club cocktails that taste so good and look so pretty at first, after the initial novelty wears off, it's a bad combination that just ends up making everyone sick to their stomach.

I recall several dinner parties in elegant Prairie Style homes where my Oak Park–bred boyfriend of that year introduces me to old class-mates, relatives, and friends of his, and the conversations always go something like this:

"Hi, you must be Anna," the friend or relative says, without shaking my hand. "Nice to meet you. Where is it you're from originally?"

"Indiana."

A tilt of the head, a blink. "*Indiana*. I see. What is it that your family *does*, Anna?

"What?"

"What *business* are they in? Law, finance? Or are they perhaps in commercial farming? Lot of that in Indiana, I hear."

"Oh. Well. Umm, my mom is a clerical worker, but she's sort of unemployed right now. Her husband's a janitor. My parents are di-vorced. My dad works for a defense contractor—"

"I see. Well, *lovely* to meet you." And the Oak Park friend or relative winces and darts off to find someone else to talk to in the farthest possible corner of whatever vast Prairie Style house the party is in.

I'll have a similar experience with Dean's Oak Park–River Forest friends, especially Raj. Raj is the son of two extremely successful In-dian-American physicians. Raj still has several relatives who occupy the highest positions of power and influence in their country, including one uncle who's a railroad baron and who lives in the former house in Mumbai of Mohammed-Ali Jinnah, Pakistan's first governor-general. Raj is related to several well-known Indian-Americans too.

Raj loves nothing more than pointing out how everyone and every-thing around him is beneath him—jobs, stores, clothing brands, restau-rants, even friends (notwithstanding the fact that Raj works only inter-mittently as an hourly computer software trainer, has taken almost eight years and four different universities to finish his bachelor's degree, and at the age of twenty-nine still lives mostly on handouts from his par-ents).

When Dean introduces me to Raj and his girlfriend Amy at the birthday party, they both seem to like me well enough at first. We bond over our shared interests in music, books, and movies, especially Asian cinema and Japanese animation. We sit around the living room with the rest of Dean and Raj's friends, watching *Crouching Tiger, Hidden Dragon* on DVD and freeze-framing the best fight scenes while we discuss the similarities between that film and Kurosawa's old-school samurai flicks. We drink beer, then scotch, then play charades and drinking games into the wee hours like we're all old friends.

I stay overnight in Dean's room after the party. We make love, then talk in bed for a few more hours before finally falling asleep just before dawn.

It's that bedroom conversation where I get my first indication that Dean and Raj's friendship, which goes practically back to kindergarten, is strained.

"Do you know when you might start working again, Anna?" he asks.

"As soon as I can find something," I say. "I'm looking as much as I can, but it's hard right now. Why?"

"Are you planning to stay in your apartment?" Dean grabs my hand, more nervous than I've ever seen him before.

"I dunno. I might need to get a new roommate if Aziz doesn't stay after the lease is up, but—"

"Would you ever consider moving in here?"

"I dunno. Why?"

Dean sits up, tosses the futon's covers aside. "I've been having trouble paying the bills here lately. Raj's not very good about paying his share sometimes, and—"

I'm stunned. Raj drives a late-model VW Jetta, wears the latest fashions from J. Crew, and has a room stuffed full of expensive electronics that he spent half the evening showing off to party guests. "I thought Raj had plenty of money."

Dean laughs. "He does. He just doesn't always spend it the way he should."

Dean then explains how he's had to pick up the bulk of the household bills for the past several months—even sometimes fronting cash to Raj that he never pays back—because Raj has trouble understanding that his $4,000 monthly allowance from his parents and whatever he earns doing software training has to go to rent, utilities, and food before it goes to plasma-screen TVs, stereo equipment, and expensive clothes. Making matters even worse, Raj's girlfriend, whom I'll call Amy, has virtually moved into their apartment, eating more than Raj's share of the groceries by herself and racking up huge, long-distance phone bills to her family and friends on the West Coast. Dean has tried meekly to put a stop to the situation, but Raj and his new girlfriend ignore him and just go on spending huge sums of money on themselves. Just last week, they purchased matching Cannondale carbon-fiber road bikes for $3,000 apiece while Dean got stuck with the full month's rent and electric.

"I thought you said this guy was your friend," I scoff.

"He is. We've been buddies since grade school."

"A real friend wouldn't treat you like his own personal ATM machine."

Dean sighs. "I dunno—I don't think Raj *really* thinks of me like that. He's—he's just had kind of a hard life, is all."

I laugh. "That's funny, since he obviously grew up on Easy Street."

Dean sighs again. "Well, yeah, his family *is* wealthy, but they have a lot of problems. Raj's dad is a bit of an asshole. He's violent too. He beat Raj and his brothers up a lot when we were growing up. Raj used to come over to my house to hide from his dad when he was on a rampage."

"My dad was violent too, and I don't use you as my own personal ATM."

Dean ignores this. "Raj has a lot of trouble knowing what to do with himself. He has trouble managing money especially. I just feel like I should help him, since he's my friend and all."

"Whatever. It's your money."

Dean looks hurt. "You're such a kind and compassionate person, Anna, I thought you'd understand."

"Dean, it's really none of my business, but Raj is not your real friend if he does shit like that. He's just using you, and helping him will only make the situation worse. I have an older brother sort of like Raj, so I know."

Dean ponders this for a minute or two. "All right. But that's all the more reason why you should move in here. I know you're having money problems right now too, and I'd like to help *you* with them—"

"Dean, *no*. We're not ready for that—"

He holds up his hand. "Hear me out. I know you're struggling right now without a steady job. If you move in with me, you won't have as many bills. It's not like I'd be paying your way. And I need some help standing up to Raj and Amy. You're strong. You could help me. We can help each other."

Red flags go up in my brain. I've craved rescue from men for my entire adulthood, but every time a man has swept into my life—promising to "save" me from ruin, to give me the stable-yet-glamorous life I've always dreamed of—I've always jumped full-throttle into the relationship, moving too fast too soon. And it's always ended badly. Just look at what happened with Dieter Franzl, for God's sake. But I just shrug those concerns off. I'm the eternal optimist when it comes to boyfriends, even if my brain is sending out all sorts of smoke signals that if I'm smart, I'll get out now. Those signals are just wrong. They have to be. Dean wouldn't be offering to rescue me if he didn't want to, right? Because I'm special. At least he thinks so, even if I don't. And I latch onto that as a drowning man does a life preserver. With the noise that pollutes my brain on a daily basis, I'll take whatever I can get.

As a young single woman who's struggled with mood disorders on and off since high school, I've often judged my value as a person solely on whether I can get a certain man to love me or not (first my emotionally distant father, then a long succession of men I sought as replacements for the one man who'd first rejected me in favor of a succession of younger wives and their subsequent younger, cuter children). The tremendously needy, vulnerable part of myself that often first charms and attracts those lovers-cum-father-replacements is also what drives them away in the end.

Dean will turn out to be the latest in that long stream of men. Our relationship will ultimately burn out in the worst way possible, and all because at the age of twenty-eight I still lack the self-awareness and insight to recognize the destructive patterns of behavior in my romantic relationships. Red flags the size of Nebraska could be plastered across Dean's forehead, and I'd still look right past them.

So I ignore all those giant red flags and decide to move in with Dean. I really think that this time, it will be different. And the truth is, I *do* need the financial help. Not two days after Dean and I have our late-night bedroom conversation, my roommate Aziz flies the coop, abandoning my apartment with nothing but a "Screw you, stupid American" note stating he's returned to Malaysia, so there's nothing I can do to make him pay his share of the three months' rent still left on the lease. It will take all the savings I have just to cover *my* share of the rent for those three months. I'll forfeit the security deposit if I sublet this late in the game, but Dean and I both decide that's the best course of action to take.

For the next two weeks I set about listing the apartment for immediate sublet and selling off almost all my furniture and household items since Dean doesn't have room for them at his place. By the time I move into Dean's bedroom at the end of the month, my worldly possessions consist of my computer, my meager wardrobe, a small CD collection, four bath towels, and three cooking pots.

It never once occurs to me that I might be putting too much confidence in my belief that moving into Dean's tiny bedroom in a cramped garden apartment he shares with another couple is equal to the stability and commitment of a marriage. But that's exactly what I do. Logic is no longer part of my vocabulary. I'm drowning in a whirlpool of repressed emotions, financial stress, and nonstop mental noise by this point, and Dean is the guiding light of my rescue ship. Or so I think. He turns out to be something else entirely.

Looking back now, I think this is when the first seeds of my later psychotic episode begin to germinate. The DSM-V defines *brief psychotic disorder* as a temporary psychotic state that lasts for at least one day, but can last as long as a month, that is not related to bipolar disorder, schizophrenia, schizoaffective disorder, or delusional disorder. It frequently occurs as a result of extreme stress. Brief psychotic episodes involve disorganized speech, thinking, and behavior; hallucinations; problems with memory; sleep disturbances; the inability to make basic decisions; and unusual behavior or dressing inappropriately. I will eventually show most of these symptoms when the situation with Dean becomes untenable. But I think the delusions first start here. I should already know by now that moving in with Dean is the worst possible thing that I can do, but I believe the exact opposite.

Still, I can see why I might have latched onto those delusional ideas. Raj and Amy (who by then is living in the cramped apartment full-time herself) are welcoming at first. And things are looking up in other ways too. I've returned to work on a short-term contract job writing grant applications for a nonprofit organization on the South Side, a job that requires I buy a car with my last remaining savings. The small women's theater company I run as a side project is offered the funding necessary to produce a play about the Rape of Nanking; I manage the production crew and even help Dean get cast in it as his first professional acting gig. I offer Raj the opportunity to run the box office on weekends to make some extra cash, and he gladly accepts my offer. Dean receives favorable reviews in the Chicago newspapers for his performance in the high-profile play, and offers from talent agents and auditions for well-paid on-camera acting gigs start to roll in for him. I encourage Dean to pursue a professional acting career—he has talent, and as one of the very few working Asian-American actors in town, he soon finds himself in demand. Dean and I spend more and more time together doing theater work, and Dean soon finds a whole new circle of friends and acquaintances with whom to spend his time. Dean spends less and less time with Raj at the Ashland Avenue apartment and more and more time out on the town with me and our new mutual theater friends.

At first, Raj is happy for Dean's newfound success. But he soon grows to resent it—especially when Dean finally puts his foot down (at my insistence) on Raj's constant financial freeloading. Within a few weeks, things come to a head in the cramped two-bedroom apartment.

It's clear how low Raj's self-esteem is when he becomes so threatened by the attention Dean is receiving for his downtown theater work that he deliberately blows off his box-office duties for an entire weekend—the very same weekend I've planned to be away in Indiana taking care of some family business. I spend almost the entire weekend at my mother's house on my cell phone, fielding calls from angry ticketholders and patrons who can't get through to anyone on the box-office line, can't get anyone to return their calls asking for directions to the theater, and can't even have their ticket purchases confirmed. Dean tells me later that the cast and crew have to run the box office themselves one night when Raj fails to show, and they have to cancel the show on another because no audience comes to see it. The production loses several thousand dollars' worth of potential ticket sales that weekend; the whole six-week run ends up a money-losing venture because of it. And so, my financial situation gets even worse as a result.

The stressors pile up, and my mental state continues to deteriorate. I start loading up on caffeine to stay awake during the day because I'm not sleeping well at night. The caffeine makes me jittery and short-tempered, and the lack of sleep gives me migraines. My eyes become bloodshot, and I somnambulate through my workdays with a facial expression usually only seen on war survivors. People begin to ask me if

I'm sure that I'm okay—coworkers, friends, even random strangers on the el platform. Everyone except Dean, Raj, and Amy. They either act like everything is normal or just look past me as you would a smelly homeless person on the street you don't want to acknowledge is there. That should clue me in that something is seriously wrong with both my relationship and my living situation, but I just ignore the warning signs. My delusions that everything between Dean and me is just hunky-dory and that my financial situation will somehow fix itself are so much more comforting.

When I arrive back in Chicago the Sunday evening after Raj botches the box-office management gig, my cell phone is still ringing off the hook with nonstop calls from angry ticketholders and the show's livid director.

I'm furious.

When I get to the apartment, Raj and Amy aren't home. Dean has just returned from the Sunday matinee performance a few minutes before, and he's in our bedroom, sulking. "I'm gonna kill him," he mutters over and over. "I'm gonna *kill* him."

"I assume you mean Raj."

"You know what happened, then."

"My cell rang nonstop about it the whole damn weekend." I sit down next to him on the bed, trying hard to bite back my rising anger, which by now is controlling almost everything I do and say. It's all I can do to keep from tearing Dean and our tiny shared bedroom apart. "Look, Dean. I know you suggested I hire Raj to run the box office, but after what happened this weekend I'll need to fire him. Which might make things a little tense around here, but—"

Dean stamps his foot. "*No.* Absolutely not."

"Excuse me? He did box office for my theater company, which means he's *my* employee to fire, even if he is only earning ten bucks a show."

Dean sighs. "Look, it's tricky with Raj. He sees any kind of criticism as a violent attack. I've known him long enough to know how to manage him. Let me deal with him myself. I promise he'll apologize to you for what went wrong and that he'll do the right thing from now on. Just let me handle it in my own way. He won't screw up again, I promise."

I mull this over for a moment. I'm beginning to see a lot of strange parallels between Raj's behavior and my older brother Mark's behavior.

The thought that Raj might be a paranoid schizophrenic whose serotonin-and dopamine-addled brain considers me a lethal threat (I've seen that kind of behavior in my brother Mark often enough) crosses my mind. But I can't trust my own emotions or perceptions by this point either. I'm plenty moody and unstable myself, with a hair-trigger temper and a life preserver of delusions that are fast becoming too little too late to save me from the violent storm that's soon to come. But I still manage to give Raj the benefit of the doubt and dismiss my notion that he just might be as crazy as everyone in my own family, me included.

Against every instinct I have, I finally agree to let Dean handle Raj in his own way. And this is the latest in my very long string of mistakes.

"All right, fine. If it'll keep the peace. But I won't tolerate any more screwups on the box-office thing. There's too much riding on that show and I don't have the funds to float it myself."

Dean goes behind closed doors with Raj and Amy that evening when they come home. They stay locked away together for almost two hours, and I overhear shouting and the muffled sounds of a heated argument. But in the end, both Raj and Amy come out and apologize for what happened over the weekend. Apparently, they'd decided going on a forty-mile bike ride together was more important than Raj's part-time box-office job. They are truly sorry, and promise it will never, ever happen again. But their smiles are forced, and they still refuse to meet my eyes. My brain sends me paranoid flash warnings that they are planning something behind my back, and this time, I think that my usual self-defeating paranoia may actually be based on reality.

But I clamp those fears down. *I will find a way to make this work*, I tell myself, even though my gut tells me to dump Dean, get the hell out of there right now, and never look back—even if it means living in an alley.

I thank them both, shake their hands, and consider that the end of the matter.

But it's not.

After the play closes deep in the red, what little spare personal money I have left goes to paying off the theater company's contractual obligations for actors' stipends and production costs. Raj's botched box-office work (his work for the rest of the run is marginal at best) has cut into ticket sales so much that I, as the company's sole fiscal board member, have to pay the bills out-of-pocket or risk being sued by the

City of Chicago, which owns the theater where we produced the show. Then my temporary grant-writing job gets cut short unexpectedly when my non-profit employer runs out of funding and can't make payroll.

Two months after moving in with Dean, I am unemployed and totally broke.

I spend my days holed up in Dean's bedroom, desperately surfing the Internet for job opportunities and mailing out resumes. I'm not sleeping much at all by that point, and most days I don't even change out of my pajamas or take a shower. Raj—who works at home when he works at all—becomes my daytime companion while Dean and Amy are both at work. He chats me up the first few days, asking me all manner of friendly questions about where I went to school, what kinds of jobs I've had during my short career, where I grew up, what my family is like, how long I've been involved in professional theater. I answer all his questions in polite, cheerful detail. In my innocence I think Raj is merely trying to mend fences over the botched box-office incident. But in reality, he's on a kind of sinister reconnaissance mission. I reveal too much, of course. My dysfunctional *nutjob* childhood is laid bare for him to see in all its gory detail. Not only that, Raj sees first-hand just what a basket case I've become myself since moving in on his turf.

After a few more days of sitting home with Raj, I get a call from an employment agency offering me another short-term contract job as a temporary research assistant at a small brokerage firm. The job has no benefits and pays way below what I'm used to earning, but I take it to just get out of the house and start earning money again. In the meantime, I notice there's an odd change in the air at the apartment. Raj and Amy start abruptly leaving the room and locking themselves in Raj's bedroom whenever I walk in. I often catch them whispering to each other and casting me sidelong glances in the breakfast nook each morning. My worst fears have come true. I should leave, but I have nowhere else to go.

Dean starts behaving strangely too.

I find him waiting for me on the sofa one evening when I arrive home late from work, arms folded, a deep frown painting his features ever downward. He's alone in the apartment. All the lights are out, and he throws an ominous question at me in the darkness.

"Did you *really* graduate from the University of Chicago, Anna?"

The words hit me like a left hook. I drop my briefcase to the hardwood floor in shock. It lands with a hollow crash. "What? Yes!"

*Where the hell is this coming from?*

My framed (and very, very expensive) master's degree from the U of C's Humanities Division, the degree I paid for with work-study jobs and massive student loans that will take me twenty years or more to pay off, hangs on the wall of our bedroom, right next to Dean's bachelor's degree from the college. We'd graduated only two years apart—I started as a grad student the year after he finished undergrad—we'd even had some of the same professors. We laughed over our shared hatred for the East German Communist comparative literature professor on our first date; we once spent an entire evening passing inside jokes back and forth about two seedy South Side bars that are favorites with U of C students. After all that, how could Dean possibly think I didn't go to school there?

I'm shocked. "Why the hell would you even *ask* me that question?"

Dean looks at the floor. "No reason."

"Bullshit. Tell me why."

Dean purses his thin lips together, sheepish, and doesn't speak for almost a full minute. "Raj says that you've been deceiving everyone about who you are. He says you're a fraud."

"*What?*"

Dean sighs, looks even more sheepish. "Raj says there is no way in hell somebody like you could ever have graduated from an elite school like the University of Chicago."

"What do you mean, *someone like me?*"

"I mean—I dunno." Dean puts his face in his hands and snuffles, obviously close to tears.

Rage starts a slow simmer in the pit of my stomach. Within days, it will boil over and explode. But that evening, I am able to keep it mostly under wraps. Mostly.

"Dean, I'm your freaking live-in *life partner* here. Answer the question, please, for God's sake."

Dean's lower lip quivers and his body shakes. Finally, he speaks. "I mean, somebody with—well—your *background*. You don't come from—no offense—you don't come from a good background. Your family is—well—odd. Not normal."

I don't contradict him. "That has nothing to do with where I did or did not go to school."

"And you come from a *low-class* background," Dean adds, his voice barely a whisper. "Don't you?"

"Yeah. In some ways. So?"

"Raj says—Raj says that somebody from a low-class background like you could never get accepted to the U of C, let alone pay for it. You know, because of bad public high schools, lower intelligence—"

"*Fuck* Raj," I hiss. "The guy doesn't know shit about shit. He's obviously a freaking lunatic. You realize that, don't you?"

Dean stares me down. "I don't think so."

"What do you mean, *you don't think so*?"

"Raj's been doing a lot of research on you. And he says you're a fraud."

"What do you mean, a *fraud*? Why am I supposedly a fraud?"

"Well, the U of C thing, for one. He said he Googled you, and—"

I stomp off to our bedroom, where I retrieve a pile of student-loan bills from a file. I toss them in Dean's lap. "If you ever think for a *minute* I lied to you about going to the University of Chicago, take a look at these."

Dean stares at the pile of bills—nearly forty thousand dollars' worth of student loans that I'd taken out to attend graduate school with zero grant funding, zero money from parents, zero trust fund. I'd mortgaged my future for a degree that Raj now says as a low-class, mentally unstable bitch I couldn't possibly have earned. The fact that my own live-in life partner is even willing to *consider* that possibility turns my stomach. I'm so livid I can barely breathe.

Dean's eyes widen at the huge balances, tears form when he sees that on every single statement is a reference to the University of Chicago.

"Jesus," he sputters. "I knew you had bills, but Jesus H. Christ. No wonder you're broke."

"Yeah, no fucking kidding. And why in God's name would you listen to a bunch of baseless bullshit from Raj over what you know yourself? Over *me*? Why?"

But I *know* why. Because I'm not exactly the picture of stability, here. I come from a broken home and a bad family. My mother is crazy, my dad is a nymphomaniac, and my older brother is a paranoid schizophrenic. I can barely hold things together myself, I'm flat broke, and I'm about three seconds away from tearing Dean to pieces with my own bare hands. Why would anyone believe anything I have to say? Why would anyone want to be with me at all? I'm not good enough, I'll never be good enough, and I'm probably better off dead. The same mantra that has plagued me and my brain for years has simply jumped out of my head and come to fruition right here in this cramped Chicago apartment's living room. Dean is drawing the same conclusion anybody in his shoes would make. And it certainly doesn't help that Raj is an asshole, either. I don't stand a chance here.

Dean looks helpless, and for a brief moment even seems to pity me. But mostly he just stares at me with contempt. "I've known Raj a long time. And he's my friend. I care about what he thinks."

"What about what *you* think? Doesn't that matter?"

"I don't know what I think," he says, his voice like a little boy's. "So I asked Raj to do more research on you. So I can figure out what exactly I *do* think."

"What the fuck—"

Dean holds up his hand. "You're not who you pretend to be, Anna. That much I know for sure. You're a different person from one day to the next. You have too many different personalities, your behavior's so unpredictable, I—I just need an outsider's objective opinion. So, I'm having you investigated. Raj and I, we've tracked down and contacted a lot of people who used to know you, people from your past, so we can investigate what kind of person you really are. Psychologically speaking. Raj's even thinking of hiring a private investigator. Thought maybe you should know that."

Investigated. They are having me *investigated*.

I feel the floor drop out from underneath my feet. Granted, I've never considered myself the portrait of mental stability—and in the interest of full disclosure, I told Dean as much from the get-go—but to say that I have *too many different personalities*? To tell me, to my face, that my behavior is so unpredictable that I have to be *investigated* as a possible *fraud*?

What the hell is going on in my relationship? Who is this man that I sleep beside every night, cook and eat meals with every day, and for all intents and purposes have settled into a reasonable facsimile of married life with—to *investigate* me?

And yet, it all makes perfect sense. I've been in a downward spiral for the past two months, ever since I met Dean. And I wasn't exactly sane when I met him, either. In the past two months I've lost my job, my home, all of my money. I live in an overcrowded apartment with people who hate my guts, and I don't even have the wherewithal to do anything about it. I don't bathe or even get dressed half of the time, and I spend most of my free time online. Sure, I've been job-hunting, but I also waste a lot of time reading newsfeeds, trolling Craigslist, and typing away in theater chatrooms. My angry tirades about how much money my theater production is losing alienates almost everyone in the cast and crew—they call me a "bitch" and a "bully" behind my back. For all I know, they think I've just blown all the box-office receipts on myself. That's something Raj would do—hell, he *already* does that with his rent money—so why wouldn't he have those kinds of suspicions about me? Besides, he has plenty of motivation to poison Dean against me since I keep telling Dean to stop letting Raj use him as a financial gravy train. I've stepped right into the middle of a perfect storm, and it's not like I can just pack my boxes and bags and move home to Mommy and Daddy's comfortable home in the suburbs. As a daughter of *nutjobs* from a broken home, I don't have that option. And so, the *nutjob* pattern of my family DNA just loops and repeats, loops and repeats.

I can't comprehend any of this right now, though. I don't have the benefit of hindsight when I'm about to make a complete psychotic break with reality.

I stare right past Dean out the living-room window and watch the traffic pass for a moment or two. I feel sick to my stomach. My head starts to spin, my heartbeat to race. I take several deep breaths, will myself not to fall apart on the spot. I've spent my whole life building an airtight outer facade around myself to hide the chaotic, empty blackness I am inside, and now I can feel that facade crumbling down right onto Dean's living room floor. I've been exposed, found out for what I really am—a borderline psychotic. It doesn't matter that at this moment, I don't *believe* that I'm borderline psychotic. It doesn't matter how much I've always tried to hide the gaping black hole in my brain, especially from Dean. The gaping, oozing, pus-covered sore of my mental illness is right out in the open for Dean to see now, whether I like it or not. It's pretty apparent that Dean is revolted by it. And who wouldn't be?

By now I'm desperate. I cannot—will not—let myself be abandoned again. I have to salvage this relationship somehow. I have to hold onto Dean at all costs. At *any* cost. *"I'm not crazy,"* I shriek, my voice high and sharp as razor wire.

Dean won't meet my eyes. "A lot of people say you are."

"Who? What people?"

"Just people that Raj and I have been talking to. People who know you."

*"Who?"*

Dean hems and haws for a moment or two, obviously trying to find a way to avoid the question. But I won't allow it. "Look, Anna, I'll tell you once I have more information. Raj is doing all the legwork," he finally says.

I start hyperventilating then. Adrenaline starts coursing through my body—it's fight-or-flight time.

I know what I have to do then. I know because I've done it so many times before whenever a domestic situation goes bad—I've done it over and over again from the time I was a child being torn between a psychotic mother and a selfish nymphomaniac father.

I run.

I dash to the bedroom, grab a backpack and start stuffing it with items I grab at random—cell phone, shirts, shoes, underwear, a half-empty bottle of cologne, a paperback novel, a pair of earrings. I pull my heavy parka out of the hall closet and head for the front door.

Dean suddenly jerks upright from where he's been sitting slumped on the couch. "Where are you going?"

"I'm leaving. Goodbye."

I dash out the front door of the building and stand on the corner, watching taxicabs and SUVs roll by for ten full minutes before I realize I have no idea where I can go.

I walk up and down block after block of dark, sleet-slick city streets, my mind's gears spinning out of control.

In my mind's ear, I hear two passionate voices—both of them young and female but neither one my own—having a rapid-fire, passionate argument.

One says, I can't stay with Dean. I *can't*. The man obviously doesn't trust me, seems to think I'm some kind of lying robot alien. Staying with him would be like shacking up with the KGB. Staying with him would mean that I believe what he believes about me. Staying with him means that I believe I am a crazy, lying, low-class, trailer-trash, borderline-psychotic fraud. This voice sounds more like a normal person. This voice makes sense.

But there's another voice in the conversation. This one is louder, faster, meaner. Shrill, scheming, and screaming. Scary. And totally mesmerizing.

*You cannot let this happen. You cannot. You will go back right now and you will fix this. You will use whatever means necessary. You will not lose this man who has become your mind, your life, your soul, your very reason for existence, because if you do, you will die. Use whatever means necessary to keep him from leaving you. Whatever means necessary, because if he leaves, you will die.*

I do not want to die.

I will go back, and I will fix this. And I will use whatever means necessary.

My mind has raced so far and for so long that I've walked almost twenty blocks north and west without realizing it. I stop short on the corner of Clark and Winnemac, and stand there staring into space for several minutes before I can get my bearings. The beginnings of a violent mood swing take hold, and I suddenly switch from a bottomless ravine of despair and terror to a mountain of manic power and pride. I have given myself a purpose—to hang on to my tiny, narrow, precarious ledge of a domestic situation at all costs. I hail a cab, my dark mood bubbling up into something brighter, sharper, and potentially lethal as the taxi heads south on Clark Street back to Dean's Lakeview apartment.

*You will fix this. You will fix this. You will fix this, or die.*

I do not want to die. I do not.

I arrive back at the apartment in a euphoria and find Dean hunched over in our bedroom. He clutches at his stomach as if poisoned. His mouth hangs open, and he breathes through it in short bursts. I can tell he's been crying.

"I'm sorry," he snuffles. "I'm so sorry."

"We need to get out of here," I say. "We need to get away from those two. They're like, destroying us." My breath comes in short bursts too. Soon Dean and I are hyperventilating in perfect unison, like Siamese twins who share the same pathetic set of lungs. "We have to get our own place. *Have* to." I grind my teeth and dig in my heels, prepared to fight to the death for that objective. But for the moment at least, I won't have to.

"I know," he says. "We'll get one. We're going to be okay."

But it's not going to be okay. Not by a long shot.

Dean and I go looking at one-bedroom apartments the next day. We find an affordable one we like in a neighborhood further north and west. We sign a lease, but we can't move in for another two months.

Dean promises he will tell Raj and Amy that we are moving out soon, but he keeps making excuses to avoid it. Meanwhile, the situation between us and them is getting downright nasty.

Every night, I take my dinner alone locked in our bedroom while Dean sits out in the living room listening to Raj and Amy rant about everything that is so horrifically wrong with me. According to them, my clothes, appearance, and behavior are slutty. I am a sex-crazed lunatic who is out to bilk Dean for money. My few remaining personal items and housewares are chintzy junk that must be disposed of—along with me—before they and I can infect and corrupt everyone in the apartment with my working-class, mentally unstable contaminants. They belittle Dean for ever wanting to take up with me in the first place, call him "weak" and a "victim." Raj and Amy have even somehow managed to get into contact with some of my old college classmates (whom I haven't seen or spoken to in years) that have all supposedly vouched for my cruel, manipulative insanity. The worst part is, I know that at least some of what they're hearing has to be true. I worry and wonder who their sources are, and whether there is anything I can do to silence them.

Dean sits and stonily listens to all of it without a hint of complaint. And not only does he not complain—after a few weeks of Raj and Amy's nightly rantings about his live-in girlfriend's purported mental and socioeconomic degeneracy, Dean begins to believe every word. He starts avoiding eye contact with me, then almost all conversation altogether. We stop having sex. He stops wanting to be seen with me in public. He even leaves some pamphlets for Stone Soup—a low-cost communal housing building for single young women up the road from our apartment—sitting out on my desk as a passive-aggressive suggestion that I consider moving there, alone.

I know then that something bad, very bad, is going to happen between Dean and me. I don't know what and I don't know when, but part of me knows it is inevitable.

Everything comes to a head a few days later—the last week of April 2002.

On Monday of that week, I go to my temporary research assistant job—a job that just a week earlier the employment agency that had placed me in it had said would soon switch to a permanent basis with a good salary and full benefits—and am summarily told by my boss that my services are no longer needed. Apparently, the job is indeed going permanent, but my boss prefers to hire one of his former colleagues recently laid off by another company than offer it to me. He gives me the choice of staying for the rest of the day and *training* the woman who will replace me, or going home.

I choose to go home. There will be no paycheck for me that week, and with Chicago's economy still in the toilet, maybe no paycheck for a very long time to come. And since I've lost a temporary job, there is no possibility of unemployment benefits. I have no savings, only credit cards that are still maxed-out from my first unemployment stint. I have only a few dollars left in my checking account and a pile of bills due by the end of the month. I have no idea what I'm going to do next, but I hold on to the hope that my live-in boyfriend will help pick up the slack until I find another job.

I call Dean at work from the apartment and tell him the news. He sucks in his breath, but doesn't speak.

"Dean? Dean, are you there?"

He isn't. There is a click, then dial tone.

Dean doesn't come home from work that evening. He doesn't come home at all, in fact. When I wake up alone in bed the next morning with no sign of him anywhere, I begin to panic.

I sit on the couch that morning, nervous and twitchy as a mother hen as I wait for word. There is none. I call Dean's parents in the western suburbs to see if he's surfaced there. He hasn't. I call his office, where a receptionist tells me he's failed to show for work that day. A hundred different scenarios run through my mind. When I have visions of Dean and his mint-green Honda Accord splattered across concrete pylons on Interstate 94—the highway he takes to and from his Japanese translator's job in the north suburbs—I start calling hospitals. I can only imagine that something terrible has happened. My *nutjob* brain is simply unable to conceive the notion that the only reason I can't find Dean is because he doesn't want to be found. To me, that is the same thing as Dean being dead.

Raj gets up around ten and finds me on the couch. He sees my dire expression and snickers. "What's up *your* butt this morning, Anna?" he sneers.

"Dean didn't come home last night."

Raj laughs and claps his hands twice. "Well, it was bound to happen sooner or later," he says. "I only wonder why it took him this long."

I have to get out of there.

I grab my cell phone and backpack, throw things inside it without thinking, and dash out the door. I forget to take my coat. When I get outside, I realize I have no shampoo or conditioner. I decide I will need shampoo and conditioner if I am going to leave the untenable apartment situation and find somewhere else to live while I search for Dean's dead body (there can be no other possible explanation for why he didn't come home last night). I will stay with a friend and figure things out. It will be okay. It will be okay. It will be okay.

I'm walking when I realize that I don't have a coat and it is very, very cold. I should go back to the apartment and get my coat, some shampoo, some conditioner. Wait, no—there's no time. I'll just go to Walgreens and buy some cheap hair products for 99 cents. Bought it. Got it. Good. Don't know exactly why I feel I need it so desperately, but I do. This is what you'd call "disorganized thinking," a classic symptom of a brief psychotic episode. I'm focusing on all the wrong things for the wrong reasons, like believing a cheap bottle of shampoo is the only thing that will keep me alive.

I exit Walgreens and walk some more. I'm getting colder and colder with every step. I walk faster to warm up. I dial Jacey. We talk. She can't help me. Not today. Maybe later in the week. I hang up and walk some more. I walk and walk and walk without seeing, without hearing, without feeling the uncontrollable shivering that has set in as I spend hour after hour in the freezing cold with no jacket, no gloves, no hat. I walk and walk until I end up somewhere in Lincoln Square. I glance at my watch and see that several hours have passed. It's almost dark. Soon it will be nightfall and I have nowhere I can stay unless I go back to the untenable apartment where Raj thinks the fact my live-in life partner has vanished into thin air is funny. I have to go back there anyway, though, because suddenly I remember that I need a coat.

I find an el station. I ride the train south-southwest until I reach my neighborhood again. I get to my building and climb the half-flight of stairs to the first floor landing. I try my key, and it doesn't fit. I try it again. It doesn't fit. I make sure I have the right apartment—I do—and try my key a third time. It doesn't fit.

I inspect the door. There's a new deadbolt on it, smaller and shinier than the one it used to have. I pound on the door several times, beg to be let in. Silence.

In the few hours that I've been gone, Raj and Amy have changed the apartment locks—illegally evicting me. I can't get inside my own home (such as it is), even to get a coat to protect me from the freezing Chicago cold. I can't get a change of underwear or contact lens solution or the small stash of cash I have hidden in a shoebox underneath my bed. Raj and Amy have finished their investigation of me, and have obviously discovered something about me so awful and sinister that they have banished me for their own protection, lest the pus-covered, gaping black hole of my illness somehow creep its way through the crack of the doorjamb and infect them too. As of this moment, I am homeless.

I am homeless. Broke, cold, crazy, and homeless.

I trudge back out onto the street. Everything is a blur, a dark, colorful blur. I try to think of friends I can call at this hour to help me, to shelter me, but I come up with nothing. I can't, for two reasons. For one thing, my brain has been hijacked into what my therapists will later tell me is a *brief psychotic episode*. For another, the very small part of my brain that is still working properly is too embarrassed to ask anyone for help. Because to do that will be to admit that Dean, Raj, Amy, the cast and crew of the play I just produced, and everyone I've ever met is right about me. They have found me out, discovered that my true self is that of a *nutjob* and a life on the cold Chicago streets is therefore all that I deserve.

And so, I swallow the rest of my pride and sanity and make for The Sunflower Arms.

Tonight, I will sleep in a flophouse.

The bed at The Sunflower Arms is lumpy and lopsided. I can't sleep. I can't even cry. I know I should feel sad, and empty, and lost, and frightened. Those would be logical emotions to feel when someone who is smart and educated and used to have a good job finds herself suddenly homeless and broke and sleeping in a flophouse. But there is nothing inside of me right now that is logical. Logic is impossible when the only emotion occupying my brain's empty shell is rage.

The rage I feel is rage in the pure, classical sense. Rage is a primal emotion. Most people never truly feel it. I know that I've never truly felt it until this exact moment. Those that do feel it often commit heinous crimes. Rage is what drives people to commit murder, violence, war, mass extermination. Rage is dangerous. And rage is real.

As I study the desiccated remains of the horsefly on the light bulb just beside my head, I wonder if my rage is real enough for me to commit a crime. It certainly feels that way.

So I do.

I dig my cell phone out of my purse. It's after ten, which means the call won't use any of my precious few remaining minutes. That leaves me free and clear to do what my borderline-psychotic brain tells me must be done.

I dial Dean's number at work. I know he's not there, but his voice mail is. I can't let my rage loose on him personally because I don't know where he is, but voice mail is the next best thing, right? There's nothing illegal about that, is there?

Dean's voicemail greeting picks up. I wait for a second or two after the tone before I let loose.

"You fucking cocksucker, *I am going to kill you*. Do you know why? Because I don't have anywhere to fucking live right now, and it's all *your* goddamn fault. You abandoned me, you fucking asshole! And now I'm fucking homeless! If I ever get you in my sights again you are gonna fucking *die. I will kill you, and you will die*."

I hang up. Ten minutes later, I leave him another, longer, even more threatening message. And so I pass the night in the flophouse this way, threatening to kill, dismember, shred, burn, annihilate Dean in every possible way and with every possible weapon until his voicemail at work is full.

The next morning, I check out of The Sunflower Arms and consider my options.

As I stand in the blinding morning light on Belmont Avenue, I realize I don't really have any options. Except one.

I decide to call my friend Sharon.[6] She and her husband Brian[7] were classmates of mine back in college. They are married now and have an apartment together nearby. Sharon is a computer programmer, Brian is a part-time graphic designer and painter of postmodern nudes that I have posed for on occasion when I needed extra cash. I haven't talked to either one of them in a while. But I know that Sharon has had problems with depression in the past and takes a cocktail of several antidepressants every morning to help her function normally. Somehow I guess that the two of them will be sympathetic to me, maybe give me shelter and aid until I figure out what to do.

It's the middle of a weekday, so when I call Sharon's house the voicemail picks up. I leave as desperate a message as I can. I'm far beyond pride or shame by this point.

I have no money on me so I go to the Chicago Public Library branch a few blocks away to wait for word. My stomach growls from lack of breakfast; my teeth are mossy from lack of brushing. I sit in the Periodicals Department, a few tables away from some smelly winos who are obviously regulars there. I am humiliated.

My cell phone rings. "Anna, it's Sharon. I just checked my voicemail at home. Look. Go to our apartment, right now. Brian is working at his studio this morning but he'll meet you there soon. He'll help you get your stuff back from Raj and Amy too. We'll take care of you. Don't worry. It's going to be OK."

"Thanks," I say. A recorded female voice interrupts and says I have no more prepaid cell minutes available, and the line goes dead.

I crash at Sharon and Brian's apartment for the next several days. They are kind to me. Brian goes over to the apartment and manages to get Raj and Amy to let him in so he can retrieve most of my belongings, including my cat, Mouse. Mouse doesn't get along with Sharon and Brian's cats, so my friend Jacey (who has returned from her downstate movie shoot) takes my cat to her place in Evanston. Brian offers me some paid work modeling for his latest painting project. Jacey offers to pay me to help her catalog her vast costume collection. Everyone is so kind, so generous, so nonjudgmental. They all say that I have been horribly wronged, that Dean is a weakling and an ass to disappear without explanation and allow his so-called friends to throw me out onto the street. Nobody even considers the possibility that the whole thing is my own fault, the inevitable result of a mentally unstable brain that exploded under the pressure-cooker of the apartment—at least, they never say this to my face. Whether they really believe those statements, or just say them out of pity I'll never know. But I'm forever grateful for their help when I'm at my lowest. Perhaps they do this for me because of their own experiences of mental illness. They know better than to judge when they could someday be judged themselves—or perhaps they already have been.

Sharon, Brian, and Jacey buy me food and toiletries and help me look for a new job, they hug me when I cry. I wonder if they would treat me the same way if they knew I leave more messages threatening to kill Dean on his work voice mail every evening before I go to bed.

"You know Anna," Sharon says to me one night over dinner. "Way back when, people like you and me, we would have been the crazy aunts that families locked away in attics and didn't talk about. Or even worse, we'd have been lobotomized and put away in institutions like Rosemary Kennedy. We should consider ourselves lucky that we live in the age of Prozac."

"I don't take Prozac," I say. "I don't take anything."

"Maybe you should," Sharon says.

I spend a few weeks at Sharon and Brian's apartment. Dean finally resurfaces at his parent's home. It turns out that he has had a nervous breakdown of his own that involved him living in his car for a while in rural Wisconsin. He takes medical leave from his job, and talks to me occasionally on the phone. I apologize for threatening to kill him. I apologize for all my voicemail rages, and for calling him a cocksucker and an asshole. He tells me that he understands, he tells me that it's not really my fault I acted that way. "You had a breakdown, I had a break-down. I know that now. I understand," he says. But he doesn't sound convinced.

I have found a freelance job doing desktop publishing and editing on a short-term contract that pays well. The time comes for Dean and me to move into the apartment we rented together in Ravenswood. Brian and Sharon help me move. Dean shows up with his furniture and speaks to me civilly. Everything seems back to normal. But it isn't.

Once Dean has moved in all his furniture and household items, he gets up to leave.

"You're not staying here?" I ask.

"I need some time," he says. "I need some time at my parents'." He will not meet my eyes. He leaves.

I plunge on. My rages and mood swings eventually even out. I go to work and get through most days without a single thought of causing harm to myself and others, with occasional lapses that I suppress with alcohol and cable TV. I send Dean dozens of apology-love-note e-mails that go unanswered. I wait for him to contact me and tell me that we will be together in our little love-nest forevermore.

He doesn't.

I settle into the apartment—a sunny, spacious one-bedroom-plus-den on a tree-lined street, an apartment with new carpeting and an eat-in kitchen and a bay window overlooking mature trees and a mailbox in the lobby that the landlord has marked with mine and Dean's names. A week or two after I move in, I get a letter.

I don't have the letter any longer. I burned it with a long-handled butane lighter in a brass bowl designed for holding incense. I don't have it any longer, but I do remember most of what it said.

Dean sends me a break-up letter. He can't face me himself or even call me to end things between us, so all I get is a laser-printed letter on cheap recycled paper, typed and folded and unsigned. He calls me a *walking disaster area*. He calls me a *manipulative bitch*. He calls me a *lunatic fringe case*. He says my personality is *borderline*, encloses a pamphlet on *borderline personality disorder* and a clipping of the anonymous classified ad he took out insulting me in the "Personal Messages" section of the *Chicago Reader*. He says that I and my mind and my body are damaged beyond repair, he says that I deserve to be miserable and alone, he says that I am solely responsible for his nervous breakdown that forced him to live in his car in Wisconsin and embarrassed his family. Dean says that with Raj's investigation help, he has spoken personally to some old college classmates of mine who say I am crazy and a menace to society.

One of those old classmates is Todd Naismith, the first man I truly fell in love with, the man who taught me about Buddhism and the Beat poets in a college dorm room that smelled of Japanese incense.

So Todd Naismith—whom I haven't seen or spoken to in almost six years—thinks that I am crazy and a menace to society?

It is this knowledge that hurts me the most.

In the letter's closing, Dean calls me a *nutjob*.

I am a nutjob. Bona fide. I have it in writing.

I burn the letter, savoring every red ember as the edges ignite and curl and float away into ash.

# 4

# 1993–2002: NINE YEARS TO
# ENLIGHTENMENT

I fall in love for the first time when I'm nineteen. And the first man I fall in love with is one of the very few I never sleep with. Anybody who says that love is sex and sex is love has got it all wrong—I've got proof. I'll call my proof Todd Naismith.[1]

When I first meet Todd Naismith, he's tall—six-foot-five if he's a day—blonde, blue-eyed, lithe and rippled of body, strong of chin. He's like a young Gen-X-grunge version of George Peppard in *Breakfast at Tiffany's*. We are chosen to be resident advisors—RAs—in the same coed dorm our sophomore year of college at a large public university in the Midwest. As recognized peer leaders of our student body, hand-picked by the university administration to serve as models of good be-havior and blossoming adulthood to incoming freshmen, RAs are sup-posed to be models of academic success, mental health, and stability. Todd Naismith and I are none of these things, so I guess that doesn't say much for our university administration. But we are two grunge-goth kids with similar tastes in dark literature, death metal, and Kurt Cobain, along with just the right amount of melancholy. Our first conversation is a brag session where we compare our favorite books to read when depressed. (Mine is Dalton Trumbo's *Johnny Got His Gun*; Todd's is Henry Miller's *Tropic of Cancer*.) We both love Led Zeppelin, the Beatles, and Violent Femmes, and we're both the product of broken Catholic homes. Todd and I are kindred spirits, and we latch on to each other from the get-go. I'm a long way from Chicago, at this point. In college I'm just another 1990s working-class girl lost in a sea of mediocrity and *Reality Bites*.

Todd and I are RAs in a dilapidated 1960s-era dorm. Todd is assigned the ninth floor of the building, and I have the tenth.

Todd and I both have "specialty" floor assignments that are matched to our own academic achievements. I have the Honors floor (with 24-hour quiet time and a private library to encourage extra studying by the floor's Honors-program freshmen) thanks to my omnipresence on the Dean's List; Todd has the Wellness floor (on which all smoking, drinking, drug use, and non-monogamous unprotected sex are prohibited) because he was active in the Campus Wellness Program (a student activity group that advocates for a healthy, active, drug- and alcohol-free campus lifestyle) during his freshman year.

Todd and I both bond during the two weeks of RA training before the school year starts largely because neither of us lives up to our assigned floor's ideals in our own personal lives. I might make the Dean's List every quarter, but that's only because I find all my classes unchallenging. I get straight As but rarely study more than a half-hour a day and never set foot in the library. Todd joined the Campus Wellness Program only to serve as cover for the fact that he consumes copious amounts of marijuana. Todd is also a connoisseur of frequent multiple sexual partners, booze, and mind-altering chemical inhalants—especially nitrous oxide, which he can get by the tankful whenever he wants at the dairy where he works on school breaks (they use it for whipping cream).

Todd Naismith and I are therefore both campus hypocrites of the highest order. So of course we become fast friends.

Todd is a history major with a minor in literature, I am a literature major with a minor in history. We therefore find ourselves in the same classes every quarter, and we start hanging out in each others' dorm rooms for long late-night hours to "study." The only thing is, we never really *study* anything, except each other. And I don't mean that sexually.

We study each others' *souls*.

No, really. It sounds trite, sure—two nineteen-year-old college kids bonding on a deep spiritual level without the benefit of sex. But that's exactly what we do. I spend three or four nights a week in Todd's room, the two of us always splitting a sausage pizza from Papa John's that's always delivered by the same Korean graduate student with English so poor that Todd and I invent a catchphrase for our frequent nightly soirees on Eastern philosophy and all things Beat Generation. One of us will call the other and say, "You-ah Order-ah Papah Jah-hans?" and the party is on.

It's Todd who introduces me to the freethinking literature and wide-open spiritual writing that I'm not learning about in my dull literature survey courses. Jack Kerouac and Diane di Prima, Gary Snyder and Allan Ginsberg, William S. Burroughs and Denise Levertov—all these writers are the stuff of our late-night pizza talks, which we mix liberally with incense, vinyl records, and mix tapes from Todd's vast postmodern jazz collection.

On the surface, Todd and I are a lot alike. We're both the offspring of divorced Irish-Catholic parents. We both grew up in relatively un-stable lower-middle/working-class homes; we were both dreamy and introspective "odd" kids who'd preferred books to toys since we were toddlers. We're both foul-mouthed, sharp-tongued, cynical, and blunt to the point of being obtuse. We have the same dry sense of humor and the same love for obscure modern jazz and minor women writers like Katherine Mansfield and Margaret Fuller. We gaze into each other's deep-set eyes and understand things we've never understood in anyone before.

I become Todd's best friend, confidante, mentor, and partner-at-arms in all things. We sit together in all our classes and trade witty barbs on handwritten notes we pass back and forth for the entire lecture, notes that start out the class period as bad jokes and end up two hours later as long strings of freeform poetry. We manipulate the RA duty roster to ensure we are both on call on the same nights, and we always make our "rounds" at night (when we walk the floors of the dorm, checking fire extinguishers and busting underage keg parties) together. I help him write term papers and teach him all my secret techniques for bullshitting through essay exams on Renaissance literature for easy As. I teach him how to speed-read, how to tell the difference between post-modern and poststructuralist, how to tell the difference between Pre-Raphaelite and Romantic poetry and art. In exchange for all these arts and culture lessons, Todd teaches me how to meditate by sitting on a black cushion and measuring out my breaths two at a time, gives me inscribed copies of *A Buddhist Bible* and *On the Road*, teaches me the Heart Sutra, and loans me his CD boxed set of live Jack Kerouac poetry readings. He makes me personalized mix tapes to listen to while I write term papers. He loans me his sex manuals when I complain I'm not having orgasms with my boyfriend. He lets me cry on his shoulder.

Todd shows me the best ways to mix drinks with bong hits without getting sick; he takes me out for my birthday and gets me drunk on blowjob shots until I'm too bombed to lick the whipped cream off my cheeks and nose, so wasted that he has to help me up to my bed and tuck me in and lock my dorm-room door behind him using his RA master key.

Todd makes me into his de facto emotion-spiritual advisor. In fact, he idolizes me. Todd tells me I'm the smartest person he's ever met, tells others that he respects me and my supposed great intellect more than anything else on campus—more than his favorite history professors. Todd even refers to me in a campus newspaper interview as "a Renaissance woman for the 90s." He consults me on all his most personal decisions, including whether or not he should break up every other week with his on-again, off-again sorority-girl girlfriend, whom I'll call Marcia. I always tell him he should, no matter how many times they manage to get back together. And why wouldn't I? I have ulterior motives, after all.

I don't understand what attracts Todd to Marcia. She's scrawny, and she has pasty skin and firebomb-red hair that always looks and smells greasy. Her teeth are vaguely brown, probably from heavy smoking and drinking too many whiskey sours at Alpha Chi Omega, the sorority house where she lives off-campus. Marcia rarely speaks above a whisper, and in true early-90s grunge-rock fashion, she never seems to wear clean clothes or to have recently bathed. Whenever her path crosses with mine, I find her conversation and personality to resemble something between expired yogurt and a rock. While Todd is witty, sardonic, well-read, assertive, and ambitious in a New Bohemian sort of way, Marcia is dull, wooden, shy to the point of disappearing into concrete walls, spoiled, lazy, and culturally illiterate.

Todd and Marcia couldn't be an odder match if they tried.

Marcia studies oboe in the Music Department, but she supposedly has tendonitis in her hands so severe that it makes playing the oboe impossible, so she's "on leave" from her music-performance major for a few quarters until her hands heal. In the meantime, Marcia is failing music theory and has withdrawn from most of her other courses. As far as I can tell, she is majoring mostly in sorority parties and fucking Todd's brains out.

I suppose what attracts Todd to Marcia is the sex. They only seem to spend time together on weekends (they're always broken up or "on a break" during the week), but every Friday and Saturday night without fail, Todd and Marcia have sex loud enough to wake the thousand-years' dead, and always just one floor below me with their windows wide open.

Todd and Marcia apparently are not the kind of couple who are into meat-and-potatoes, missionary-position sex either. As far as I can tell, they most enjoy doing the deed standing up, preferably while banging against a heavy, stationary object that crashes loudly upon each impact. I hear each and every thud, crash, shout, and sigh through the cheap dorm drywall and cinderblock. I even follow their sexual role-playing scenarios from one weekend to the next like a Hispanic telenovela—I have the pleasure of overhearing a running bedroom gag going for several weeks that involves Todd playing the role of a milkman and Marcia playing the role of a desperate housewife who relies on his "special deliveries" for sexual sustenance. Every time I hear Todd shout "SPECIAL DELIVERY" through my dorm-room window, I try to match up his nymphomaniac weekend bedroom habits with the cool, detached man I share pizza with almost every night during the week, and I come up with nothing.

There's no accounting for taste, I suppose.

Maybe I'm so attracted to Todd because he's like my dad in that respect. Some psychology schools of thought say that every girl wants to grow up and marry her father.[2] If I'd ever managed to marry Todd, I'd have come pretty darn close to achieving just that.

Todd's romps with Marcia get so wild during winter quarter that the freshmen residents on his floor start coming up to my room on weekends, asking if I would mind telling Todd to either keep it down or get a motel room off-campus. "I know you're his friend," a shy, pimpled young woman whispers to me late one Friday evening. "Make him stop. I can't sleep and I can't study with all that racket. Plus, it's kind of embarrassing."

A pudgy young fratboy puts it a little more bluntly the following Sunday: "My parents came to visit yesterday and asked me why my RA's room sounds like a porn film soundtrack."

"I'll talk to him," I promise. But I don't.

Up until this point, I've felt like I can talk to Todd about anything. We've touched upon plenty of sensitive subjects in our late-night private pizza parties already—like the fact that I'm not at all sexually satisfied by my current boyfriend, a chemistry major named "Bob" whom I met last year when I was a member of the university's marching color guard, for one; the fact that I always teeter precariously on the edge of clinical depression, for another. Todd tells me the solution to managing both issues is to look inside myself—therein, I'll find the answer. He gives me a book on walking meditation by Thich Nhat Hanh, blows pot smoke at me, and then asks with a straight face what *does* turn me on in bed. But no matter how hard I try to build myself up to it, I can't confront Todd about his own wild sex life, even as a favor to the timid college freshmen he's hurting with it. I just can't.

It's around this time that I realize I'm in love with Todd.

I don't know what to do. I'm already dating somebody else. And Todd is my closest friend and Platonic soulmate—I don't want to do anything that might jeopardize our near-perfect friendship. Still, listening to him fornicate wildly really begins to bother me—and yet, I can't bring myself to tell him how I feel. I also can't help but notice the parallel between Todd's exhibitionist sexual behavior and what I endured in my father's house as a child, and that realization starts making me feel ill. I know by then that Todd is probably bad for me, but being the young woman exploring her independence for the first time that I am, that knowledge just makes me want him all the more.

Yet in a strange paradox, I find myself inhibited by my desire to please Todd, in much the same manner as I'd stifled myself around my father in childhood and adolescence. Todd idolizes and adores me as no man ever has before, and all without ever laying a finger on my body.

Todd has given me the gift of true emotional intimacy for the first time in my life. And yet, I'm incapable of appreciating that intimacy as long as it exists without sex, without *love*—I think (erroneously, of course) that the two things are interchangeable. Do I dare risk spoiling the cozy relationship we share by telling him the truth?

In the short term, the answer is no.

I stuff my growing physical attraction to Todd into a tiny, compact area just underneath my spleen, where it slowly festers. I break up with my boyfriend Bob, who takes it so badly he begins stalking me. Todd tries to be supportive, but he's getting distracted by his constant week-day fights with Marcia, which he tempers by sleeping around with some of his floor residents—including a deranged, plump self-mutilator named Lisa who comes to Todd's dorm room seeking peer counseling and gets herself some good-old-fashioned sexual healing instead. I start having trouble with my accelerated French class, and my grades threaten to slip below straight As for the first time ever. And probably worst of all, our dorm inherits a pyromaniac "problem" resident who's already been kicked out of two other dorms for setting fire to pizza boxes stuffed in trash chutes. So for the second half of winter quarter, twice-nightly fire alarms and hours-long evacuations into the frigid night air so firefighters can clear the smoke-choked hallways mean nobody in our dorm sleeps more than two hours a night for several weeks. Our residence hall director puts his foot down a week before spring break and kicks the pyro out himself, but by then I'm crashing and burning into a major stress-induced depression.

The stress and mood disorders that are keeping me up nights, killing my appetite, and making me lose focus in class are a bigger threat to me than just making me feel bad or sorry for myself too—I'm attending college on a full academic scholarship, which I'll lose if I don't maintain at least a 3.5 grade-point average. My dad is now on his third marriage and has two new babies at home, so it's not like I can move back in with him, and my mom lives on welfare in a one-room apartment miles off-campus. I don't have a car, and all my money goes to pay for school. I've lost track of what my brother is doing now entirely—the last I heard he was living in a rented house full of other college dropouts like himself. I know I should probably go seek therapy, but I don't. I use my part-time job and full course-load as an excuse, telling myself I just don't have the time required to spend two or three hours a week meeting with a therapist. But the truth is, I just don't want to face the truth. It's the same choice millions upon millions of other people with mental illness make—if you just ignore the symptoms, if you hope and pray and deny it enough, maybe it will just go away.[3] Besides, seeking help will publicly brand you with the scarlet letter of being crazy, and no nineteen-year-old girl wants that. I certainly don't.

Todd notices my melancholy mood the weekend before spring break. He's broken up with Marcia that week, so we go out for dinner and a movie—*The Remains of the Day* with Emma Thompson and

Anthony Hopkins—with our friend and boss Regina LaChance,[4] a graduate student who works part-time supervising the dorm's RA staff. The film's plotline centers on the tragedy of unrequited love, and it affects me tremendously. So tremendously, in fact, I can't get up from my seat to follow Todd and Regina out of the old Esquire Theater when the credits roll. I've struggled so hard to bottle up sobs in the second half of the film that the entire lower half of my body is temporarily paralyzed.

Todd and Regina have both left the theater already, and in the clutch of departing people they don't notice I've remained behind. When the theater is empty I manage to release a couple of choking sobs that come out more like whimpered coughs, and that's enough to unlock my frozen legs and waist. I put on my sunglasses to hide my red eyes and tearstained cheeks, make it out onto the street, and find Todd and Regina waiting for me on the sidewalk. They don't seem alarmed at all to have lost track of me; they probably both think I just went to the bathroom or something.

Todd and Regina want to go to a nearby street cafe for after-dinner drinks. It's a laid-back place that never cards underage drinkers, so Todd and I are sure to get served. I shrug and follow Todd and Regina down the block to an empty cafe table. I feel as if my whole body is under pins and needles—like the heavy, tingly feeling you have when coming out from under anesthesia. I walk along the sidewalk and sink into a wicker cafe chair as if moving slowly through Jell-O.

Todd and Regina talk between themselves for awhile without noticing me much. I've suspected for some time that Todd might be sleeping with Regina too—which if true, means he has at least three different sexual relationships going at once—but my perception could certainly be distorted by my growing depression. To me, any attractive woman I run across is my potential competition. It's no secret that Todd sleeps around on Marcia, but why won't he choose to sleep around on her with *me*? If I'm good enough to be his best friend, why am I not good enough to be his booty call? That unanswered question tortures me without end. I'm pretty enough to get plenty of date offers from other guys—all of which I turn down—because Todd is the only one I want, and he doesn't want me. And still, he sends me mixed signals all the time, flirting with me, talking to me frankly about sex, asking what my hopes and dreams are. I don't know what he wants from me anymore, except to make me feel awful about myself. And yet, his behavior is pretty typical for most guys his age. He's immature and self-centered, sure—but so is just about every other nineteen-year-old college kid. That doesn't make him special at all, even if I think he is.

My moods blacken and my grades slip. I anger easily, and I lose a couple of friends over it. Regina LaChance takes me aside after the weekly RA staff meeting and tells me I need to work on controlling my temper. I try to run for president of the university women's choir and lose to a bubbly airhead who'd joined only a couple of weeks before the election, and the grapevine says I lost because I'm "too bitchy." But I don't believe any of it, and I swear my problems are someone else's fault, not mine. I've just had a string of bad luck, that's all. I don't even want to consider the possibility of what's really going on.

I can no longer see the forest for the trees. After all, almost everything my eyes see this spring just get twisted into yet another reminder of how I am not a woman Todd finds worthy of his sexual attention. Nothing else matters to me, not even sleeping or eating. Small wonder that I fall apart.

Back on Ludlow Street after the movie, I tune out Todd and Regina's lively conversation and stare out into space—for how long, I don't know.

I return to earth when I feel Todd jab me in the shoulder. He looks genuinely concerned—scared, even. "Anna? Anna, are you okay?"

I run my finger around and around the rim of a highball drink I don't remember ordering. "Yeah," I sigh. "I'm fine."

"You sure? You seem really . . . well, distant."

I shrug my shoulders. The pins and needles take over my body again. I feel as if I'm soaking up ether from some invisible source. My field of vision goes wavy, then black clouds sink in and obliterate it. I think for a moment that I've passed out, but this feeling of sinking into nothingness is simply the raging beast of my chronic illness returning from hibernation to poison me, paralyze me with its toxic venom, capture me and drag me forcibly back to its lair to be consumed and swallowed whole. I don't know what to call it yet—back in high school my high-school guidance counselor and a child psychologist I saw for five sessions said I suffered from "mood swings," but they never gave me a diagnosis. They might have given an official one to my dad, my legal guardian at the time—but he never shared it with me. And I'm still too frightened to

seek help on my own. All I know now is that my mind is filled with a
dark poison that makes me feel tired, nauseous, disembodied.

Somehow I manage to gather my senses enough to mumble to an
increasingly wary Todd and Regina that I'm not feeling well and need to
go home.

Once safely back at the dorm, I know what I have to do.

I sit down at my desk, take out a pad of paper and a sharp new
pencil, and write Todd a letter. It covers nine pages, front and back, in
my slanted, looping feminine script. The letter gives each and every
angst-ridden, sappy, hormone-drenched detail of the kind of love only a
nineteen-year-old woman can feel for a man who obviously doesn't love
her back—at least, not physically. I write and write without reading
over what words my pencil forms, I write while tears fall on the page,
smearing those words before they're finished. The act of writing that
letter becomes almost a sexual act in and of itself; when I finally set my
pencil down, I am sweaty and spent as if I've just had an orgasm. I'm
wildly euphoric too, as if I've just snorted six lines of cocaine off a
Manhattan toilet seat. In the warped parallel universe of my illness, I
think that the letter I've just written will solve everything—in that respect, it's just another delusion, not to mention a passive-aggressive cry
for help. It's sexually explicit and asks that he do things to me that I'm
embarrassed to admit now. I offer to do plenty of things to him too—
things I think any red-blooded nineteen-year-old boy would love to
have done to him, but I am wrong. With that letter, I cross lines that
should never be crossed.

I fold it into a compact packet, seal it shut with a price sticker I peel
off the back cover of a history textbook, and slide it under Todd's door.
I honestly believe that letter will break down all the barriers between
having emotional intimacy with Todd and having sexual intimacy with
Todd and bring the two together into some kind of interstellar explo-
sion. I believe those nine soggy sheets of folded paper will somehow
bring that impossible, cosmic fantasy to life.

Of course, they don't. Why would they? The letter is filled with the
nonsensical, hormonal rantings of a moody nineteen-year-old girl who
has mostly lost touch with reality, and its intended recipient is a self-
centered, immature, and randy jerk who prefers to do things his own
way and on his own damn time. I could have predicted it would all go
badly, but I'm far too deep into my state of denial to expect anything

other than wild success. Surely, he and I will be jetting off on an all-expenses-paid trip to the Caribbean for spring break, where we will make love on the beach and plan our future lives together. No other possibility even crosses my mind.

I wait for word from Todd with great anxiety—I crave and fear his reaction so much that it makes my body ache as if stretched on a rack. I hear nothing for the rest of the weekend; Todd seems to have disappeared from the dorm entirely. The following week is finals. The only time I see Todd is at our Survey of American Literature exam, before and after which he will neither talk to me nor meet my eyes. I try to follow him out of the exam, but he ducks into the student union and I lose track of him in the midday crowd. I have two more exams that day. By the time I make it back to the dorm, it's late afternoon and the hall director tells me Todd has requested permission to leave campus for spring break two days early.

I finish my exams and leave for spring break in a depressed trance. I don't remember much of what transpires over the next nine days of break, but I remember what happens when I return to campus all too well.

The RAs have to be back at the dorm two days before the start of spring quarter to undergo refresher training and to redecorate our assigned floors for the spring. At the first back-to-campus meeting with our hall director, Todd makes a point to sit as far away from me as possible, and he refuses an assignment to head up a social-program committee with me. The hostility leaking from his body language is as viscous as used motor oil.

I can't take it anymore. After the meeting, I march up to Todd's room and confront him. He answers the door wrapped in a bedspread. It's obvious he wears nothing underneath. I hear Marcia's voice in the background, behind the half-closed door, wanting to know "why that crazy bitch is bothering us again."

"Yeah, I got your letter, Berry," he says. "Still kind of mulling it over."

"What do you mean?"

Todd wraps the bedspread tighter around himself. "Well, you know. I totally get what you're saying and everything, and I feel like we do have this like, strong *spiritual* connection, but I'm not sure I wanna go physical with it. 'Sides, I've still got a pretty good physical thing going on with Marcia."

It's exactly the reaction I expect. And yet, it makes me feel as sick as I would if I'd just learned that Todd is dead. And he is, in a way. The soul-to-soul communion that we've shared over so many late nights is gone, in an instant.

"What should we do now?" I ask. "How can we go on now?"

"We'll just keep on as usual," he says, and lets the bedspread drop enough for me to glimpse his rippled, hairy chest. That only makes things worse. "Keep on meditating, Berry. Self-reflection. That's the way for you to even yourself out. Meditation and sutras. Enlightenment is the answer, Berry. Enlightenment. 'Night, Berry."

Todd shuts the door in my face.

Todd and I try to keep on as usual, but it's torture. Our late-night rap sessions become a cruel joke. He goes out of his way to flirt with me—to even touch me suggestively by "accident" whenever possible—only to pull away the minute I feel the inkling of a physical connection form between us. The resulting emotional roller-coaster ride only makes me feel even worse. I become like the walking dead. I stop fulfilling my RA duties. I file no weekly reports with the hall director. I forget all my floor residents' names. I drop two classes and take a less-than-full course-load for the first time ever, and even flunk two midterm exams because I've lost all motivation to study. The dean calls me in to his office and asks if anything is wrong, and I of course say no, because to admit that something is wrong could put my scholarship at risk right away, even before I've had a chance to pull up my grades. I stop talking to my mother by phone once a week. (I've become close to my mother again during this time. I also think it's probably my mother who finally calls my bosses at the dorm and asks them to intervene.)

In the middle of spring quarter, Regina and the senior hall director take me aside. "We're worried about you, Anna," Regina says. "We think you need professional help."

My bosses refer me to an on-campus counseling service and tell me I have to start going or I'll lose my RA job, which provides me with free room and board. It's the same service I've referred my own floor residents to when they're depressed and anxious—at least, I did it when I still gave a damn about being an RA. I have no choice but to get help, but that doesn't mean I'm happy about it. In tribute to how little I care for the whole system by that point, I show up for my first counseling session ten minutes late.

My therapist is a middle-aged bearded man who wears badly wrinkled polyester suits. I'll call him Dr. X.

Dr. X asks me why I'm so depressed.

"Because I can't get Todd Naismith to have sex with me," I tell him. Over the course of several sessions, I give him the details of our entire friendship, from the late-night pizza-and-Beat-poet sessions to the cruelly manipulative physical flirting to the angry outbursts he's been having with me lately whenever we're assigned RA duty rounds together. I leave out the sordid details of the letter I wrote him, because I'm too embarrassed to admit the truth. My story is skewed heavily in my own favor, which I'm sure doesn't help me, but I'm too selfish and immature at the time to care. I'm angry at Todd, and what I say in this tiny, confidential room is the only chance I'll ever have for revenge.

"This Todd Naismith person is obviously a narcissist," Dr. X says after he's heard the whole long, sordid story. "He enjoys toying with you. You're nothing but a plaything to him. Don't you think so?"

I shrug. "He tells me all the bad feelings will go away if I just meditate."

Dr. X laughs. "And he's right, ironically. But that doesn't mean you should take his advice. As I said, the man enjoys toying with you. Women are toys to him. You see this sort of thing among young men a lot, and it's a phase most of them fortunately outgrow. But don't wait around for him to outgrow it. I advise you to cut off all contact with him."

Dr. X gives me a free copy of M. Scott Peck's *The Road Less Traveled*, and he tells me to read it. He says it will make me feel better. He also says I need to find another man, a man who is interested in having sex with me. He says that will make me feel better too.

"Can't I just have some antidepressants?" I ask. "That would be easier."

"No," Dr. X says. "I don't trust them. Read the book. Find a man who is interested in you and wants to satisfy you sexually instead of just playing mind games. And no matter what you do, don't let Todd Naismith toy with you ever, ever again."

I skip my last two appointments with Dr. X. I don't like him very much. But I do take one piece of his advice—I end my friendship with

Todd Naismith, who responds by slipping long handwritten letters about how much of a histrionic bitch I am under my door.

We're a real pair, Todd and I—two self-centered, dysfunctional teenagers who try to act like mature, sophisticated adults but just end up devolving into silly tantrums delivered by letter. We're no better than seventh-graders with a Slam Book at a weekend house party, jumping up and down, loading ourselves up on junk food and soda, and blowing everything out of proportion until we finally make ourselves throw up.

And he's right—I *am* a histrionic bitch. But I can't admit the truth to myself or anyone else. Instead, I tear the letters up and toss them down the trash chute. Damned if I'll let him toy with me like that ever again.

And yet, almost a decade later, in a breakup letter from Dean—a man Todd Naismith has never even met—that relies on Todd Naismith's third-hand opinion of me as a crazy, histrionic, menace-to-society bitch is black-and-white proof that toy with me like that (from several hundred miles away and sight-unseen, no less) is exactly what I've let him do.

It reminds me yet again of why I've always worked so hard to hide the truth about myself and my family from everyone—because mental illness can brand you for life, and creep back up on you in the worst possible ways, even years later. But running and hiding from the truth is also what got me into this mess to begin with.

*To hell with people who don't understand*, I think. To hell with anyone who won't accept me for who and what I am. It's high time to turn this ship around and leave those who don't understand back on the shore for good.

I'd abandoned my half-hearted attempts at Buddhism around the same time that Dr. X told me to cut off all contact with Todd Naismith. I've dabbled here and there in the years since, but the knowledge that the man who introduced me to Buddhism and Eastern philosophy in general is still disparaging me from hundreds of miles away stirs something in me. I am finally ready to stop being a victim. I am finally ready to take responsibility for my own actions and to take the steps I need to learn to manage my illness. I am finally ready to do the hard work necessary to find my own inner peace.

Todd and Dean were right about me all along, you see. I *did* have something wrong with me that I wasn't willing to acknowledge. Maybe their assessments were cruel, vicious, and exaggerated, but at the heart of them, there was some truth. My illness was expressing itself in the unhealthy ways I carried out my relationships—not to mention in whom I chose to have my relationships with. I knew all along I had something bad going on in my brain—the black hole, the blinding feelings of confusion, the short temper, the memory lapses. Perhaps if Dean and Todd had been more informed about mental illness they would have helped me seek the aid and treatment I needed instead of condemning me. But since young men are not always known for their compassion and insight, they behaved instead as some young men behave. That's life, and I don't necessarily hold it against them. And as hurtful and unhelpful as their treatment of me was, in the end my illness was not their fault or their problem; I was not their responsibility. The responsibility fell only to me.

Most experts on borderline personality disorder believe that like substance abusers, people with BPD need to hit a "bottom" before they can ever truly begin to heal. I've hit my bottom, all right. In the past month, I've lost my job, my live-in life partner, my home, and my dignity. I'm broke and only a hair's breadth away from being destitute. An old friend, someone I once trusted, has said some deeply hurtful things, and to top it all off, I've so badly harassed and threatened someone I love that if he really wanted to, he could get me charged with a felony. I've got nowhere to go but up.

It is time to take my first serious steps toward enlightenment—real, concrete steps, not bullshit platitudes shared over modern jazz and cheap pizza in a dorm room. And with enlightenment will come my first steps on my long journey out of the gaping black hole of my illness and into the bright light of health.

I start by meditating for an hour every day before I go to work. Real meditating too—not teetering on a secondhand futon while stoned, as Todd used to do. I learn how to do it properly, and I do it every single day with discipline. I go every Sunday to a local Buddhist temple that offers hour-long, structured Zen Shin meditation sessions, and I learn how to control my breathing by counting from one to ten, how to do walking meditation by focusing on every minute sensation my stocking feet make in contact with the temple floor, how to prostrate and bow in sets of twenty to relieve tension in my back after an hour of sitting without breaking my mind's cleansing concentration. I chant in English,

Japanese, and Sanskrit. I learn how to accept whatever thoughts come and go in the busy, cluttered, and filthy train station my mind has become after years of sex addiction, booze, drugs, dysfunctional relationships, and self-pity. I take up yoga. I learn to breathe deeply and stand on my head. I learn to surrender the self and dwell in the moment and only the moment, to let everything before and after the moment slip into nothingness. I pay out of pocket for therapy sessions with a licensed clinical social worker who believes in the power of spiritually integrated talk therapy instead of psychotropic drugs for counseling, seeing him once a week for six months, even though the cost is a financial hardship.

But it's money well spent. I've finally learned to let go.

After several months of dedicated self-study, I feel the fog of my lifelong mental illness begin to lift. I have developed a level of self-awareness I've never known before. I find myself apologizing to store clerks when I snap at them. When I feel a rage attack coming on, I sit down, count to ten, and take long, slow, deep breaths until the urge to tear everyone within arm's reach to shreds passes. I start to feel compassion for strangers on the street. I sleep better than I have in years, and even find I can wake up for meditation every day at 5:30 a.m. on the dot without the need for an alarm clock. I have a focus and presence of mind I've never thought possible. The top of my head opens wide and lets in the sky, which gets brighter each day. A life of meditation and mindfulness has literally changed my brain chemistry, in a way no amount of medication can.[5] I've discovered that Buddhist meditation is as effective, if not more so, as Western-style cognitive and pharmacological therapy in changing the behavior and brain chemistry of practitioners, up to and including increased sense of well-being, increased cognitive performance, greater longevity, higher levels of empathy, and increased levels of insight.[6]

I learn to make better relationship choices too. I end friendships with longtime theater friends who have raging drug and alcohol addictions; I stop associating with people and places who reinforce any of my former destructive patterns of behavior, like going out on the town looking for one-night stands, and spending money like water on shopping trips and expensive lattes; and I ditch those who trash-talk others behind their back too much. I stop going to bars and clubs altogether in favor of the occasional cup of tea at Kopi, my favorite coffeehouse. I meet my closest, most loyal friends for lunch or to watch movies, never for drinks. I cut up all my credit cards and learn to live below my means. And in perhaps the ultimate act of self-awareness, I decide that from this point forward, my days as a needy, self-destructive sex addict are over. I will never sleep with a man again until I am married and he is my husband.

Some of my friends find that last life-altering decision a bit too austere and old-fashioned, but I've never once regretted it. Shortly after I make that decision, after all, I meet the man who will later become my husband.

A few weeks before I am to be married, I call Dean and tell him he can come take away all his abandoned furniture and belongings from the apartment, where his name is still on the lease; if he doesn't, I plan to toss it all in the Dumpster behind the building. I won't be needing anything of Dean's in my new life—his junk is nothing but pieces of worn baggage from a me that no longer exists.

Dean comes over with a van to pick up his things one night. He stares at my new engagement ring with palpable envy, and flirts with me just as he did when we were first dating. I can tell he regrets how things ended between us.

When we're in the basement storage unit, rummaging around to separate his belongings from mine, we come across a battered leather briefcase. "Here, I think this is yours," I say, and hand it to him.

"No, that's not mine," he says. "It was Raj's. I don't know how it got mixed up in my things, but—" He stops, takes a moment to collect himself. "Throw that piece of shit in the garbage. I never, ever want to see anything of his ever again."

"I'll let you throw it out then," I say, and smile. "I think you'll enjoy doing it a lot more than I would."

Dean appreciates that. There is peace between us from then on.

Several people have asked me over the years what's it's like to be enlightened. To be honest, I don't know. I'm not even sure that I am. Like learning to live and thrive with a mental illness, enlightenment is a never-ending work-in-progress, after all. The minute we stop working at it is the minute we cease to exist. But whenever anyone asks, I tell them only one thing.

"I'm awake. I was asleep for a long, long time, but I'm awake now, and that's all that matters."

It's been over ten years since my life-changing, bottom-hitting relationship catastrophe with Dean led me unwittingly away from an unstable, self-destructive life and into a healthy one. I now know what it's like to have a relationship that lasts, as my husband and I will be celebrating our eleventh wedding anniversary this year. I have plenty of money in the bank, a solid retirement plan, and I no longer worry about where my next paycheck is coming from or how I'll make the rent. I own my own home, am debt-free, and I am successfully self-employed with a freelance writing business. I have a wide circle of friends, many of whom look up to me and regularly come to me for advice on how to address their day-to-day problems as well as how to respond to friends and family members who are struggling with mental illness. I work as a novelist and journalist, and many of my articles for newspapers and magazines focus on wellness—mental wellness, specifically. What I write resonates with my readers because unlike some other reporters covering that beat, I've actually *lived* through the very types of situations and tribulations I now report on.

Each year since, I've celebrated May 25—the anniversary of the first day I spent actively trying to change my borderline behaviors—as a second birthday of sorts. I've come a long way in ten years. I've gone from being broke, unemployed, abandoned, self-loathing, and homeless to becoming a happily married wife and mother with a stable home, a loving husband, two beautiful children, sound finances, and a successful career. I am here to tell you that no matter what anyone says, mental illness does not mean you can't have a good life. You can, and I'm living proof.

When I put my kids to bed each night, I watchfully gaze over them, stroke their tiny foreheads, and say two little prayers. One, that they will never know the pain and anguish of the mental illnesses that have plagued their mother and her family for seven generations. And two, that if (God forbid) my kids ever do have to suffer under the weight of mental illness, that with my love and support, they'll be able to find their way out of the darkness and into the light. I am not my parents, who were unable to help me because they were too busy dealing with their own struggles. But I don't hold that against them. I was able to help myself, and I will teach my children to do the same.

I say these prayers knowing that many, if not most, of the people in this country who struggle with mental illness haven't been so lucky. I say it knowing too well just how unlucky my own family members are in managing their own illnesses. To this day, my mother and brother struggle on—mostly in vain—to survive and thrive under the weight of their afflictions. The remainder of this book is their story—and my own, as both their survivor and their caretaker.

# 5

# MOM: A RELAPSE

The thing I remember most about my early childhood is visiting my mother in the psych ward.

By age eight or so, I believe that all mothers spend at least part of the year locked up in psych wards. It's that normal to me. At eight years old, my child's mind begins to believe that all mommies are crazy, and the job of all daddies and kids is to help take care of their crazy mommies. It takes me a few more years to understand that mommies who are locked up in psych wards are not normal mommies and that the daddies and children who have to help take care of them aren't normal either.

As any child of a mentally ill parent can tell you, there will always be a time when the traditional parent/child roles are reversed. It has come for me many times—the first when I was eleven years old and my mother threw away clothes and furniture in an obsessive/compulsive fit one day then collapsed into a zombie-like state the next. Back then, I'd "parented" by scolding my mother when she trashed my prized possessions and then cooking my own dinner and doing my own laundry. I thought that when I moved out of my mother's house as a young teenager and into my dad's home I'd be finished with that role forever. I was wrong.

In the spring of 2004, when my mother begins to relapse into her worst drug-addiction and clinical depression/anxiety pattern in twenty years, there's little I can do to "parent" her from three hundred miles away. That doesn't stop her (or the authorities) from relying on me for all sorts of supervisory intervention, though.

In early 2004, I am newly married and my husband and I have just purchased our first home, a three-bedroom two-bath rehab condo on Chicago's North Side. My new husband George,[1] a hardworking immigrant to this country from Hong Kong, knows a little about my family's (and my own) history of mental illness, but not much. George has made it clear he accepts my family's many psychological foibles, but he also doesn't want to get directly involved in any impending crises, either. As my mother begins a rapid meltdown in the months immediately following our marriage, however, I find it more and more difficult to shield George from what is going on back in Indiana.

At this time I have a job doing technical writing for a library-cataloging software company. The job is stressful and tedious and the company isn't doing well financially. I know I have to find a better job soon, but with a marriage and a mortgage to consider, I can't do anything to jeopardize even this crummy job until I have another one lined up. The Chicago economy is only starting to bounce back from a long recession, and I know it could take six months to a year to find anything at a comparable salary. In the meantime, I have to be on my best behavior at work.

Mom has trouble understanding this.

Every day for a week in mid-April, I show up for work promptly at 9:00 a.m. to find at least thirty voice mails on my work phone, all from Mom. Her voice changes modulation and speed every few seconds, like an old reel-to-reel tape that's been heat-damaged on playback.

"Anna, it's Mom. I j-j-just need to know if everything is g-g-going to be all right with my Social Security. I submitted the papers but now I don't know. I don't know I don't know *Idunnnnnoooo*. Is everything going to be all r-r-right with my Social Security? I need to know. I NEED TO KNOW. Is everything going to be all right? Is. Every. Thing. Going. To. Be. All. Right. *Iseverythinggoingtobe ALLRIGHT?*"

I always delete everything after the first message, knowing full well there will be another twenty-nine just like it. It takes me almost twenty minutes to clear out my voice mail some mornings—Mom leaves me more than fifty voicemails on my work phone one night this week, the very same night that I call the phone company and have Mom's number blocked on my home phone after she calls almost sixty times in less than two hours, frightening my husband and infuriating me.

When I come into work the next day, there is a Post-It note on my computer screen instructing me to go meet the head of HR in her office immediately. My desk phone rings as soon as I sit down. I glance at the caller ID screen and recognize my mother's Indiana area code. I ignore the phone; it rings four times, then stops. A moment later, it starts ringing again, the Indiana area code back on the phone's digital screen. The phone rings four more times, stops, then starts again. I switch the ringer off.

The HR department secretary walks sheepishly up to my cubicle, and hands me a pink slip of paper telling me I have to report to HR *now* ("now" is in capitals and underlined three times in red ink).

I know exactly what's coming.

"Anna, we are concerned that you may be abusing your telephone privileges," my employer's HR director says after she shuts the door to her office and sits down. "The information services department tells me you have had an unusually large number of voice mails lately, and it's been causing problems with the telephone system. And the receptionist tells me that whenever she transfers clients to your extension in the early morning, the line is busy and your voice mailbox is full. What's going on?"

I fiddle with my hands. "My mother is mentally ill," I say, my voice barely above a whisper. I say this without fear of retribution or judgment because it's just a fact I've lived with and accepted since childhood. I say it as matter-of-factly as I would a remark about the weather or the Chicago Cubs' current losing streak, and I think nothing about how my frankness about my mother's condition could somehow come back to haunt me at work. And yet, I soon find out I will pay a heavy price for my honesty.

"Mom's having a—well—an attack of her illness right now, and one of the things she does when she's having an attack is dial the phone incessantly. She's been calling me at work. I've told her to stop it several times, but—" I sigh and stare at the floor.

The HR director just stares blankly at me. I notice with some amusement that the framed diploma behind her desk says she graduated college with a degree in psychology.

"I've told her several times to stop calling me at work," I repeat. "But she's just not listening," I say. Trying to appear the model employee, I add a little white lie. "I was actually planning to come talk to you about this today. I want to get some more information about the employee assistance program. I remember from the brochures I got when I was hired that it has a support program for dealing with family mental illness issues."

The HR director just keeps up her blank stare. She picks up a pencil from her desk, puts it down again, but says nothing.

"I'm also wondering if there is any way I could have my mother's number blocked from the phone system," I go on. "I was able to do that on my phone at home, and—"

The HR director blinks. "You mean to tell me that you blocked your own *mother's* telephone number?" Her tone is cold, judgmental. "Why on earth would you want to do something like that? I mean, she's your *mother.*"

"I know that, but—"

The HR director raps her knuckles on her leather desk pad like a schoolteacher. "You are just going to have to tell your mother that the calls must stop," she says. "We don't have the capacity to block calls here. We are a business, and as such we are in the business of receiving telephone calls from our clients and from the public. I don't want to hear about any more inappropriate personal calls coming in after today, Anna. All right?"

"With all due respect, it's just not that simple."

The HR director—an attractive, well-dressed woman in her middle thirties; I'll call her "Stella"—shakes her head and sighs. She receives a six-figure salary for processing insurance forms, mediating manager-employee conflicts, and discreetly escorting fired workers off the premises, so I'd think that if anyone at the third-rate software company I work for writing technical manuals and the occasional press release is capable of helping me, it's her. But it appears that supposition is wrong.

"Frankly, I don't see what's so difficult about telling your mother to stop calling you at work," she snaps. "Especially considering that our company policy is to keep personal calls to a minimum, and *never* to allow them to interfere with company business." Stella's perfectly waxed eyebrows raise, and her hazel eyes bear into mine. "*And* especially considering the complaints I've been getting about *your* abrasive, forceful personality, Anna. From what I understand, it hardly seems as if you have a problem ordering people around."

My jaw drops. I have absolutely no idea what Stella is talking about. Sure, I've had problems with that kind of behavior before, but I've been going out of my way not to engage in it for years now. I'm so self-conscious of my past problems with my short temper that now, if anything, I go out of my way to be so nice to people that they find my upbeat, bubbly, and overly helpful nature annoying. I frantically think back, trying to remember anything I could have done or said that might even remotely have been misconstrued as rude, nasty, or unhelpful. The only thing I can think of is the fact that I turned down a coworker from the Java-coding department for a date (he didn't realize I was married), and that I spend all my lunch breaks reading books instead of socializing. Do they think I'm a snob? Do they not like the way I dress? Did I look at someone the wrong way? Did I ask the lead programmer for the newest library software too many questions when I got a difficult proposal-writing assignment for a library in Bogota, Colombia? The possibilities race through my mind all at once, and my eyes glaze over.

Stella picks up on this. "You see, Anna? This is exactly what I mean. Your boss just told me about how you daydream in meetings too much. I didn't believe her at first, but *wow.*"

Then a sinister thought occurs to me. I wonder if perhaps Stella has noticed I'm seeing a psychotherapist based on my medical insurance claims. I see the psychotherapist not because I'm feeling unstable or even mildly ill, per se, but simply because I periodically go back to therapy as a sort of "tune-up." Just like your car needs regular oil changes and maintenance, so too does someone like me who has successfully overcome crippling mental illness. It's just a long-term management strategy. My current therapist even asked me the other day why I feel the need to keep seeing her when I'm doing so well, but I told her it's mostly to help me deal with the stress my mother's mental illness is causing for both me and my husband, rather than my own issues.

Besides, it's not like I get a lot of opportunities to "order people around," as Stella says. I'm a low-level technical writer, for God's sake— all I do all day long is read mind-numbing software code and translate it into intelligible English for use in sales and marketing materials. There are sometimes entire days when I don't speak to anyone except to ask one of the programmers what a line of Javascript means. Where is all of this coming from? I take a long, deep breath before jumping to any conclusions, and instead I ask a polite question, just as my therapists have taught me to do. "I'm sorry, Stella, but could you please be a little more specific about what you mean by my *abrasive personality*?"

"Your supervisor will be talking to you more about that," Stella says curtly. "But between you and me, you should really watch your manner around people, Anna. You tend to rub people the wrong way."

I'm still drawing a blank, but I try to steer the conversation back to the positive. "How, exactly? Can you be specific? You know, so I can be *aware* of how I might rub others the wrong way? I can't change my behavior if I don't know how—"

Stella chuckles. "Frankly, if you even have to *ask* me that question, that's a pretty big measure of what the problem is." She takes a booklet on the employee assistance program out of a drawer and tosses it at me. "Now if you'll pardon me, I have a new employee starting this morning and I need to go do an orientation. Good day."

I feel as if I've been punched in the stomach. It's clear to me what is happening here now. My employer has gotten wind of my family's mental health problems, and they want me out the door because of it. They're just looking for an excuse to fire me, and now I've given them one. I *really* need to find another job, and fast.

I go back to my desk and sure enough, my voicemail light is blinking. I log in to the voicemail system and discover that Mom has left me eight new messages during the ten minutes I've been in the HR office. I know they're all from her because her home number is stored in my caller ID eight times.

I delete all eight messages without listening to them.

I try to immerse myself in my latest writing assignment, a business proposal to provide cataloging software services to a foreign national library. But I can't concentrate. I keep bracing myself for the next time the phone will ring—and I know it will, it is only a matter of minutes— with Mom talking in her gritty, rapid-fire, drug-addled slur, a voice that sounds like a defective electric typewriter that won't shut off.

I analyze and reanalyze the scolding I've gotten from Stella in HR, and I feel all the old anxieties and insecurities of my worst borderline personality disorder days creeping back. How exactly do I "rub people the wrong way?" What am I doing wrong? Am I not doing enough at work to hide the fact that Mom's latest relapse is really getting to me? Has Mom perhaps started dialing my coworkers' extensions at random and asking *them* if everything is going to be all right? Am I in the early throes of a *brief psychotic episode* myself? Have I verbally abused a coworker recently and somehow forgotten about it? Do my inescapable *nutjob* genes and resulting chemically defective brain doom me to fail at any nine-to-five job I undertake?

Or do I perhaps just work for a crappy third-rate company staffed with paranoid, gossipy, and immature people? Is it that perhaps I'm abrasive at times, but that my coworkers are also highly sensitive, not to mention miserable at work? Maybe we're all a little abrasive at times when we're unhappy. It's certainly possible. I glance over the top of my cubicle wall and see two of the other tech writers—both librarians by training, not professional writers per se—whispering and nodding in my direction when they think I'm not looking. Most of my coworkers at the software company are less than enthusiastic about their jobs, and I get the feeling during weekly staff meetings that my two cowriters resent the fact that I usually complete my assignments a full week ahead of deadline and then go off in search of writing projects from other departments to keep me busy until our managing editor assigns me something new.

I have, again, fallen victim to my own extraordinary efficiency—a skill I've developed over the years out of necessity because I'm never sure when either a family mental health crisis or my own depressive/borderline psychotic behaviors will kick in. It's a skill I cultivated in college and grad school and mastered at my first job out of school as a financial editor at the high-pressure brokerage firm. Any day that I feel reasonably coherent and stable, I have to get all my work done at lightning speed because there is no guarantee I'll still be reasonably coherent and stable enough to finish it the next day. (Either that, or I'll have to go jetting off to Indiana to help my family deal with my mother's or my brother's latest nervous breakdown.) As a result, I can type over a hundred words a minute, read faster than 99 percent of the population, and copyedit complex, hundred-page documents written in the most mind-numbing technical jargon imaginable in an hour or less.

That monomaniacal efficiency worked well enough for me in school when it came to making sure I still got decent grades even when I was on the verge of a nervous breakdown. But it hasn't worked so well in the corporate world, where I soon learn that the average office drone doesn't like to be upstaged by the new kid on the block, especially when the new kid on the block is younger and prettier than they are. I've lost jobs because of it before, a Machiavellian victim of my own competence, and my own fear of relapse. And it appears that after only six months on the job at the library software company, it is happening again.

Mom isn't helping matters. The phone rings again—Mom's Indiana phone number appears on my caller-ID screen for the umpteenth time. I know I have to take this one, there's just no avoiding it.

I pick up the receiver. "Mom, I know it's you," I say, not even bothering with hello. I make sure to keep my voice low, lest I give my meddling coworkers anything else to whisper or gossip about. "Listen to me very carefully. You *cannot* call me here at work anymore. You *cannot* leave me any more phone messages. You are getting me into trouble at work and if you don't stop, *I am going to get fired.* Do you understand?"

"A-A-Anna, I just need to know if ev-ev-everything is going to be oh-kuh-kuh-kay—"

"Mom, I am only going to say this once. If you call again, I will call the local life squad and have them take you straight to the state hospital psych ward. And I *know* you don't want to go back there." The state hospital's emergency psych ward is infamous. Mom stayed there once, several years ago when she had no health insurance, and the experience still gives her nightmares. Mentioning it is a cruel and manipulative tactic for me to use, I know, but she's left me no other choice.

"Well, Mom? Are you going to stop calling?"

Silence. I take that as a yes.

"Good. I'm hanging up now." I return the phone to the receiver without saying goodbye. Tough love at its best and worst.

With that, I'm able to shrug off the whole affair for the rest of the morning and actually get some real work done. I complete the bulk of my current writing assignment and send it to the managing editor for review, then take off for lunch. When I get back, I'm relieved to find no frantic, slurred voicemail messages waiting for me. I think that my tough-love statements just might have worked, and I picture my mother sitting alone in her two-bedroom bungalow in that cheap, gritty, working-class Indiana town, idly watching daytime television, drinking diet soda, and chain-smoking. Maybe she's telephoned her therapist or perhaps her Social Security disability caseworker and they were able to calm her down. Whatever the reason for her silence, I'm thankful for it. I can't afford to lose my job over her obsessive-compulsive, anxiety-laden telephone habits. Not now.

My relief is short-lived, however.

Shortly after I return from lunch and open the PDF file that contains my newest writing assignment—a request for proposal for cataloging services from a prestigious university library—my phone rings again. I notice from the caller ID that the number has an Indiana area code and exchange, but I don't recognize the extension. I consider ignoring it, figuring my mother might have gone to her next-door neighbor's house to make her call to try to trick me into thinking it isn't her. But something in my gut tells me to pick up the receiver, so I do.

"Hello, this is Anna Berry speaking."

"Ms. Berry, this is Officer James Caruthers."[2]

I feel the bottom drop out of my stomach. "Yes?"

"Ms. Berry, I'm here at your mother's house. She called us asking for help. We've got the fire department here as well. We don't know what we can do to help her. She told us to call you."

I swallow hard, willing my voice to keep itself low and businesslike. I glance across the aisle and see that two of my coworkers are eyeing me suspiciously. I have to somehow make this end of the conversation sound to them as if I'm conducting a business call. "Is ahhh, is *your client* well at this time?" I ask. I feel like a callous idiot referring to Mom as if she's a random business associate and not my own mentally ill mother. Officer Caruthers must think I'm as nutty as she is.

I hear some muffled conversation in the background. "Ma'am, the fire personnel have paramedics with them on the truck and they've taken your mom's vital signs. They say she's fine physically, but—"

I cut Officer Caruthers off. "I would encourage you, sir, to advise *your client* that our company cannot assist her in this matter, and to thank her for contacting us." I say this ridiculous statement loud enough for my coworkers to shrug off my phone call as business-related instead of personal; they stop eyeing me and get back to their work. As a bewildered Officer Caruthers hems and haws on the phone, I lean down below the level of my cubicle wall, cover the lower part of the receiver with my hand, and whisper, "Officer Caruthers, I'm very sorry about that just now, it's just that I can't be dealing with this . . . *situation* on the phone while I'm at work. I've already told my mother to stop calling me here. The only reason she called the police was to get you to call me for her. She's just being manipulative, is all. I'm sure you understand."

Officer Caruthers coughs. It's pretty clear he doesn't understand any of it. "Well, what do you want us to do, ma'am?"

"Tell my mother to stop calling me. Then leave."

Officer Caruthers coughs again. "Can do, ma'am. But your mother needs to understand that she can't call the fire department and the life squad and the police department out to her house all at once for no reason. That's a false alarm, and it's a misdemeanor. We'll let her off with a warning this once, but if she does it again, there'll be a fine, plus we'll bill her for the officers' time—"

"Tell my mother what you've just told me. Maybe then she'll learn. If she calls you again, just take her over to the psych unit at the state hospital and let them deal with her. Good-bye, Officer Caruthers."

I hang up.

That night when I come home, I tell George what happened. My new husband already knows that my current job security is shaky at best, and he can't understand why my mother would do anything to jeopardize my job there even further. George—who grew up in a tiny three-room Hong Kong apartment with his parents, five brothers and sisters, and a grandmother; and who is the product of an Anglicized Cantonese culture that values hard work, a good income honestly earned, and family stability above all other things—can't fathom the pathetic state my mother is in either.

"Your mom is very selfish," he says that night at dinner. "Very, very selfish." I can tell George is angry because his Cantonese accent always thickens to the point that he sounds just like Martin Yan from the PBS cooking program *Yan Can Cook* whenever he gets mad.

I sigh. "No, honey. She's sick."

He scoffs. "Well, then she's in some kind of sickness that makes her selfish. She needs to stop. She needs to stop acting like a stupid selfish woman."

I sigh again as I dribble too much soy sauce onto the shrimp lo mein George has so lovingly prepared for us in his prized Joycook wok. "I wish it were that simple," I say. "But it's just not."

"Why?"

"I don't know." And if I did, I probably could have figured out by now how to permanently cure my mother, my brother, and myself of the illness that has plagued us all since the beginnings of our lives.

As I finish eating my dinner that night in silence, I think over the past several years of my mother's life, trying to piece together where or when she might have begun her latest downward spiral back into clinical depression and obsessive/compulsive anxiety. Mom had done so well for so long, I took for granted that she would *always* be well.

But of course, I should've known better. You never really recover from mental illness. Like cancer, or alcoholism, mental illness isn't ever "cured"—it merely goes into remission. Like a savvy cat burglar, mental illness always lurks somewhere in the depths and crevices of the afflicted's brain, and it can pick its time to jump out of the shadows and back into your life whenever it wants to. That's why I continue to go to psychotherapy even when I don't need to; it's why I constantly meditate and study how mindfulness can manage your emotions; it's why I constantly second-guess myself and my own behavior; and it's why I tried to choose my polar opposite to marry too. George and his family seemed to me the picture of stability and wellness—they seemed everything that my family was not.

There are things you can do to keep the cat burglar at bay, sure. Psychotherapy, medication, meditation, a supportive social network, a loving spouse, a twenty-four-hour crisis hotline can all help. But just like alarm systems and deadbolts on a house, all these precautions can still fail. Especially when the cat burglar in your brain is a master thief, the kind capable of stealing a Michelangelo right out from under the nose of a team of armed guards. That's the kind of cat burglar that lives inside my mother's brain, and in the spring of 2004, the cat burglar very nearly manages to steal her brain away permanently—and her body along with it.

After spending much of the 1980s and early 1990s going in and out of psych wards, collecting disability checks, and taking loads of psychoactive drugs—interspersed by periods of brief lucidity in which she manages to hold down menial jobs (cashier in a bakery, assembly-line worker at a plastics factory, bank teller)—my mother makes a substantial step toward total recovery in the winter and early spring of 1994.

I am twenty years old in 1994 and finishing up my sophomore year of college. Mom and I were not very close during my high-school years—she was either too ill to see me or so clingy and smothering during our infrequent visits (my brother and I were then living with my father) that she made me feel like a coddled three-year-old. But we've gradually grown closer during my first two years of college. I take a cab from campus over to Mom's tiny apartment (she doesn't have a car) on weekends and spend the afternoon sitting at her kitchen table, gossiping about the boys from campus who have crushes on me and telling her about my English literature classes, a subject Mom has always dreamed of going to college to study herself.

Mom has spent the past two years living alone in a two-room apartment in a dilapidated, subdivided Victorian-mansion-turned-rooming house, where she shares an ancient bathroom with an elderly schizophrenic man who lives across the hall. She and her second husband Bob, a janitor at the local YMCA, are separated during this time, but they remain amicable and visit each other frequently. Bob soon takes the attic apartment in the same building to be closer to her.

Mom and Bob very nearly divorced following a major depressive episode in 1990–1991 that landed Mom in a hospital psych ward for an extended lockdown stay that rendered her completely dependent on a potent mixture of multiple benzodiazepines and sleeping pills. At the height of this period of illness, Mom and Bob got into physical fights a few times, and Mom also overdosed on a mixture of antianxiety drugs and alcohol—an event which brought about a second hospitalization that just increased her drug intake even more. She'd already been unable to work for almost a year when the breakdown happened, and the combined strain of their resulting extreme low income, Mom's volatile behavior, and her massive, unpaid medical bills led to a near-collapse of their marriage, progressing as far as the filing of divorce papers and the hiring of attorneys. Mom and Bob remained estranged until late 1993, when they decided not to complete the divorce proceedings but to continue living apart.

One of Mom's therapists thinks it will be good for her to try to live entirely on her own for the first time in her adult life. Bob agrees, and together they decide to be just platonic "friends" for a while, without necessarily having the ultimate goal of repairing their marriage.

The arrangement does end up being very good for Mom. Because she married out of my grandparents' house almost immediately after high school and depended on my father financially throughout their marriage and then for alimony and child support after their divorce (all the way up to the day she married Bob, in fact), Mom has never been completely responsible for herself—financially, emotionally, or otherwise. She's still unable to hold down a full-time job, but she can take on odd jobs and still receive her Social Security Income (SSI) disability as long as she doesn't earn more than $900 a month. With the help of a caseworker, Mom collects and deposits her own disability checks, takes a bus to group therapy at the county Mental Health Department three times a week, and takes a cab to and from her private sessions with her new psychiatrist once a week. She finds a part-time babysitting job for the couple who lives next door to the rooming-house; they soon befriend Mom and use her as their primary source of weekend and evening child care for the next several years, even after my mother returns to full-time work.

Her psychiatrist at this time, Dr. Friedman,[3] is one of the few old-school Freudian psychiatrists left in her area and also one of the very few psychiatrists who ever treats Mom with total compassion, respect, and sound medical ethics. Dr. Friedman works for QCB,[4] a social-work agency contractor that does Mom's case management on behalf of the Mental Health Department and administers her SSI disability checks. When Mom becomes a full-time staff member at QCB a few years later, Dr. Friedman also becomes her colleague.

The first thing Dr. Friedman does when Mom goes for her intake session is tell her she's on way too many drugs. Mom tells me that when Dr. Friedman first reads her file after her hospital transfers him her records, he goes white as a sheet. "I don't know who the hell put you on all of this shit, but they should be shot," he tells her. And Dr. Friedman is right—given my mother's family history of substance abuse, not to mention her own problems with prescription drug addiction and frequent alcohol abuse, she should *never* have been considered a good candidate for taking any psychoactive drug on the federal controlled substances list, let alone six or seven or even ten at once.

Dr. Friedman promptly reduces Mom's meds to a moderate "little cocktail," as he calls it, of two tricyclic antidepressants in relatively small doses. One will help with both her depression and obsessive-compulsive disorder, and the other will regulate her sleeping patterns. Dr. Friedman's "little cocktail" is a work of pure psychoactive genius, and it keeps Mom happy and healthy for several years. He then not only helps Mom get enrolled in the county's intensive group-therapy sessions and a high-level case-management program for indigent patients, he also facilitates getting Mom registered for a government-supported job-re-training program designed especially for mental health "consumers." This very progressive program trains mental health consumers (a politically correct term for psychiatric patients) for jobs in healthcare administration, drawing in part upon their experiences having to navigate a complex and often hostile healthcare system while seeking treatment for their own mental illness. The program's graduates go on to good jobs in medical records administration, insurance claims processing, patient advocacy, and mental health social services. Dr. Friedman is able to see through Mom's thick, bloodstained layers of emotional scar tissue built up by her years of mental illness to see that she is an intelligent, empathetic, and potentially capable healthcare employee.

Mom will have to remain on a waiting list for at least three months to get into the training program, but once Mom shows that she's responding well to his "little cocktail," Dr. Friedman gets her a volunteer position at a local hospital's Psychiatric Department where he has admitting privileges and where she was once a patient herself. Mom volunteers there three half-days per week, answering phones, greeting visitors, and pulling charts. It gives her something to look forward to, and it also makes her feel useful—two key components to any successful recovery from advanced clinical depression and anxiety disorders.

One day in early spring I go over to Mom's two-room apartment to find a woman living there whom I barely recognize. She no longer trembles like a quaking aspen. Her eyes are no longer glazed over and drooped, but look brightly out onto the world. Mom greets me with a smile, a handshake, then a light hug, and tells me a funny story about the two neighbor children she babysits two or three nights a week while their parents work second shift. She tells me about all the interesting people she meets working behind the reception desk at the hospital. She tells me how excited she is to be on the government training-program's waiting list, and she shows me notes she's made in a spiral notebook on the kinds of jobs she'd like to have once she graduates from the program.

For the first time in almost fifteen years, my mother has hope. For all intents and purposes, Dr. Friedman and his "little cocktail" have worked a miracle.

Another miracle happens shortly thereafter. Someone drops out of the job-training course unexpectedly, and this makes room for Mom a full three months earlier than planned. She gets the call from her caseworker late one evening saying that if she wants the slot, she'll have to agree to be at the training center downtown the next morning at seven; if not, it goes to the next person on the waiting list. Mom calls me at my dorm with the news, then asks if I can help her figure out which bus routes she'll have to take and when. I throw a sweatshirt over my pajamas and go to the student union to get a bus schedule, then I call Mom back to tell her there's a bus she can pick up two blocks from her apartment that stops right in front of the job center. But it's a long, winding route that will take almost an hour to get downtown, and she'll have to be on it no later than six in order to be on time.

"Oh, I'll be on it at *five*," she giggles in a voice easily twenty years younger than her actual forty-four. "No way will I risk being late. You never know with these city buses. I can just bring a book to read if I'm there too early."

Mom is at the training center too early the next day, and every weekday thereafter for four months. I don't see her much for the first month or so because I'm busy with exams and my job as a resident advisor in my dorm, but I promise to visit her for a few days during my next school vacation.

I finish my last final exam early on a Friday afternoon. I pack a knapsack and hop a cab over to Mom's building. I wait for her on the front steps until she arrives home from classes herself around three-thirty.

She gives me a big hug and leads me upstairs. I notice that she's lost some weight since I've last seen her, and she's dyed her graying hair back to the deep auburn I remember from my childhood. Her clothes are neat and pressed, her makeup perfect. "I've got so much to tell you," Mom says while she pours both of us glasses of sweet iced tea from a pitcher. "Here, let me show you some of my school papers. You'll be proud of me—I'm getting straight As, Anna. Just like you do."

She takes a manila folder out of her satchel and opens it proudly. I flip through several mimeographed tests on medical terminology, office administration, and typing skills and see that Mom has achieved perfect or near-perfect scores on all of them. They're emblazoned with gold stars and red smiley faces and "GREAT JOB!" is written in red ink everywhere. "This is fantastic, Mom," I say, and hug her. "I knew you'd do well."

"We do a lot more than just job training at the center," Mom says. She beams as she rummages around in her satchel. "We do group counseling too. Every week one of the students gets to do a presentation on how she copes with her illness and stays focused on work. Our teacher asked me to give an extra-special presentation next week on what I do. I've come up with a whole plan based on some things I've learned from Dr. Friedman and some stuff I've come up with on my own. It's called 'Living in the Moment.'"

This piques my interest. I'm deep into my infatuation with Todd Naismith and all things Beat Generation and Zen at the time, and I can't help but see the connection. "'Living in the Moment,' huh? You mean Zen."

Mom looks bewildered. "What's Zen?"

"Never mind. Just show me what you've put together."

Mom presents me with a handwritten draft of a detailed study guide she plans to pass out to her classmates when she gives her presentation. I glance over it and find that Mom has essentially recreated all the basic tenets of Zen Buddhism—moment-by-moment awareness, humility, finding peace in the mindful enjoyment of simple daily tasks and service to others—without ever having been exposed to these ideas.

I'm first filled with awe, and then rage. There I am, spending inordinate amounts of time reading books and taking college classes on Eastern philosophy and zazen meditation, hanging out in Todd Naismith's dorm room pining over both my affection for him and my envy of his easygoing brand of devil-may-care Buddhism while I strive with every fiber of my being to achieve some modicum of enlightenment—and my mother has managed to find it completely by accident. If my mother is any example, all one needs to do to become enlightened is pop a hundred milligrams of antidepressants a day and then take some free typing classes designed especially for lunatics. It's ironic—my mother, who has been mentally ill for as long as I can remember, is doing so well when I'm an emotional wreck. It doesn't seem fair, and I hate myself for that.

It's so hard to be happy for her when I'm so miserable, but I try my best—and still come up short.

I hate to admit it, but I'm jealous. All at once I feel like chucking into the trash the paperback copies of Kerouac's *The Dharma Bums* and Suzuki's *Zen Mind, Beginner's Mind* I always carry in my knapsack.

Mom picks up on this right away. "Hon, is something wrong?"

I shake my head, cheeks smarting. "Go ahead and show me the rest of your presentation."

She does. The whole thing takes about forty-five minutes. She explains how to "live in the moment" and what it means, how doing so can relieve anxiety and fear, how it can make even the dullest of office tasks meaningful and enjoyable. She's included inspirational quotes from Mahatma Gandhi and Norman Vincent Peale, and she displays posters on which she's pasted up drawings and watercolors she's done of flowers and seascapes to help relieve anxiety. She even demonstrates a deep-cleansing, monitored breathing technique that I recognize as identical to that used in Zen meditation. Mom concludes the presentation with a guided imagery exercise that leads her participants to an island of serenity in a calm blue ocean, and she finishes with the Serenity Prayer. It's a truly beautiful thing to behold, and yet I can't bring myself to feel anything about it but jealousy.

"Well?" Mom asks as she put the papers and posters she's prepared back into a cardboard box. "What do you think?"

"I think it's very nice, Mom," I say through gritted teeth. "I'm sure you'll get a good grade for it."

"I didn't do this for a grade, hon."

I have difficulty understanding this. It just doesn't fit into my black-and-white thinking patterns at the time. "Then why do it at all?"

Mom just smiles. "Sometimes we just do things for the sake of doing them, hon. And that's reason enough."

My jealousy of Mom's sudden mental and spiritual awakening soon subsides. It's simply impossible not to be awed by her rapid transformation. She's gone from zombielike pill-junkie to productive citizen in a matter of a few months. She graduates with flying colors from the job-training program a month earlier than the rest of her class and soon lands a full-time job as a medical-records coordinator at QCB, the social-services agency where her caseworker and Dr. Friedman both work. QCB has hired Mom in part based on the success of her Living in the Moment seminar, which has been so well-received at the job-training center that several local social-service agencies have asked her to present it to their clients. She is earning a real middle-class salary for the first time in her adult life, and she's a celebrity among the local clinical-depressive set to boot.

By the end of the summer, Mom has moved out of her two-room, shared-bathroom apartment (in our family's long tradition of psychiatric irony, Mom sublets it to Mark, who's recently dropped out of his third junior college in as many years due to his inability to cope with school and schizophrenia simultaneously) and into the much larger attic apartment Bob has leased upstairs. They rekindle their marriage. They start saving for a down payment on a house. They are happy.

And they stay happy, for many years. Mom and Bob buy their first house together in the spring of 1996, a two-bedroom 1920s brick bungalow on Evansville's northwest side. I'm able to spend a couple weekends helping her strip ancient wallpaper from the kitchen and hall before I move to Chicago for graduate school, and I track the progress of her and Bob's loving, room-by-room restoration on holiday visits. Mom calls me in Chicago at least three times a week, monitoring my exciting big-city life (and my not-so-exciting emotional ups and downs) with a healthy, doting mother's perfect combination of concern and detachment. Just like when I was back in college, she's doing so well when I'm barely scraping by, and that can be hard for me to take. She sends me care packages, and she takes Greyhound buses to Chicago at least once a year for mother-daughter visits. She wires me grocery money when I'm out of work, even when her own money is tight. I worry sometimes when I'm at my lowest points if I'll end up like she used to be, driving a jalopy around town searching for dead bodies in my bathrobe and curlers. But Mom doesn't dwell on her sick, dysfunctional past. She lives in the present, and she does very well.

But it doesn't last.

Mom remains the picture of good mental health until the winter of 2004, when everything my mother has built for the past nine years begins to fall apart.

Mom's been working at QCB and thriving under Dr. Friedman's care for almost nine years when a major change in management occurs. QCB changes from a non-profit social-services agency to a for-profit entity when it merges with PRI,[5] a rival agency with which it has often competed for government contracts. PRI's policy prohibits any employee from seeing any psychiatrist or psychologist who is also a PRI employee; that policy forces Dr. Friedman to sever his patient relationship with Mom—unless she quits her job.

Mom is heartbroken. Dr. Friedman is far and away the best psychiatrist she's ever had, and now the job that he helped her get is taking him away from her. She can't quit, either—with the consolidation of the region's two largest mental health agencies into one, there isn't anywhere else she can go in town now to receive both a good salary and on-the-job counseling.

PRI's new executive director tells Mom she'll have to find a new psychiatrist and gives her a list of names to choose from. Mom scans the list until she sees a name she recognizes—Rumanna J. Agarwal, MD.[6] Dr. Agarwal is a middle-aged Indian Sikh woman whom Mom encountered some years ago during her 1986–1987 hospitalization stint. Mom wasn't under Dr. Agarwal's care at the time; without any private insurance, Mom had to see whichever psychiatrist the Medicaid program assigned her. But back in 1987, Dr. Agarwal had stopped Mom in the hallway toward the end of her hospital stay and offered her free private counseling if she wanted it after her discharge. "You pay a few dollars if you can, otherwise free," Dr. Agarwal had said in her thick Bengali accent. Dr. Agarwal's office wasn't on any bus line and Mom didn't have a car in 1987, so she hadn't taken up Dr. Agarwal's generous offer. But Mom hasn't forgotten Dr. Agarwal's kindness, so she chooses Dr. Agarwal as her new agency-approved psychiatrist.

Dr. Agarwal's office is in a converted Victorian mansion in an upscale Evansville neighborhood. Mom describes Dr. Agarwal's office and waiting room as "super-duper ritzy," with Spanish leather-on-mahogany furniture and Ralph Lauren wallpaper with matching curtains. Mom and I have since speculated as to why it's so lavish, though based on the experience Mom has during the six months she is Dr. Agarwal's patient, I think it's likely that Dr. Agarwal gets a significant proportion of her practice income from under-the-table pharmaceutical kickbacks, otherwise known as "consulting fees," which Big Pharma pays physicians in exchange for giving public lectures and writing journal articles promoting the use of certain drugs over others and also for favoring certain drugs with their patients.

Mom has to wait almost a month before she can get an intake appointment with Dr. Agarwal. In the interim, Mom is under heavy pressure at work. PRI has laid off all of QCB's Medical Records Division management and replaced them with its own people, and my mother's new direct supervisor—I'll call her Louise—is not satisfied with Mom's work. Mom has received stellar performance reviews ever since starting at QCB, and she has even helped design a more efficient system for archiving and pulling patient files. On busy days, Mom often stays after hours, without pay, to make sure the records remain in perfect order; she frequently takes work home with her too. She rarely calls in sick and never takes more than two or three days of vacation at a time. My mother is, by all accounts, a model employee.

None of this matters to Louise, however. As a product of PRI's institutional aversion to hiring former mental health "consumers" as employees, Louise dislikes Mom from the start.

"I don't like no crazies on my staff," Louise tells Mom every morning. Then Louise follows Mom around wherever she goes, admonishing her for not pulling files fast enough or not refiling them in a way that Louise likes. Louise complains that the entire Records Division is put together "by crazies like you." Mom tries to explain that the records filing system was approved by the agency senior management and done according to precise specifications. Louise tells Mom to shut up and work faster, belittling her every step of the way.

Mom calls me almost every evening during this period, giving me detailed play-by-play descriptions of what's going on, asking for support and guidance. I am newly married and therefore preoccupied with other things, so I'm not much help. But I encourage her to report Louise's behavior to the senior management. "What she's doing is probably illegal, Mom. After all the years of hard work you've put in, I'm sure the agency will back you up."

How naive of me to think so.

When Mom complains to PRI senior management about the way she's being treated, they tell her "to find a way to get along with Louise, or else." Mom then seeks Dr. Friedman's help, but he tells her they both risk reprimand—perhaps even termination—if he does anything on her behalf now that the PRI policy is expressly against employee/staff-psychiatrist relationships of any kind. Meanwhile, Louise has stepped up her on-the-job belittling until it has become all-out harassment.

Under the increasing pressure, Mom's anxiety levels increase for the first time in almost nine years. She starts having trouble sleeping, and the familiar black cloud of clinical depression looms. Mom knows that she needs an adjustment in her medication, but until she can get an appointment with Dr. Agarwal, she self-medicates with alcohol instead.

By the time Mom finally gets her intake appointment with Dr. Agarwal over a month later, she's a mess.

Mom asks Dr. Agarwal if she can readjust the dosage in Dr. Friedman's "little cocktail," which has worked so well for her for so many years, to help her cope with her job stress. Dr. Agarwal refuses. Not only does she refuse, she takes Mom off Dr. Friedman's "little cocktail" entirely, and puts her on a heavy mix of addictive benzodiazepine anti-anxiety meds and sleeping pills—the same drugs Dr. Friedman detoxed her from. The side effects of these heavy meds are many—including uncontrolled trembling, weight gain, blurred vision, and mouth problems, along with walking around zombie-like in a deep, drug-induced haze. Unlike Dr. Friedman, Dr. Agarwal gives my mother no cognitive therapy or counseling of any kind; her sessions with Mom consist of asking a few rudimentary questions, scribbling on a prescription pad, and walking out the door to see her next patient, as if she's on a psychotropic assembly line. Pens, notepads, posters, and brochures advertising the latest psychoactive drugs litter Dr. Agarwal's office at every turn, even in the bathrooms.

For the next six months, Mom sees Dr. Agarwal at least once a week. And every week, Dr. Agarwal changes Mom's medication.

"She never gave anything a chance to work," Mom says now. "I don't even remember all the stuff Dr. Agarwal had me on." Mom only remembers the drugs she took for more than two weeks at a time—there weren't many—under Dr. Agarwal's care. Sometimes Dr. Agarwal puts Mom on an antidepressant-benzodiazepine cocktail one week, then switches to an antipsychotic-sleeping-pill cocktail the next, then switches back. With all the random switching and replacing of meds, Mom's brain soon becomes a chemically-induced firestorm.

Almost all the drugs Dr. Agarwal prescribes are known to cause drug-seeking behavior even in small doses, especially in persons with a history of substance abuse. Soon Mom is mentally and physically

hooked on all these drugs, and whenever Dr. Agarwal switches a prescription or takes away a bottle of leftover pills—only to re-prescribe
them again two or three weeks later—Mom finds ways to "seek" the
meds her brain and body now desperately need to survive. Mom learns
how to "clue" Dr. Agarwal into reissuing a past prescription by using
her personal copy of *Physicians' Desk Reference* to research which
symptoms to rattle off in her weekly checkups. Since it's evident that
Dr. Agarwal gets financial incentives from the drug companies to push
their meds as much as possible anyway, this strategy usually works just
fine.

On the rare occasions that it doesn't work, or when Mom can't get
the dosage that her mind and body increasingly need to prevent withdrawal symptoms, Mom finds other sources to feed her addictions. She
does research on the Internet and discovers that over-the-counter antihistamines produce a sedative effect (and sometimes even pleasant hallucinations) when taken in large doses or combined with alcohol. Indeed, Mom finds that all the drugs she's on seem more potent when
mixed with large doses of antihistamines and cheap beer. She buys so
many allergy meds from the CVS pharmacy down the street from her
house that the pharmacist becomes suspicious, takes it off the regular
store shelves, and places it behind the pharmacy counter, refusing to
sell her any more of it. (I learn this months later, when I visit Mom in
Indiana and she makes up a story about having an allergic skin rash that
requires oral antihistamines and sends me down to the corner CVS to
buy her three boxes of the stuff.)

As Mom becomes more and more medicated, she has more and
more difficulty performing her job. She shakes so much that she can't
hang onto medical files, and she spills their contents all over the place.
Her vision gets so blurry she can't read the charts correctly and she
starts pulling the wrong ones. She starts calling in sick at least one day a
week, and soon she finds herself unable to work for days at a time.

Her supervisor Louise loves every minute of it. She sees Mom's
deteriorating job performance as her chance to get Mom fired. However, taking Mom's many years of loyal service under consideration, the
executive director allows Mom to go on short-term disability instead, as
long as she keeps seeing Dr. Agarwal and comes back to work within
three months.

That condition, however, dooms Mom to failure. The longer Mom is under Dr. Agarwal's care, the sicker she gets.

In February 2004, I get a call one night from my brother Mark. Mark and I have never been close as adults, and he never calls me at home, outside of Christmas and birthdays, unless (1) he wants money, or (2) Mom is sick.

The phone rings during dinner. At thirty-one, Mark is back in college for the umpteenth time, though this time it looks like he might actually graduate. He calls from his campus apartment. "Hi Anna, it's your brother," he says in his usual singsong baritone, slurred as always by the cocktail of heavy antipsychotics he takes for his schizophrenia. "Wanted to let you know Mom is in the hospital."

"What?" I feign surprise, but I've known for months that this was probably coming.

Mark sighs. "I took her over there myself. She had a pretty bad episode with Bob over at the house, and he called me to come deal with her. They've got her on those benzo drugs that she likes, so she's calming down. And they gave her a sleeping pill—"

"Mark, *Mom cannot be on any benzodiazepenes or sleeping pills*. You know that."

"Dr. Agarwal called the hospital and *told* them to put her on that stuff. Said that she needed to be stabilized."

"Mark, Mom is a *junkie*. Those meds are like *heroin* to her. You need to tell her doctors to stop giving her that dope."

Mark sighs again. "I tried, Anna. But they aren't listening. At least she's in the hospital where somebody can keep an eye on her—"

I cut him off. "Mark, you need to get Mom the hell away from Dr. Agarwal. Dr. Agarwal's got her hooked on all kinds of shit. And even if Mom gets out from under Dr. Agarwal, you know she's gonna start doctor-shopping for drugs—"

"Anna, I understand all that. But it's complicated. And I have finals coming up—"

"Don't give me that bullshit, Mark. If you're taking Mom to the hospital yourself, the least you can do while you're there is tell the ER docs that Mom is a pillhead junkie who's just manipulating them for prescriptions."

"Anna—" Mark raises his voice, then sucks in a deep breath. "Look, it's not that simple. Mom's married, and that means the only person who legally can do that kind of thing is her husband. And Bob doesn't want to get involved. He's pretty mad at Mom right now because she grabs him and drags him down onto the floor whenever he tries to leave the house for work. He's almost ready to move out because of it. She's afraid he's abandoning her whenever he tries to go somewhere—"

"Oh, good Christ."

"Anna, Mom is legitimately sick. She *needs* to be in the hospital right now."

"She'd be *fine* if Dr. Agarwal hadn't doped the crap out of her," I shoot back. "She'd be *fine* if she was still seeing Dr. Friedman. You need to get her the fuck away from Dr. Agarwal, do you understand me? That lady is the Dr. Feelgood from hell."

"I'll see what I can do," Mark says, and hangs up.

But he does nothing. Mom is discharged from the hospital after two days with a hefty benzodiazepine prescription. Mark and I have never agreed on how to handle Mom's issues, and we never will. Mark is too sick to even take care of himself half the time, so it's not like I can rely on him to make sound decisions anyway. And it's not like we can do anything to get Mom off the runaway train she's on, short of a court order—which as Mark pointed out in a rare moment of lucidity, we can't even legally obtain for her against her husband's wishes. It's a disaster waiting to happen.

The next few months go something like this. Mom takes too much of Dr. Agarwal's latest prescription, then runs out of pills early. She tries to call Dr. Agarwal for more, but often can't reach her on weekends and off-hours. She then drinks too much beer and pops too many antihistamines as she tries to mask the withdrawal symptoms, then she has an "outburst" with Bob (or the neighbors, or my grandparents) and eventually winds up in one of the area's many ERs. Over time, the ER physicians at all the area hospitals learn that Mom is an addict engaging in drug-seeking behavior, and they refuse to admit her.

The three months PRI gave Mom to get better come and go. She asks for long-term disability, and it is granted, but only for three more months. If Mom doesn't improve and return to work within that time, PRI will terminate her employment.

Mom is well into the third month of her long-term disability when it's clear she won't be returning to work anytime soon. PRI fires her. The only good thing to come out of the whole mess is that without private health insurance, Mom can no longer afford Dr. Agarwal. She'll be under the care of a state-appointed Medicaid psychiatrist from now on. There's of course no guarantee that psychiatrist will be any better, but I don't think anyone can possibly be worse for Mom than Dr. Agarwal has been.

Mom petitions for SSI disability again, but with the advent of welfare reform, the process has grown a lot more complicated since her last application ten years earlier. It takes almost three months for her application to go through, and then she faces further delays as she and her caseworker navigate more and more red tape. Apparently a computer glitch leads Social Security to believe Mom is still receiving private disability from PRI when she isn't. In the meantime, no money is coming in save from Bob's twelve-dollar-an-hour job as a maintenance man. The bills are piling up.

Making matters worse, Mom is pissing away all of her money and racking up huge debts besides.

Mom calls me every evening without fail, frantic and hysterical, wanting to know if I can tell her why her credit cards are all maxed out and her checking account is empty.

"Mom, why are you asking me this?" I always say. "I don't have any control over your money."

"I-I-I don't know where all the m-m-m-money went," she says, her teeth grinding from all the drugs. "Where duh-duh-did all my m-m-money go?" Sometimes this same conversation loops and re-loops, ad infinitum.

"I don't know, Mom. Did you read your credit-card statements? Go get your statements and read them to me."

Mom goes to get her bills and reads long lists of credit-card transactions that she doesn't remember making, but I recognize them as anxiety-driven manic spending habits—the very same kind of destructive behavior that once plagued me.

There are the familiar liquor-store and drugstore binges I know are the result of Mom's self-medicating ways. There are occasional spending sprees at local discount stores. But the bulk of the manic spending is in the form of cash advances, drawn on several different credit cards in large amounts and totaling almost $20,000 in debt.

"Mom, why did you get all those cash advances? What the hell did you spend that kind of money on?"

"I duh-duh-don't know, A-A-Anna."

"What do you mean, *you don't know*? Think! Try to remember! Surely you've got some receipts or something lying around—"

Mom starts to cry. "I *dunnnnooooooo*! I d-d-don't know what *h-h-happened*, Anna, and I nuh-nuh-need you to fuh-fuh-find that money for me!"

"Mom, you've spent this money on something, and you need to figure out what. I can't just magically get it back for you. If you bought stuff at the store and still have the receipts, maybe they'll take it back and you can get a refund." I doubt that's the case, though. My guess is Mom has spent the bulk of the money on booze, possibly also frivolous things like nice dinners out or pay-per-view movies that she and Bob can no longer afford.

Or it might well be a symptom of something much more sinister. I think back to a time in the early 1990s when my mother told me she'd started getting mysterious phone calls from people looking for someone named Edith Morehouse. There were blocks of time that she blacked out and couldn't remember any details of, and there was always money missing from her purse afterward. She was afraid to mention the issue to her therapists, but she mentioned it to me. I told her she might have multiple personality disorder, but Mom scoffed at the idea. "That kind of thing doesn't really happen to people except in the movies," she said then. "I'm sure it's just my memory playing tricks on me. My nerve medication makes me forgetful, you know." Now, ten years later, it seems the same thing is happening again.

"Mom, I want you to cut up all your credit cards," I instruct her. "Your ATM card too. Give the checkbook to Bob. You shouldn't be handling any money in your condition."

"Buh-but Bob says he doesn't like to h-handle the m-m-money—"

"Well, then he needs to shut up and get used to it," I hiss, and hang up.

I immediately dial my grandparents. Papaw Jones answers the phone. "Papaw, it's Anna. I need to talk to you about Mom—"

"I'm gonna git your Memaw," Papaw drawls in his thick Southern accent before I can get another word out.

Memaw comes to the phone. "Yes, what is it, Anna?"

"Memaw, I need you and Papaw to keep an eye on Mom and her spending habits."

"What do you mean, hon?"

I sigh. "Just keep an eye out. If you notice she's suddenly got a lot of new clothes or Bob has a bunch of expensive new tools or something like that. You know Bob doesn't like to deal with money and then just leaves Mom to make a mess of it. Let me know if she's eating out a lot, or seems to be carrying a bunch of cash around—"

"Anna, honey, your Papaw and me are mostly trying to steer clear of your Mom these days."

My jaw drops against the receiver with a *thud*. "What? Why?"

"We're just fed up with her, hon. She's been sick on and off like this for going on thirty years, and we just can't deal with it no more."

"But Memaw—"

"Anna, sugar, your Pap and me, we're getting too old, and we can't deal with it no more. Hell, Bob's her damn husband, and *he* don't even wanna deal with it no more. And Mark—well, you know how Mark is. Don't think 'bout nothing but himself. Your Mom's fifty-some years old now, and she's just gotta learn to take care of herself. So that's all I know to say, hon."

Memaw Jones hangs up without another word.

I'm furious. My mother is disintegrating back in Indiana, and the people who should be taking care of her there have all washed their hands of her. And there's little I can do from Chicago but watch the whole thing unfold from afar.

I try to help Mom as best I can for the next few weeks, but with all the other members of her family shutting themselves out of her life, I become Mom's anxiety receptacle. She starts her incessant, histrionic telephone calls, causing problems for me at work and home. She gives no consideration to the fact that by doing so she jeopardizes my job and my marriage, and instead she makes me feel guilty when I become angry with her for it. In short, she uses her illness as a weapon, uses her status as a victim of a terrible disease to inflict pain upon everyone around her, perhaps in an unconscious effort to force those she loves to endure the same emotional hell she herself lives with every day. It's familiar territory, and not just because Mom has behaved this way in her past episodes.

I recognize the behavior for what it is because I have done all of these things myself.

Experts on clinical depression and other forms of mental illness have stated time and again that the afflicted person is not the only one who suffers. Families and friends suffer too. And they are often just as powerless against the raging torrent of emotions that inevitably result from dealing with a mentally ill family member as their afflicted loved ones are themselves. Some of this is from the deep social stigma mental illness carries, even in a society that is more open and educated about it than ever before. But mostly it's due to the way mental illness has a succubus-like effect on the afflicted's loved ones—it simply drains the lifeblood out of the family, the accidental caregivers who often just have to stand back and watch the growing catastrophe like a cameraman does a plane crash. Friends, spouses, and colleagues can walk away from the afflicted (and often do), but blood family cannot—at least, not permanently. That doesn't mean we are any better equipped to help our loved ones than a stranger on the street, though. We often have no choice but to feel helpless.

Sometimes we caregivers—who are all too often survivors of mental illness ourselves—have no choice but to stand back and let the horrible happen, let the afflicted find his or her own way out of the abyss. By the fall of 2004, I've been fired from my job at the library software company and I'm back to doing freelance writing work instead. Angry and frustrated, I join the rest of my family and walk away from Mom, leaving her with nothing but a silent prayer that she won't kill herself or end up a crazy bag lady. I will be happy if she merely stays alive and off the streets. But I consider the chance of her ever getting better as likely as a winning lotto ticket or a Chicago Cubs World Series win.

I stop taking Mom's calls. I stop trying to monitor her health from afar, stop combing the Internet for the next miracle cure for depression, stop dedicating my yoga and meditation practice to her health and well-being. I stop everything. I sever all contact.

In short, I give up on Mom.

When you and your family are all *nutjobs*, you learn to manage your expectations.

# 6

# MARK: THE LOST CAUSE

**M**y brother, Mark Landon Berry,[1] is an enigma.

I have never known what to make of my brother, and neither has most of the rest of the world. And Mark doesn't seem to know what to make of himself either. Over the past fifteen years, he has flitted between many different personas, never settling on any one of them for long—liberal atheist, flunking college student, U.S. Army medic, Catholic priest-in-training, ultraconservative Republican Party canvassing volunteer, pyramid-scheme salesman, Dungeons & Dragons devotee, social worker, volunteer who supposedly helps veterans win disability benefits, server of legal subpoenas, all-around general con artist, doctor, lawyer, Indian chief.

My brother, Mark Landon Berry, is a paranoid schizophrenic.

The DSM-V and other major psychiatric tomes describe schizophrenia as a mental disorder characterized by impairments "in the perception or expression of reality and/or by significant social or occupational dysfunction." My brother fits both of these criteria with such perfection that his profile could serve as a case study in any college freshman's Psychology 101 textbook. He first got the official paranoid-schizophrenic diagnosis by our family psychiatrist Dr. Nickelback as a teenager, and it's stayed with him ever since, though he's somehow managed to convince some questionable doctors that he's perfectly normal, or just ever-so-slightly bipolar. The one thing that has remained consistent about Mark is that he has never lived the life of a stable, functioning adult. He's never maintained any kind of employment, he's always on antipsychotics, and he seems unwilling or unable to grow up. His life revolves mostly around playing computer games, visiting the VA psychiatric department on a near-daily basis, and exploring get-rich-quick schemes. He gets by mostly by manipulating others to his every whim.[2] Mark is very good at getting everyone around him to agree to do ridiculous things in the name of keeping him from falling apart.

Throughout his life, though, it was difficult to determine what Mark's actual illness was, or if he really even had one. The 2007 school shooting at Virginia Tech, however, helped put my brother's lifelong illness into sharp relief for me. The shooter in that tragedy had allegedly undergone some psychiatric evaluation but had had no actual diagnosis or real treatment of any kind beyond a few brief consultations with non-MD psychologists, according to news reports. Reportedly, his Korean immigrant family had essentially abandoned him due to his severe mental illness. And his parents obviously lived in a state of denial about that severe mental illness, going so far as to say that the only thing wrong with their son was that he was "quiet" and "had difficulty fitting in." But to my mind, he wasn't "quiet" or even a little eccentric. He seemed to me to be the worst extreme of what an adolescent paranoid schizophrenic can become when he isn't properly treated, when he is written off completely by his family and society. While I watched the shooter's "multimedia manifesto" on *NBC Evening News*, I recognized him for exactly what he was—an untreated, unmanaged paranoid schizophrenic. I could see that so clearly because my own brother has been the exact same thing for most of his life.

I sat frozen on my living room sofa, feeling rivers of ice flow through my veins as I saw the shooter's vacant, staring eyes, listened to his rambling monotone, heard him rage against the "you" who supposedly forced him kill thirty-two people without explaining who that mysterious "you" was—and I saw my own brother's vacant, staring eyes looking back at me, heard my brother's own rambling, raging monotone coming out of my plasma-screen's stereo speaker. (Unmedicated paranoid schizophrenics are remarkably alike in their behavior—like clones, even.)[3] I stayed up half the night watching CNN, and I shuddered as I realized that only a few random strokes of luck separated me from the paranoid schizophrenic who went wild with two handguns on a college campus and my own paranoid-schizophrenic sibling, the one person on this planet who shared the biggest component of my DNA.

Mind you, most paranoid schizophrenics are not violent or dangerous, and my brother has never been violent. But knowing that even a tiny fraction of people with that illness are capable of such heinous acts if left untreated terrifies me to the core—especially since I know firsthand what a poor job the American mental health system does of caring for them.

I'll itemize Mark's schizophrenic characteristics—and there are many—before I get into how his schizophrenia has affected his relationship with the world, with our family, and with me.

*Significant Social Dysfunction.* Mark was odd practically from birth—needy, prone to violent tantrums, unable to play normally with other children from an early age. He had a series of medical problems and hospitalizations from birth (crooked legs that required casts, severe allergic reactions to penicillin and vaccinations, extreme high fevers), and he was a difficult child to control even when healthy. He couldn't make friends. He was the frequent target of bullies, large and small. He failed at school from kindergarten on; he often couldn't grasp the most fundamental norms of social interaction either in school or on the playground, and he got into frequent conflicts with teachers. In one case, a teacher specifically asked that he be transferred out of her class because she simply didn't know what to do with him. The principal tried putting Mark in Special Ed, but he didn't fit in there either (despite his behavioral problems and failing grades, he had high IQ scores), so he bounced around from class to class until he fell so far behind there was no way for him to catch up. In fourth grade, Mark's teachers decided to hold him back a year, and he ended up in the same grade as me, which only made his behavior patterns worse. So the school bumped him back up to fifth grade in the middle of the year, mostly as a peace offering. If born today, Mark would probably be diagnosed (incorrectly) as autistic.

Childhood-onset schizophrenia is extremely rare but not unheard of. I've often wondered if my brother had it, if perhaps his schizophrenia merely matured along with his body, rather than emerging at puberty or late adolescence, as it does for most male schizophrenics.[4] There were certainly plenty of indications during Mark's formative years that he was destined to a life of severe mental illness.

Growing up, Mark often had difficulty with basic hygiene. I remember many late-night conversations between my mother and father on what to do about Mark's refusal to use toilet paper when he defecated (he was almost ten at the time—old enough to know better). In high school, when most young men are fastidious about their appearance, Mark had to be reminded, cajoled, and sometimes even forced to brush his teeth, use deodorant, even bathe. My father spent an inordinate amount of time emphasizing the importance of shaving with a sharp, clean razor, to no avail—Mark's face was always a mess of razor burn and infected cuts from ancient, rusty blades.

Psychiatrists call the poor hygiene and poor social skills typical of many paranoid schizophrenics symptoms of "disorganized behavior."

Mark's behavior was very, very disorganized.

His taste in clothes was odd. When most kids our age wore jeans, T-shirts, and sneakers for both school and play, Mark preferred to wear stiff gray corduroys, button-down Oxford shirts, and loafers—just like a miniature Alex P. Keaton. In the 1980s this wasn't necessarily odd, but it *was* odd when you considered the fact that Mark wore these formal clothes, unwashed, day in and day out for school, play (and sometimes even sleep) until they formed stiffly to his body like a reeking second skin. The colors and styles of clothing he wore never changed from year to year, even during his teens. Every fall, when Dad took us to the local mall for our school wardrobes, Mark always picked out four identical pairs of gray corduroys and four identical blue Oxford shirts from the men's department, and he wore them until they fell apart. Mark refused to let anyone buy him anything else to wear during regular day-to-day life, and any clothes he received as gifts other than his preferred corduroys and blue Oxfords would sit untouched in his bureau drawers.

One day in junior high, I take Mark aside after I witness him receive a particularly bad bruising from a pack of jocks, and suggest that he let Dad buy him at least one pair of normal, boring jeans. "You might not get beat up so much that way," I say.

I'm only trying to help.

"I can't wear jeans," he snarls.

"Why not?"

"Because they don't stay on my body," he says.

I laugh at this. "What do you mean?"

*"Because they won't stay on my body,"* he all-out screams. "My body won't *hold* them. They won't *hold* my body." Mark then pats himself down, as if he needs to check that his body is still there.

This is probably the first example of Mark's *impaired perception or expression of reality*. His brain has conjured up the idea that his very existence is somehow tied to wearing identical gray corduroy pants every day.

My mother swears to this day that she never could have managed Mark and me as babies (we were born barely a year apart) if I hadn't been the standoffish, quiet infant that I was, a "good" baby who slept through the night almost from birth without coddling. I preferred to feed and entertain myself from the very moment I was able. I was a dreamy and introspective child, happy to be left alone all day in a playpen while my mother devoted every waking minute to trying to keep Mark from tearing the house down, and himself with it. I had a factory-loaded stronger personality and fierce, independent streak from the get-go, and Mom indulged both by ignoring me while she cosseted my needy older brother and met his every demand and whim.

I was strong. Mark was weak. And in parenting us the way she did, my well-meaning-but-naive young mother—barely an adult herself, with two babies by age twenty-three—strengthened the strong and weakened the weak.

There's a *Simpsons* episode that illustrates the circumstances of my early childhood exactly. In it, Lisa Simpson is shown in flashback as a baby, lying face up on a diaper table. Marge and Homer Simpson are in the middle of changing her diaper when Lisa's brother Bart sets the curtains on fire, then runs his toy car through the wall, then shreds the carpet. Marge and Homer drop everything and ignore Lisa to try (in vain) to control the out-of-control Bart. Baby Lisa ends up rolling her eyes, sighing, and changing her own diaper.

Scientists disagree on what exactly causes schizophrenia, though it seems to have a much stronger genetic component than other forms of mental illness. However, a strong genetic predisposition to schizophrenia still isn't a definitive predictor of who will develop symptoms of full-blown schizophrenia. Multiple studies have concluded that childhood psychological trauma, especially in adolescence, can awaken the unique orchestra of genes that then work in concert to produce the cacophony of brain noise that is insanity.[5]

My brother was never what you'd call a "normal" child, but he didn't become seriously ill until he was about sixteen, around the time that Dad's marriage to his second wife, Martha, began to fall apart. By then my dad had begun an affair with Martha's best friend, "Tracy," and when Martha found out, she threw Dad, my brother, and me out of the house. The three of us stayed in a cheap motel for a couple of weeks, then Dad found a house for us to rent in the same school district. Tracy soon left her own husband and moved in with us. Mark, who unlike me had gotten along well with Martha, hated the whole arrangement.

Mark and Tracy never got along, and after a year or so of constantly butting heads, Mark finally suffered an all-out mental breakdown. He refused to attend school, ripped man-sized holes in our rented, suburban-tract home's prefabricated particle-board doors with his bare hands, kicked down drywall, and made himself throw up all over the dinner table more than once—all because he thought Tracy was a member of an "alien KGB" who was supposedly trying to kill him. He hallucinated alien attacks in our backyard and threatened Dad at his job multiple times. For reasons I've never understood, Dad finally called Dr. Nickelback—the "Dr. Feelgood" shrink who first got my mother hooked on heavy psychotropic meds—and Dr. Nickelback recommended that Mark be immediately admitted to the brand-spanking-new private mental hospital for adolescents that Dr. Nickelback had just opened with a partner. Not surprisingly, Mark didn't get better—in fact, he moved out of Dad's house shortly thereafter and they remained estranged for years. Meanwhile, Dr. Nickelback's private mental hospital later got shut down by the state for fraud, and Dr. Nickelback and his partner both lost their licenses to practice medicine due to their unethical drug-prescribing practices.

Mom was pretty much out of our lives during this period, though she does say that Dr. Nickelback did call her shortly after Mark was admitted to his private hospital and informed her that her only son was "schizo," as Mom not-so-politely puts it now.

Although I believe my brother would have succumbed to schizophrenia at some point regardless, I believe our unstable family life didn't exactly help matters, and it probably hastened the onset of his illness. To this day, both Tracy and I also believe that Dr. Nickelback's questionable medical practices probably did permanent damage to Mark too.

What is schizophrenia, really?

I'm no clinician, but growing up with my brother makes me an expert in the condition by default. Psychiatrists describe two major symptom categories for the disease: *positive* symptoms and *negative* symptoms.

*Positive* symptoms are the obvious ones, the symptoms we see caricatured on television and in the movies: hearing voices; delusions; fear of everyone, and everything; vacant, staring eyes; rage, anger, and violent verbal and physical attacks on loved ones and random strangers alike; extreme self-involvement; strange speech patterns (rambling monotones are typical); the inability or all-out refusal to adhere to societal norms; poor hygiene; and poorer social skills. My brother has them all, even when he's on antipsychotics.

*Negative* symptoms are a little harder to discern. Essentially, *negative* schizophrenic symptoms are the *absence* of the subtler cognitive abilities that are present in normal people—that is, *affective flattening* (lack or decline in emotional response); *alogia* (lack or decline in speech); and *avolition* (lack or decline in motivation). Mark has displayed all of these at one time or another, but the negative symptom that plagues him the most is *avolition*. Despite having a high IQ, a college education, and the additional vocational training he received while serving in the military, Mark has refused to hold down a real job for his entire adult life—and not for lack of employment opportunities. Offered literally dozens of good, professional jobs with solid-middle-class salaries over the years at employers ranging from the VA and Disabled American Veterans to local social-service agencies and even the local university, Mark always either refuses those job offers or works at the jobs no more than one or at most two weeks at a time. His reason is always the same: "I have to have the *perfect* job, and this job wasn't perfect, so I quit."

Instead, Mark relies on others—his family, the Catholic church, his wife—for financial support. He has mastered any number of manipulative tactics to maintain a support system that will cater to his every need, tactics that he first learned by monopolizing every second of my mother's time when he was a toddler. You might say he's a professional moocher.

Mark is also a notorious hypochondriac. I'll even go so far as to say that Mark has a mild case of *Munchausen's syndrome*, a mental illness classified by the sufferer's relentless fabrication of false physical and emotional illnesses to satisfy an emotional need for attention and sympathy. Whether Mark's supposed multiple ailments are deliberately fabricated or merely another set of schizophrenia-induced delusions has never been entirely clear, but he has consistently engaged in heavy-duty hypochondriac behavior since his early teens.

To wit, Munchausen's is most common in persons with schizophrenia and other severe personality disorders. My brother was first diagnosed as a paranoid schizophrenic in his late teens, though he has never received an official Munchausen's diagnosis to my knowledge (the very nature of the illness means that few Munchausen's sufferers do).[6]

Starting around age twelve—and continuing to this day—Mark's life has always revolved around what kind of mysterious ailment he can come down with (or more accurately, come *up* with) next.

Throughout his adolescence and early adulthood, Mark "came down with" food poisoning, hypoglycemia, diabetes, kidney failure, impetigo ("caused" by his relentless scratching and picking at mosquito bites and pimples), fainting spells, heart arrhythmias, migraines, Lyme disease, West Nile virus, malaria, and a host of other ailments that disappeared and were replaced with something new almost as soon as someone figured out he was faking it to get attention.

Today Mark uses his advanced hypochondria to control others most of all—making manipulative demands on where everyone in our family can go, and what we can eat, watch on television, wear, and even wash our hair with in his presence because all of these things might in some way aggravate his (supposed) asthma, gastric-reflux disease, vertigo, seasonal-affective disorder, heart arrhythmia, restless-leg syndrome, fibromyalgia, or whatever other ailment he's concocted for himself this or that week. Mark's hypochondria is so convincing to strangers that he's managed to manipulate unnecessary prescriptions for drugs (including several controlled substances)—and even unnecessary surgery—for these nonexistent ailments. I've often wondered why so many physicians—who have surely examined his medical history of paranoid schizophrenia and the long list of odd diseases that mysteriously appear and disappear, one after the other—don't put two and two together. A convenient consequence of Mark's constant "illnesses" is that it provides him with another excuse not to get a job, which serves to satisfy his schizophrenic avolition.

There's an incident that illustrates both Mark's avolition and his delusional hypochondria perfectly. I'll go so far as to recommend that psychiatry and psychology professors use it to teach their students, in fact.

In mid-2004, Mark and his much younger new wife (an intelligent, kind, and highly-paid-but-naive computer systems engineer) decide to make a trip to Chicago to visit my husband and me. I speak with Mark's wife, Stephanie,[7] at length on the telephone in the days leading up to the visit, and she expresses her and Mark's desire to see some Chicago theater and sample some of its best ethnic restaurants. I'm an avid connoisseur of both, so I promise I'll show them both a good time.

I ask Stephanie what kind of food and theater she and Mark might like to see. (Mark's extreme political conservatism limits the subject matter he will tolerate—that's yet another tactic he uses to manipulate others.) I suggest a production of Woody Allen's lighthearted religious satire *God*, which is being produced and directed by some friends of mine at Chicago's Chemically Imbalanced Comedy, and a trip to Devon Avenue for some authentic Indian food. Stephanie says she thinks that will be fine, but she'll have to check with Mark first.

Over the next several days, I field several more phone calls from Stephanie, who is serving as a sort of go-between for Mark's many demands. "Mark says that Indian food is okay as long as it's not too spicy, and we can't go to any restaurant that has candles on the tables," she says. "The candles aggravate his asthma. The last time he was around a candle, I had to take him to the emergency room."

I have to stifle a laugh. Mark and Stephanie were married only about six months ago; I stood up at their wedding in a small Catholic church where burning candles were plentiful. They'd even lit a unity candle on the altar together. As far as I could recall, Mark claimed to have asthma at the time of their wedding, and as a member of the wedding party, I was made to refrain from wearing perfume and to wash with unscented, hypoallergenic shampoo and soap that Mark had pre-approved as not aggravating to his asthma. No mention was made then of candles being a problem; this is obviously some new delusion Mark's brain has manufactured.

"Well, that might be kind of hard," I say. "Most nice Chicago restaurants have candles on the tables."

"Mark says there can be absolutely, positively, *no* candles or open flames of any kind at any restaurant we go to. That includes Sterno heaters."

Then I really do laugh. "Well, that will knock out most Indian restaurants. A lot of them use Sterno on the buffets, sometimes even on the tables to heat curries."

"I'm sorry," Stephanie replies. "No candles, *no* open flame. That's just what Mark says we have to do. But he really has his heart set on Indian no matter what, so he can get tandoori chicken. Do you think one of the Indian places might put away their candles and stuff if they know we're coming ahead of time?"

"All right," I sigh. "I'll see what I can do."

I call around to the numerous Indian restaurants on Devon Avenue where George and I like to go for dinner. One of them where my husband and I are regular customers agrees not to set candles out on the night we're coming or seat us around any Sterno heat, provided I can guarantee that we'll spend at least $100 on our meal. That's not a problem—knowing Mark's ravenous appetite for food and booze, I know he'll probably rack up that much by himself. The manager promises to seat us off by ourselves as far away from the Sterno cans on the buffet as possible. I call Stephanie back and tell her about the arrangements I've made, and she tells me they are probably fine.

Things seem to go all right at the restaurant until we're about midway through the meal. There's a half-wall dividing the semiprivate dining room we occupy from the main dining room. Mark sits facing the half-wall, so he can see what the people on the other side of the restaurant are eating. Someone orders a sizzling tandoori dish that requires a cast-iron pan be set on a rack over a can of Sterno. The family eating the sizzling dish sits a good ten yards away—and Sterno has no smoke or odor anyway. But Mark sees his opportunity, and he takes it.

"We have to leave now," he shouts, and stands up.

I try to keep the scene from getting out of hand. "What? Why?"

"You *told* me there'd be no open flames!" he shouts, louder this time. "There's an open flame!" Mark starts huffing and puffing, and pretends to be lightheaded. I know he's pretending because it's the exact same act he used to pretend he was having a hypoglycemic attack when we were kids. He starts pacing up and down, wheezing and moaning. People on the other side of the restaurant turn to stare.

My husband balls his napkin and tosses it onto the table, furious. I promised him I wouldn't let something like this happen tonight, and less than an hour into the evening, I've already failed.

Stephanie immediately goes to comfort her husband. It's clear Mark has her trained; she falls hook, line, and sinker for his manipulative act.

I pity her.

Stephanie ushers Mark out of the restaurant and out onto the busy street while George and I settle the huge bill—Mark has ordered himself the most expensive spiced roast lamb-and-chicken dish on the menu, along with two giant Taj Mahal beers, which he emptied right before pulling his dramatic-asthmatic act.

Things only get worse when we get to the theater. I've reserved four tickets for us to the sold-out Saturday show at Cornservatory on Lincoln Avenue, where the latest Chemically Imbalanced Comedy play is running; the only reason I've been able to get tickets on such short notice is because I know the show's producer. Since we've blown out of the restaurant early, we are an hour early for the show and can't sit down yet, but the producer is already setting up the box office when we arrive. I've promised to pay cash for the tickets on arrival, and I dig $60 out of my purse to cover the cost of four tickets—but as I do, I see out of the corner of my eye Mark giving the ramshackle theater lobby a look of disapproval.

Just as I'm handing the cash over to the show's producer—Megan, a personal friend I've known for years—Mark makes a scene.

"Has somebody been *smoking* in here? Because if somebody's been *smoking* in here, I'm not staying."

I suck in my breath. I know what's coming.

Megan goes to greet my brother and his wife, all slick customer service. "We don't allow smoking in the theater," she says. "Chicago city ordinance prohibits that. But there's a Korean barbecue restaurant next door—maybe you're just smelling their cooking."

"Somebody's been SMOKING in here!" Mark yells, and starts pacing. "Somebody's been SMOKING in here! I can't stay here if somebody's SMOKING!" He paces, fake-wheezes, and then hits the wall with his fist. "Goddamn it! *Goddamnit!*"

Mark stomps out of the theater.

Megan's jaw drops. Stephanie just looks helpless. "I'm sorry, Anna, but if Mark smells smoke in here, we can't stay and watch the show." She dashes out onto the street after her husband. Meanwhile, my own husband clearly wants to disappear.

"Anna, I promise you, I don't let *anybody* smoke in the theater," Megan stammers, trying in vain to fix the situation. "That's—that's like, against the law."

"I know you don't," I reply with a sigh. "I'm really, really sorry about that. That's my brother and he's just—well, he's mentally ill, and he just has a lot of problems."

Megan frowns. "I guess you'll need a refund on the tickets then," she says, and she hands me back my cash in a huff.

I apologize several more times, but Megan is clearly upset. She held those tickets as a personal favor to me, and now she probably won't be able to resell them. And all because a chemical imbalance in my brother's brain insists there is smoke in a theater when there is, in fact, none.

Since there's apparently no entertainment venue in Chicago that will meet Mark's asthma-safety criteria, we spend the rest of the evening driving Mark and Stephanie around Chicago's most exclusive neighborhoods, pointing out interesting architecture and hot blues clubs through my cramped old Hyundai's dirty windows. But Mark grows impatient with that after an hour or so, claiming his restless-leg syndrome is acting up. (That's a new one; I'm sure he's picked it up from all the restless-leg-syndrome pharmaceutical commercials that litter the TV airwaves.) Mark angrily demands that I drive him and Stephanie back to their hotel, which is on the other end of town. Stephanie gently reminds him that they've left their car parked in front of our condo building. He keeps quiet for the rest of the drive back to my neighborhood, but he makes a point to shift a lot in his seat, kicking my dashboard hard with every move he makes.

As my brother and his wife head off toward their car without so much as a thank you for the expensive dinner I've bought them or all the trouble I've gone to, I slam my car into park and put my head down on the steering wheel.

"Why the hell do you put up with him?" George asks, livid. "What a fucking asshole."

"He's my brother," I sigh. "And he's not an asshole. He's just very, very sick."

I would add one more negative schizophrenic symptom to the accepted list based on my years of observing Mark's behavior: *a high degree of suggestibility*. My brother has fallen victim to religious cults, pyramid schemes, and borderline criminal enterprises, all promising to make him rich quick. The fact that someone as intelligent as Mark is should fail to see through the flim-flam and emotional manipulation of these kinds of organizations time and time again is only explained, I believe, by a profound lack of skepticism.

Skepticism is a subtle emotional trigger that kicks in for most of us without our having to think about it at all. But when a person's mind, however intelligent, is clouded with the incandescent firestorm of schizophrenia, any and all sorts of potentially life-saving emotional triggers and gateways simply don't work.

Scientists have devised several different tools to measure a person's suggestibility (e.g., the Harvard Group scale, and the Stanford scale). I don't think Mark has ever been subjected to one of these tests, but I believe he'd score high on them. Because of his schizophrenic tendency to "split" the world around him into all-or-nothing, black-and-white situations, Mark is particularly vulnerable to any scheme that promises fast riches and a tight-knit social network that will "take care" of him. (I'm actually surprised he hasn't fallen victim to the Mafia yet.)

I first note Mark's high degree of suggestibility in high school when Dad's soon-to-be-ex-second-wife Martha decides to take advantage of it and use him as a tool in her divorce battle against Dad. Somehow, Martha manages to convince Mark that Dad has stolen money from him (what funds exactly I have no idea since Mark is a teenager with no job, and the only money he possesses is whatever allowance Dad gives him). Martha encourages my brother to file suit against my father in small-claims court. He does, and the results aren't what I'm sure he and Martha had in mind.

I'm not present at the hearing, but what occurs there becomes the stuff of Evansville donut-shop gossip for years. Supposedly, Mark presents a case claiming that not only has Dad failed to pay him some kind of remuneration for his yet-to-begin college education, Dad has also physically assaulted him. Dad admits to the judge that he manhandled Mark during an argument, but only after Mark attacked him first in a fit of uncontrolled schizophrenic rage.

Mark presents no corroborating evidence for the stolen money or the alleged assault other than my dad's own admission that he was just trying to defend himself. The exasperated judge throws the whole case out, and he admonishes Mark for bringing private family disputes into his overloaded courtroom and wasting his valuable time. Mark reportedly then launches a string of shouted obscenities at Dad and the judge, and Dad manages to subdue him before the bailiff has a chance to throw both of them out.

It was Martha and Mark's goal to publicly humiliate my father, but the opposite ends up happening. I'm sure it will give Martha pause if she ever considers engaging an unstable schizophrenic teenager to do her dirty work for her in public again.

My brother bounces around from place to place over the next several years. Most of what I know about this time comes to me third-hand through relatives since Mark essentially cuts himself off from me, Dad, and the rest of his immediate family. He attends college at the local research university for a while but abruptly leaves after he unsuccessfully sues a male psychology professor for sexual harassment. The university ombudsman dismisses Mark's initial complaint as being without merit. I have no doubt whatsoever that the alleged sex harassment occurs only in my brother's mind. I can't say for sure, but I think Mark was only partly complying with his doctors' antipsychotic medication orders during this time—if he was taking his meds at all.

From age eighteen to twenty-one, Mark moves around constantly, sleeping on friends' couches or getting kicked out of apartments because he doesn't pay the rent. He holds no job, and he flunks out of whatever college he's attending at the time. Dad dutifully pays Mark's tuition bills even though Mark gets straight Fs and incompletes, but that is the extent of their relationship; they don't communicate except through other relatives, like my Memaw and Papaw Jones.

I'm in the middle of my college sophomore year when Mark manages to matriculate as a third-year freshman at a competing college nearby. He is only about forty miles away, but I rarely see or speak to Mark during this time other than the annual Christmas and Thanksgiving gatherings at my grandparents' house. (While Mark stayed in Memaw and Papaw Jones' basement for a time when he was still a teenager, they've mostly washed their hands of him too, except to serve as an occasional relay station for messages.) I only keep up on what he's up to through my mother, whom Mark frequently manipulates for cash and favors.

Mom calls me in my dorm room at least once a week with news of Mark's latest shenanigans.

"Anna, I'm very worried about your brother," Mom says on one late-night call during midterms week early in my sophomore year.

"Yeah, so what else is new?" I'm wired on No-Doz, Mountain Dew, and chocolate when she calls well after eleven, while I'm cramming for an exam. Mom is up late studying herself—preparing for a test the next day at her mental health job-training program.

"Anna, your brother just called me to say he's about to get kicked out of his apartment." Mom is snuffling and biting back tears. "He has no money! He had to sell all his school books to buy *food*!"

"Mom, *please* don't tell me you're going to fall for this line of bullshit," I say. "You know he's just making it all up to get money out of you."

"Anna, your dad doesn't send your brother *anything*," Mom croaks. "The divorce agreement between me and him requires that he pays for you kids' education, but you know how your dad is—he just won't."

"Mom, Dad pays Mark's tuition," I shoot back. "Way more than he pays for *my* tuition, in fact. When Mark sends him the bills he does, anyway. Although I don't know why, with how Mark just flunks out of everywhere. He's probably going to flunk out of this new school just like he flunked out of all the others before, and then maybe he'll sue some more professors on the side just for fun."

"Anna, there's no need for you to be so mean."

"I'm just stating the facts, Mom. Can I go now?"

"But your Dad doesn't send Mark any *money*!" Mom is all-out crying now. "Just a few dollars here and there, not enough for Mark to live on! And he's *starving* because of it! His roommates are going to throw his stuff out on the street tomorrow if he doesn't pay them rent soon—"

I laugh. "Dad doesn't send *me* any more money than that, Mom. That's why I have a job. Maybe if Mark just got a *job* he could afford to pay his bills." I say this although I know that the more money Mark has access to, the more he will blow it on wasteful eccentricities like medieval mead-making equipment and handpainted Dungeons & Dragons figurines. Mark always has difficulty understanding the concept that one has to pay for rent and food before loading up on expensive hobby materials. I'm sure he's in whatever situation he claims to be because of that, and not because he's a starving victim of miserable circumstance.

"Well, you know your brother has all kinds of *learning disabilities*, Anna. He can't go to school full time and hold down a job at the same time like you can."

(Mom is in serious denial about my brother's mental illness. What everyone else calls *paranoid schizophrenia*, my mother calls *learning disabilities*. She's never been able to accept that he's a paranoid schizophrenic, no matter how many times she's been told by both clinicians and family members, even referring to Dr. Nickelback's "schizo" diagnosis as nothing but bunk that he made up just to make money. No matter that other doctors agreed with the diagnosis—it's just too much for my mother to take given her own constantly fragile mental state.)

"Whatever, Mom. Is there something in particular you needed? I'm kind of studying for an exam right now."

"I was calling to see if you could afford to send Mark some money."

I scoff. "No way."

"You're being selfish!"

"No, I'm being realistic. I'm not going to fall prey to Mark's lies and manipulation, and neither should you."

Mom cries harder. My heart goes out to her—I can't imagine how horrible it must be to stand by, helpless, and watch your only son destroy himself and try to take everyone in your family down with him. At one level I can understand why my mother thinks sending my brother a few hundred dollars that he'll just piss away on foolish junk will help him. But at another level, I don't want her to become the latest victim of my brother's mental illness, especially when she is fighting her own battle with clinical depression and anxiety disorders. "Mom, *please* don't ask me to send Mark any money. He needs to learn to take care of himself."

"You know I can't afford to send Mark very much out of my disability check!" she shoots back. "I need you to do just this one small thing for me. Send your brother whatever you can afford—fifty, a hundred dollars—"

"No!" I scream into the phone, then sigh. It's futile. Either I send Mark money to appease my mother and enable his manipulative schizophrenic behavior, or I hurt my already very fragile mother by ignoring her desperate pleas. It's a no-win situation, one that any member of a mentally ill family faces on a near-daily basis.

"I'm sorry Mom, but I can't help you. I'm hanging up now. Good luck on your job-training stuff."

It's the right decision for me to make, but that doesn't make it any easier. It's no wonder that I try to avoid every member of my immediate family as much as possible. There's no point in admonishing Dad for continuing to pay Mark's bills when Mom could just sue him for contempt of court for violating their divorce decree. There's no point in trying to reason with Mom about Mark when she's in total denial about Mark's illness in the first place. These kinds of inter-sibling conflicts are hard enough to weather in a normal family, but when you add our family's *nutjob* DNA to the mix, they become next to impossible.

I slam the phone into the receiver, then cry for an hour. I'm not able to get back to studying until well after midnight.

Despite all my best efforts to avoid it, I fall victim to my brother's suggestive financial manipulation a few times myself. The combination of Mark's spendthrift habits and his schizophrenic avolition—in other words, his brain's profound aversion to work of any kind because it might put him under further mental stress—has always made him susceptible to pyramid schemes and dodgy, commission-only sales positions.

The first time I fall victim to Mark's seductive "sales" tactics is my junior year of college, when Mark has finally dropped out of college altogether and is trying in vain to find a job that will pay him as much as possible while involving little to no actual work. Mom has found him a part-time job doing entry-level case management at QCP to help him cover his rent, and they're happy enough with Mark's work to promise him a full-time position by the end of the year. However, Mark doesn't see the low-paying, unglamorous world of social work as a viable career path. He wants money, power, and success. Mark wants more than anything to one-up our father, to be able to afford a better house and car than the man he views as the root of all his problems. Mark wants

these things, but doesn't really understand what it takes to get them—
or at least, how to get them honestly.

Desperate and naive, Mark starts responding to want ads in the
newspaper that say things like "INSIDE SALES: $100K+ YOUR
FIRST YEAR!" and "ARE YOU READY TO BE A MILLIONAIRE?"

He tries a few of these questionable job leads, and most of them
don't pan out—some are even boiler-room-type situations that require
he hustle unsuspecting customers for cash with empty promises when
no actual product exists. Mark usually quits those jobs within a day or
two.

After several weeks of trying, Mark finally finds one inside sales job
that looks promising.

Mark is going to sell vacuum cleaners door to door.

Mom is excited about this job. "I think Mark might have found his
calling," she tells me on the phone. I'm living off-campus by then, and I
have a small studio apartment near the university. "You should let him
do his sales pitch for you, Anna. He is really good. He'll get that nasty
carpet of yours all spic-and-span, just you watch. Your Memaw Jones
was so impressed that she might buy one of his vacuum sweepers for
her house."

"All right, but *I'm* not buying anything from him. I'm poor and those
vacuums are really expensive."

"Oh hon, he knows you can't afford one. They're meant mostly for
rich people. Your Memaw's only gonna buy the cheapest one, if she
buys one at all. Just let him do his sales pitch for you. You're into acting
and theater and stuff—maybe you can give Mark some pointers on how
to be, you know, entertaining."

"Fine. Tell him I'll be home all day Saturday if he wants to come
over."

Mark arrives at my building that Saturday at two, lugging a gigantic
chrome upright vacuum up the three flights to my tiny studio apartment, a sort of triangular alcove carved out of the attic in a rundown
Queen Anne clapboard mansion. The living-dining-sleeping room has
hideous deep-shag carpeting that looks like a bad acid trip from Grace-
land on its best days; that day, it looks like dried-up, crumpled baby
puke from all the dirt, dust, and snowmelt salt that I've trampled in. I've
purposely refrained from vacuuming with my beat-up, secondhand
Hoover all week to give Mark something to really work for during his

demonstration. I've even tucked a full bottle of baby powder behind a bookcase, which I plan to sprinkle around to see if Mark's machine can pick it up just when he thinks he's "sold" me on his product. Like any good theater director, I want to make Mark's performance as difficult as possible in order to make him a better performer.

Mark gives his demonstration. I have to admit it's impressive. Mark is organized, he proves knowledgeable and confident in his product no matter how much I pepper him with questions, and he explains the vacuum's many features while vacuuming up every mess I put in front of him with grace and poise. He makes a few messes of his own—confetti, dog hair, even a box full of tacks—that the vacuum makes quick work of with barely a growl. He then detaches the main suction unit and clips it to a hand attachment, runs it over my mattress and loveseat, then shows me the filter full of something he calls "putrefied ash"—dead skin cells and dust-mite poop, he says. "You wanna sleep on a mattress full of dead skin cells and dust-mite poop?"

"No," I say with a mixture of revulsion and awe.

Mark spends another full hour cleaning every square inch of my studio apartment, and he even shampoos my hideous shag carpeting until it reveals its true color as lime green, not baby-vomit green.

"Well, Anna?" Mark asks, pulling out a clipboard loaded with order forms. "How many can I put you down for?"

"Mark, you know I can't afford one of these. I'm just here to critique your sales pitch, and truth be told, you did great."

Mark does a double-take, then balls up his fists. I can actually see him fight to stifle a fit of rage, can see the waves of barely-contained anger undulate up and out across his torso and into his quivering arms. But he does it. He takes a deep breath, smiles, and his near-outburst evaporates without a trace.

Seeing this, I am both surprised and proud. Is it really possible for my brother to function in normal society without erupting into violent, delusion-fueled insanity at any moment? If what I've just witnessed is any example, it certainly seems so.

"I know you can't afford one, Anna." Mark speaks carefully, enunciating the vowels and consonants with the slow precision of someone learning to speak English for the first time. "That was just part of the sales pitch, is all. They taught us to say that. I was just practicing, is all."

"I know you were, Mark. And you did a good job. I wish there was something I could do to afford your vacuum cleaners, but I just can't right now. I'm sure you'll sell a lot of vacuums to other people, though."

"Thanks. But there *is* something you can do for me," he says. "It will really help me out. You see, I need to buy some nice suits. I can't sell vacuum cleaners in anything but suits, and they even stipulate what kind of suit you can wear out on sales calls, your accessories, that kind of stuff. Corporate policy, and all that. But I can only afford to buy part of what I need. Do you think you could lend me some money to help me get the clothes and accessories I need to start working? I'll pay you back out of my first paycheck."

A red flag goes up immediately in my brain. After all the stunts I've seen Mark pull over the years, I know better than to entrust him with money, even a short-term loan—especially considering the budgeting gymnastics I have to do every month to cover rent, utilities, food, and school expenses on the meager earnings I get as a work-study desk clerk on campus. But I still can't deny the marked change in him. This time, it seems that Mark just might have found something he can do well and that he obviously enjoys, something that very well might earn him a good, steady living. As corny as it might seem, I really believe that selling vacuum cleaners door to door just might be the means by which my brother saves himself from himself. He's so vivacious, so full of light and optimism, I can't help but be carried away by it right alongside him.

"All right, Mark, I'll tell you what. Rather than me giving you the cash, why don't you and me go to the store together with a list of the things the company says you have to wear for sales calls. We'll buy them together. I'll keep the receipts, and you can pay me back from your first paycheck. I can't afford to spend more than a hundred bucks, though, and you'll need to pay me back no later than the first of the month so I can afford to make rent. Will that be okay?"

Mark hesitates, then nods. Clearly, he expected me just to fork over the cash, but with his newfound ability to control his temper, he bites the bullet and settles for what I offer.

Mark drives us to a nearby Sears department store in the beat-up, half-rusted-out Honda Civic he bought a year ago with some leftover student loan money. We make a beeline for the men's department, where Mark immediately begins pulling white Oxford shirts off a rack. "I'll need a bunch of these," he says, breathless as a society housewife on a Rodeo Drive shopping binge. "And these too." He grabs six or seven pairs of black wool-poly-blend slacks off another rack, then he makes for the necktie section.

"Mark, I'm *not* buying you all of this," I call after him. "Just pick out one or two outfits, enough to get you started." He ignores me and grabs a handful of plain black silk ties from a rack and adds them to his pile. He pulls two or three black polyester suit jackets off a clearance rack without bothering to check their size, then he waltzes up to the checkout counter, where he drops the whole pile in front of a stunned clerk.

"We'll take all this," he says proudly.

"No, we won't," I contradict, trying hard to keep my voice steady.

The clerk glances from me, to Mark, then back to me. "Are you going to buy this stuff or not?" she asks.

"He's going to try some of it on first," I reply, already more embarrassed than I've ever been with Mark in public. "Aren't you, Mark?"

Mark grabs up the pile of clothes again and skulks off toward the fitting rooms. The fitting-room attendant will only allow him to bring in four items, forcing him to narrow down his selection. Instead of putting the unwanted clothes on the rack provided for the purpose, though, he simply tosses them on the counter in front of the exasperated attendant, an elderly woman wearing thick glasses on a chain. She stares at both of us with contempt through her purple-tinted, concave lenses, sighs, and shakes her head.

After a few minutes behind the fitting room's louvered doors, Mark finally emerges with two sets of shirts and pants, one jacket, and two ties that satisfy him. I inspect the price tags and after totaling them in my head find that I can only afford to pay for one jacket, one pair of slacks, two shirts and one tie and still stay under my hundred-dollar budget. "I'm only paying for these," I tell him, and set the approved items on the counter in front of the bewildered checkout clerk. "If you want more than this, pay for it yourself."

The clerk totals up the bill. It turns out the suit jacket has an additional at-register markdown, shaving about $10.00 off the total. It all adds up to $89.99.

"You still owe me ten bucks," Mark hisses as I pay the clerk.

I snatch up the shopping bags in a fury. I already regret what I've done for Mark, who's fast slipping back into the prototypical entitlement-and-manipulation behavior I recognize from our childhood. "I don't *owe* you anything," I snap. "This is a loan, remember?"

"Yeah, yeah, I know," he mumbles. He stops short, seems to collect himself. "Sorry. I really do appreciate what you're doing, sis. Seriously." Then he envelops me in a huge bear hug.

Mark hasn't hugged me since we were little kids. My hardened heart melts immediately—as I'm sure Mark wants it to.

"There's just one more little, eensy-weensy thing that I need for my job," Mark whispers as he releases me from the bear hug. "We need to go to the bedding department for it."

"The *bedding* department? Excuse me?"

Mark doesn't answer. He's already taken off for the escalator.

By the time I catch up with him, Mark is pulling oddly packaged, suspender-like contraptions off a rack. "What the hell are those?" I ask. "And why do you need them to sell vacuum cleaners?"

"They're linen clips," Mark explains as he loads his arms with Sears' entire stock of the springy-looking things. "They're designed for keeping sheets in place on mattresses. But they're great for clipping pants cuffs closed too. I need to clip my pants cuffs closed on sales calls so my legs don't get sucked into the vacuum."

I blink. Clipping pants cuffs with linen appliances to prevent a grown man's body from being sucked into a vacuum cleaner sounds a lot more like something my brother's schizophrenic brain would conjure up than any corporate policy. I glance at one of the clips' price tags; to my shock, I see that they cost $12.00 *each*. "I really don't think you need these to sell vacuum cleaners," I snap. I take the pile of elastic springs out of Mark's arms and start putting them back on the rack.

He reacts immediately. "I *have* to have at least two of these," he shrieks, and grabs my arm to stop me from putting them back on the rack. "*Have* to. So I don't get sucked in. I don't want to get sucked in, Anna. *Please* don't let me get sucked in."

Mark stares me down with a look of such deep, primal horror that I cave.

Without another word, I snatch two linen clips off the rack, take them to the counter, and pay for them. I feel dirty inside doing it, but the power of Mark's persuasion is just too great to resist. Buying those two stupid elastic gadgets puts me way over budget, and I'm not even sure that Mark won't try to fleece me for more.

In less than twenty minutes, I've blown almost two weeks' part-time student pay on clothes and pants cuffs for my brother to wear for a shady door-to-door sales job he has yet to receive a single paycheck for. And all at once, the realization that I'll probably never see a cent of that money again leaves me icy-cold.

How could I be so stupid? How could I have let this happen, knowing all that I do about Mark and his wild schemes? The answer is simple. Mark has a disease, and sometimes that disease—schizophrenia—is a lot more powerful than any one person, however smart or street-savvy. It's like a steamroller, flattening everyone and everything in its path, including its victims, who become mere vessels for its outward destruction. The only thing that keeps me from slapping him across the face right in the middle of the Sears bedding department is the knowledge that the person grifting me for two weeks' pay isn't really my brother—it's the overload of serotonin and dopamine in his brain that does it, not him. And sometimes I'm as powerless to fight the force of that chemical imbalance as he is. He can't even be relied upon to take his prescribed antipsychotic meds with any regularity, so how can I possibly expect him to behave like a normal, responsible person? So I cave. The pity I feel for him makes it impossible not to.

It's this very same knowledge that even today makes me reluctant to judge any person (or family) for enabling a family member's mental illness. Often, it's impossible not to—the illness doesn't just afflict the afflicted, it afflicts everyone the afflicted knows and loves too.

Mark only ends up selling vacuum cleaners for about a week. Apparently selling is hard work, and hard work has never been something Mark has been capable of. The idea of schlepping heavy chrome vacuums into little old ladies' homes and grifting them with usurious installment plans twelve hours a day doesn't sit well with Mark's body or mind, and he quits within a few days. And since he doesn't complete at least two full weeks of door-to-door selling, the terms of his sales contract require he forfeit all pay.

It's the outcome I should have expected. Still, it stings. Especially when the end of the month comes and I'm a hundred-odd bucks short of making my bills.

In desperation, I call my father and explain what happened.

There's a long pause on the phone as my father ponders Mark's latest gaffe. Dad clears his throat several times, something I know he does whenever he's angry.

Finally, he speaks. "So, how much are you out?"

"About a hundred twenty-five," I reply.

"Well, it could have been a lot worse, I suppose. Do you have enough to tide you over this month?"

"Not really. I put in for some more hours over at the dorm but I won't get paid for them for another two weeks. Rent's due, plus electric, and I need to buy a few more books for my Indian History class—"

Dad clears his throat again. "I'll wire you a hundred-fifty tomorrow. The full amount Mark took from you, plus an extra twenty-five for your trouble. Don't worry about paying me back—I'll go after Mark for it myself. Just don't give your brother any more money, or buy him anything, ever. No matter what he tells you. Got it?"

"Yeah, got it."

Dad hangs up. I only wonder why he doesn't follow his own advice when it comes to Mark. But I know better than to say that aloud.

This experience is my first glimpse into Mark's ongoing fascination with multilevel marketing, get-rich-quick schemes, pyramid scams, and all things shady and slick. But it won't be the last.

Albert Einstein once said that the definition of insanity is doing the same thing over and over again and expecting different results. That aphorism fits Mark's fascination with pyramid scams perfectly. Year in, year out, Mark involves himself in scams and schemes that are different in name only, each time expecting that the latest commission-driven, upfront-initial-investment sales system he's discovered will lead to the riches and Easy Street life he so craves. And year in, year out, all Mark gets out of those schemes are lost initial investments, dashed hopes, and alienated friends and family.

There are insurance schemes, and a couple more boiler-room outfits that hire Mark to "sell" nonexistent gutters and aluminum siding over the phone. None of them ever pay Mark a dime, even when he puts in hours and hours of cold-calling and product selling.

And then there's a dodgy investment-products sales scheme run by a major banking institution. Even if it looks legit on the surface, it's basically a pyramid scheme that relies heavily on cult-like indoctrination methods for its salespeople and sales directors. New recruits are first made to recruit friends and family to become the scheme's clients. Those friends and family are then encouraged (if not outright bullied) into shifting their entire savings and investment portfolios over to complete control and management by the company, whose investment products are targeted at lower- and middle-class people without substantial financial knowledge and are structured in a way that transfers most of their investment returns into the pockets of salespeople.

Mark gets involved with this latest scheme shortly after he returns from his brief stint in the Army. I've spent the past year working as a research reports editor at a major Chicago financial institution, where I have to pass the Series 7 and 63 exams required for stockbroker licensing, so I'm hardly a neophyte when it came to asset management—at least in theory. That doesn't deter Mark from hard-selling me when I come home to Evansville for Christmas 1999, however.

Mark grabs me by the arm at Memaw Jones's buffet table and pulls me aside. "Anna, you really need to roll your IRA and 401k into my new company's products."

I yank free of his grip. "I don't really need to do anything with my money right now, Mark. Least of all give *you* control of it." Given his track record, I might as well just hand my life savings over to the Mafia and hope for the best.

Mark sighs, balls his fists, folds his arms across his chest in his now-trademark gesture of impudent offense. "I'll have you know that *Dad* came to an investment-product presentation with me, and he was *very* impressed. *He* says it's great I'm getting into financial services."

I sigh. With two ex-wives, five kids by three different women, and spendthrift habits himself, our father isn't exactly the picture of sound financial advice. And Dad has always had a bit of a blind spot where Mark is concerned, anyway—even his current wife thinks so. But I don't remark on this. Instead I just narrow my eyes at him and say, "I think you should stop this get-rich-quick crap and get a real job. I've read up a bit on this company you're with, you know. It's basically a pyramid scheme. Haven't you learned your lesson on those yet?"

"It is *not* a pyramid scheme. I'll show you everything—"

"Tell me something, Mark. Mom says you've been doing this investment-sales stuff for what, six months now? Six months, and you haven't actually been paid anything yet. Isn't that right?"

"Well, *technically* that's true, but I have to make my manager's quotas first—"

I laugh. "So basically, whatever commissions you earn go to your manager, and you get nothing."

"Well, for *now* I'm just an unpaid apprentice, so I'm doing the sales for training purposes only, but later *on* I'll be making a lot—"

"You know Mark, I'm pretty sure that's called slave labor, and it's illegal. Why don't you buy a clue already and just get a real job like everybody else?" I turn on my heel and walk away.

It's easy to see now why Mark would fall for these schemes over and over, even though it was hard to understand and accept at the time. What's harder is understanding why my family members fall for them over and over again too, and provide Mark with free rent, food, and utilities until the latest scam "gets him on his feet" (as my mother does time and time again), sinking money into his schemes until he "just gets a break" (as my father, grandparents, and even I do more than once). Tough love is hard, I guess, but I'm not sure the alternative does anyone any favors.

There has been a fair bit of research into the psychology of people who repeatedly fall victim to cults, scams, and pyramid schemes. Sociologists and psychologists who have studied religious cults, multilevel-marketing scams, and the like have consistently found that these organizations not only tend to attract persons with schizophrenia or schizotypal personality disorder as their members (or "victims," as the case may be), but the *leaders* of these organizations are quite often schizophrenic personalities too.[8] Like breeds like, in other words.

As susceptible as Mark and his schizophrenic brain are to get-rich-quick schemes, Mark also craves something else: stability. And not only stability, but the complete surrender of all adult responsibility to a governing body that will feed him, clothe him, meet his every need, and even make every life and career decision for him. I suppose that's why about a year after Mark drops out of college, he decides to join the Army.

There's only one problem. Mark's status as a diagnosed paranoid schizophrenic makes him ineligible to enlist.

It's 1998. Mark moved out of his on-campus apartment and into my mother's basement about six months ago. He has the part-time social work job at QCB, which he couples with the occasional non-paying pyramid-scheme job. But despite that modest income, he isn't contributing anything financially to my mother's household, while continuing to consume massive amounts of food, soda pop, and electricity (he keeps his personal computer and stereo equipment running constantly), and running up enormous long-distance telephone bills (he spends long hours on the phone calling his old college friends, who by then have largely graduated, gotten real jobs, and scattered across the country).

"I don't know what I'm going to do about your brother," Mom laments on the phone to me in Chicago. "The Army won't take him because of—well, you know, because of the *learning disabilities* he has."

"Kick him out," I say. "Practice tough love."

"I *can't* kick him out, Anna! He'll end up on the street if I do that."

"The street might do him some good," I snap. I've just finished my master's degree and I'm working my first real job as a financial editor at a big-city brokerage firm. I am young, cocky, and arrogant with my newfound success—I have yet to taste the cold reality of the streets, though I'll face the very real possibility of living on them myself in a few years.

"Anna, you're so cold-hearted. I swear, I don't know what to do with either one of you kids," Mom sneers, and hangs up.

Things come to a head at Mom's house not long after that. Mom tells Mark he needs to move out or join the Army by the end of the year, or else she'll throw him out. Mom even helps pull some strings at QCB to help Mark find a psychiatrist who might be willing to reevaluate him in a way that will be satisfactory to military recruiters. "It's the only thing I know to do to help get Mark out of my basement," she says, though she concedes getting any qualified psychiatrist to declare my brother fit for military duty—or even take him off his meds—is probably impossible.

Ha. Apparently not.

Mark hooks up with a psychiatrist who, for a fee, gives him a certified clean bill of mental health and immediately takes him off his prescribed antipsychotic meds. Mark takes that certificate to his Army recruiter, who enlists him the same day. Even after all of these years, I still don't know how this could possibly have happened given the

Army's strict rules about recruiting anyone with even a hint of mental health problems, but it did.

The U.S. Army gives my unmedicated, severe paranoid schizophrenic brother a uniform and a gun. Not only that, they make him a medic. An ambulance driver, as a matter of fact. My brother spends a little over a year in the Army (albeit two-thirds of it he's off-duty in Army hospitals for "ailments" that range from *E. coli* food poisoning at Fort Sam Houston to a supposed back injury and asthma in South Korea to "service fatigue" once he gets back stateside, and he eventually gets a medical discharge that entitles him to veterans disability pay of $800 a month for life).

The relatively little time Mark isn't in military hospitals or scheming for ways to get a medical discharge, my brother the unmedicated paranoid schizophrenic drives an armored ambulance in the demilitarized zone between North and South Korea—arguably the most dangerous two-mile strip of land in the world.

God help the United States of America.

Oh, and it gets better.

When Mark joins the U.S. Army, he's a quasi-liberal committed atheist. When he comes out, he's an ultraconservative Maronite Roman Catholic. I don't know exactly when or how his conversion (or reconversion, since we were raised Catholic until Mom and Dad divorced) occurred, but the almost medieval Catholicism Mark spouts from the minute his feet are back on U.S. soil proves that hell hath no fury like a schizophrenic religious convert.

Mark proclaims all kinds of outrageous religious edicts, as if he is personally channeling a fascist version of the Holy See: all non-Catholic religions should be banned; possession of birth control should be made a felony; women who have abortions should be executed; all non-Orthodox Jews should be converted by force to Catholicism (but Orthodox Jews can continue practicing "pure" Judaism as a historical referent for "true" Christians). He says a global war should be fought to force all of this to happen, a war that he will personally orchestrate and oversee, no less.

Mark's VA physicians put him back on antipsychotics around this time.

Within days of returning home to Indiana, Mark announces he's joining the priesthood.

"I'll believe it when I see it," I scoff at Mom when she calls me with the news.

"I really think he's serious about this," Mom replies. "He's hooked up with a program at one of the parishes here in town aimed at recruiting new priests. They're doing all sorts of things to help Mark."

"What kinds of things?" As if I can't guess.

"Oh, they're giving him money," Mom says. "An allowance. And housing assistance I think, and some other nice things while he takes classes with the priests there at the church that will help prepare him for seminary. Oh, and they want him to finish college too. Some of his Army money will pay for it, but the church will help him out some too. I don't know all the details, but—"

"The Catholic Church must be pretty hard up for priests if they want Mark," I say, and hang up.

Now nearly thirty, Mark returns to college for the umpteenth time. He gets a car and a studio apartment just up the road from my grandparents. His degree will be in psychology with a minor in theology, and if all goes well he'll finish it within two years and then go on to seminary.

Whatever time he isn't spending on campus or studying, Mark spends either at church, socializing with priests and parishioners, or at a local Irish pub, where he drinks gallons of Guinness and listens to Celtic music. He doesn't work a part-time job; as far as I can tell, Mark lives on a combination of his military disability payments and largesse from the Catholic Church designed to tempt him into the priesthood.

I'm suspicious of Mark's motives from the start.

Against my mother's wishes, I take Mark aside when I come home for Christmas that year. "Why do you *really* want to be a priest, Mark?" I demand. "I don't believe for a minute this is about God. You and God have just never been very tight."

I expect Mark to express outrage at my question. But he doesn't. He mulls it over for a moment, then he grins. "I want to be a priest because I want to be rich. And being a priest is a great way to get rich. A lot of priests are millionaires."

I'm floored. I know Mark is interested in the priesthood mostly for financial reasons, but I'm stunned he thinks he can actually become a *millionaire* as a Catholic priest. It's clear his delusions are getting the better of him.

"Priests take a vow of poverty, Mark. You know that, right?"

"Oh, that's just a formality," he says. "Priests get very generous compensation packages, investment portfolios too. Plus, you have basically no living expenses, since the Church pays for those. All the money you make is yours to keep. I'll be a millionaire, and retire early. It'll be great."

"Fine, whatever. What exactly are you basing the priest-millionaire thing on?"

"Oh, I've figured that out for myself. Too bad you're a female, or you could be a priest-millionaire too."

"Fuck you, Mark," I seethe, and dig into the macaroni salad.

Mark's future as a Catholic priest seems assured until about eighteen months later, when he starts dating a much younger computer-engineering coed named Stephanie O'Reilly. Stephanie is an academically brilliant but socially naive young woman from an ultraconservative, ultra-devout Catholic family. Even though she has two more years to go for her engineering degree, she already has a high-paying job at a major defense contractor's jet-engine division waiting for her upon graduation. Stephanie lives at home with her parents (who still impose very strict rules on her despite her adult age), is still a virgin, and has never dated anyone before my brother, who is eleven years her senior. When it becomes clear to Stephanie's parents that Mark is seriously interested in their daughter, they forbid her to see him, and they even go to extreme measures (like locking her inside her bedroom on weekends) to prevent them from seeing each other.

At one level I can understand why the O'Reillys don't want their only daughter to date a paranoid-schizophrenic, unemployed student eleven years her senior who also has no means of sustainable income beyond the handouts he gets from the government and the Catholic church. I also suppose as devout Catholics, they don't want Stephanie to ruin Mark's chances for becoming a priest, either.

After a few more months, however, Mark switches allegiances. He decides he doesn't want to become a priest anymore; he wants to marry Stephanie instead. He and Stephanie get engaged, and Stephanie even announces her intention to support Mark financially when she graduates—he plans to be the full-time "homemaker" in their marriage since he (supposedly) has multiple physical disabilities that prevent him from working.

Stephanie's parents promptly disown her. Her mother starts incessantly calling the priest who plans to marry them, threatening him with bodily harm if he doesn't put a stop to the wedding. Stephanie's mother even threatens to throw herself on the altar in the middle of the ceremony. I wonder who's craziest—Stephanie's mother for harassing priests and locking up her adult daughter; Mark for being the lazy, manipulative, paranoid-delusional schizophrenic he's always been; or Stephanie for marrying him.

Then I figure, being a certified nutjob myself, I'm in no position to judge anyone's sanity. I agree to be a bridesmaid, buy my brother and future sister-in-law a wedding gift, and shut up.

Mark and Stephanie marry. The years pass, and they eventually have a child, which worries most of us in the family because we all know Mark isn't exactly good parent material. He's never held down a job, he often sleeps well past noon, and when he isn't sleeping or playing computer games well into the night, he either drives around town aimlessly or drinks with friends in bars. He's also heavily medicated on antipsychotics that make him sluggish and overweight, and he's fallen into some of the drug-seeking patterns our mother once did. When Stephanie is pregnant, George and I drop by to visit them at their new house when we happen to be in town, and we find Mark doped out of his mind—slurring his words, staggering, and at one point falling down on the floor. At first we think he's drunk, but we later find out he fell and bruised his elbow on a patch of ice then went to the emergency room where he managed to extract an oxycodone prescription from the ER physician. He shouldn't be taking heavy meds like that with his antipsychotics, which makes me suspect he didn't tell the doctor he was on them. George and I become uncomfortable at my brother's drug-addled state and soon leave.

Stephanie seems to understand that Mark isn't a reliable parent. When their newborn daughter is only six weeks old, she places the baby in full-time daycare despite the fact that Mark is unemployed and could therefore theoretically serve as stay-at-home dad. Stephanie simply doesn't trust him to be his own child's caregiver, and I can't say that I blame her. After all, the one time my brother held my own infant son at a family reunion (against my wishes; I was in the other room at the time, and I was livid afterward, to say the least) he almost dropped my two-month-old baby on his head.

Mark's VA psychiatrists keep him pumped full of drugs but don't seem able to help him secure employment or otherwise manage his life. Stephanie frequently pleads with Mark to secure some kind of job, and she even threatens to leave him multiple times, but he never holds down any kind of employment while continuing to spend his wife's hard-earned money on travel, electronic gadgets, and partying with friends. Stephanie never makes good on her many ultimatums though, and they somehow manage to stumble on, albeit massively in debt. Stephanie even takes on a second job teaching math courses at a local community college to help make ends meet.

There comes a point, though, where Stephanie does seem on the verge of leaving Mark. The only thing that saves their marriage at the time is Mark's promise to complete a paralegal certificate program, which Stephanie pays for, on the condition he find work as a paralegal once he's finished. I'm skeptical, of course, but the rest of the family is convinced that this might be what finally pushes Mark into the work force.

The paralegal certificate program lasts about three months. Predictably, Mark finishes it, passes the certificate exam, and then doesn't get a job. Some months go by, and then Stephanie demands that Mark find some kind of paying work or she'll throw him out of the house. She even helps him find something: an attorney her family is acquainted with who helps veterans obtain VA disability benefits needs a paralegal. And since Mark has successfully (if somewhat questionably) obtained VA disability benefits himself, he's the perfect candidate for the job.

Since I never speak to Mark unless I absolutely have to, I hear all of this third-hand from Mom. She's cautiously optimistic, but she's still taking a wait-and-see attitude. But when Mom calls me a month later with a report on how Mark is doing with the paralegal job, a big red flag goes up. Of course.

"Anna, can you answer a question for me?" Mom says on one of our weekly calls.

"Sure."

"Have you ever worked for a lawyer?" Mom pronounces it "LAW-yer," one of the many ways her now mostly hidden Southern Appalachian accent pops up at random.

"Yes, I have. I have done a lot of freelance and contract work for attorneys over the years," I say. "Legal writing and research, that sort of thing. And when I worked as a health policy analyst, most of my colleagues were attorneys. Why do you ask?"

"Well, something about this job Mark is doing for the lawyer seems strange, is all."

I heave a sigh. "How do you mean?"

"Well, I asked how Mark was doing with his new job. Money-wise, and everything. And he told me he hasn't been paid anything yet."

I blink. "Well, he's been there less than a month. Maybe they just screwed up the payroll or something." Though I have a sneaking suspicion that's not the reason at all.

"No, Anna, that's not it. Mark says that he only gets paid when he wins a case. He says it's something called—I don't know—continual, continuation, something—"

"Contingency?"

"Yes, that's it. What does that mean?"

The wheels turn in my head. I am having real trouble grasping how somebody who isn't a lawyer somehow ends up working on a contingency basis. I'm guessing that's probably quasi-legal at best. "Mom, contingency means that a lawyer takes on a case without pay unless a paying settlement is reached, then the lawyer splits the winnings with the client on the back end," I explain. "But Mark isn't an attorney, so he shouldn't be able to do that. Paralegals are administrative staff, and attorneys generally have to pay them either a salary or by the hour no matter what."

"Well, Mark says he's working on contingency."

I cough. "I think that's called practicing law without a license, Mom. He could get into very big trouble for that. So could the lawyer who's supposedly employing him."

"But Stephanie *knows* this lawyer! He's a friend of hers."

"So Stephanie's friends with a crook."

"But Anna, Stephanie knows this person, she helped Mark get this job, it can't be like, *wrong*, can it?" I can tell that Mom is trying really hard to believe that things are different with Mark this time around, even when they quite obviously aren't.

"Mom, listen to me very carefully. I don't know what kind of lawyer Stephanie's friend is, but he's taking advantage of Mark. Paralegals are staff. They are supposed to be paid either an hourly wage or a salary. They aren't lawyers and they can't act like them. Mark is just being used as free labor."

"Mark says he has the potential to make a lot more money working on contingency. He's doing all the legwork and research for the attorney, and even meeting with clients. He's—"

"He has the potential to end up in jail too. I'm pretty sure what he's doing is illegal. Or at the very least, highly unethical." I shake my head and sigh again. "Why does Mark always get sucked into this sort of thing? Why doesn't he just get a real job like everybody else?"

"Anna, he says this *is* a real job. By the way, I wanted to let you know that Mark is going to call you later today. He wants some advice on where to buy some kind of legal books or something."

"Fine, whatever. But I can't guarantee I'll answer the phone." I absolutely hate talking to Mark, which is why I try to limit it only to about once or twice a year, at Christmas and on his birthday. I brace myself for the call, expecting I'll get some kind of sales pitch or be hit up for cash.

The call comes about an hour later, as expected. It's the first time I've spoken to Mark in about six months. "Hi sis, how're ya doin'?" he says in his singsong antipsychotic-laden voice. I notice that his Southern Indiana accent sounds a lot thicker than it used to. Probably another side effect of all the meds he takes. "Got a question for ya."

"Go ahead."

"Anna, you know a lot about medical terminology and healthcare policy and such, right?"

"Well, yes I do. I work as a healthcare journalist, and I used to do a lot of policy work for organized medicine—the AMA and such."

"Do you use like, books and stuff to help you find out things about law and policy?"

"To a certain extent, yes." I'm losing patience with the conversation already. I'm tempted just to hang up and then blame a bad connection, but I don't.

"Well, my boss wants me to do some research for her on a certain medical condition and I don't know where to look. Can you um, help me?"

I have to bite my tongue hard to keep from spewing out a string of profanity. True to form, my brother has called me only because he wants something. And what he wants could easily take him months to find—you don't exactly become a competent medical policy expert in one afternoon, and I already know he lacks the necessary focus and discipline to do what's required. But rather than berate him, I decide just to give him a gentle nudge in the right direction. "Well, you could go to your local bookstore and look in the health and medicine section," I suggest. "You could buy the *AMA Stylebook*, which covers how to do citations and how to write up medical research reports, and some other general reference titles. For more substantial information, like the latest medical journals and such, you're going to have to visit a good medical library. You can probably get a public access card to your college's library for free, since you're an alum. Or drive to Indianapolis and go to the main public library downtown."

There's a pause on the line. "That's it?" Obviously this wasn't the answer Mark was expecting.

"What do you mean, *that's it*? I'm not going to do your job for you, if that's what you're implying."

Mark clears his throat several times, as if he's trying hard to stifle a smartaleck reply. Finally, he speaks. "Well, Anna, that's helpful. I'll look into it." He hangs up.

About two weeks later, I get another call from Mark. Or rather, a voicemail message. Several of them, actually—each one more frantic than the last.

All the messages are the same: "Anna, it's your brother. Please call me." Only the tone becomes different after the third or fourth one. He sounds upset and scared.

I call him back on his cell, half-dreading that he'll be bearing bad news about our mother or grandparents. But that's not it at all.

He answers the phone on the first ring and starts talking right away; he recognizes my number on the caller ID so I don't even need to identify myself. "Anna, something's happened," he says. Then he starts rambling, the words falling out of his mouth at such a breakneck speed I can't make heads or tails of any of it.

"Mark, slow down. I can't understand a word you're saying."

He pauses, takes a breath. "I just found out something," he says. "I just got a look at my VA file. It says I have some [medical gobbledygook term I've never heard before that likely doesn't exist] neuropathy. Nobody told me this. My psychiatrist didn't tell me. My boss didn't tell me, and he has my file. He's hiding my file from me now. I think I got it in Korea from breathing VX gas. I—"

He rambles on, making no sense. Something about nerve gas, and poison, and his shady attorney "boss" (who has yet to pay him anything) hiding information from him. Another psychotic episode, I'm sure.

I listen to his rambling nonsense, mutter a few meaningless words of encouragement, and hang up. There's not much else I can do.

Predictably, a week or so later Mom reports that Mark is no longer working for the attorney Stephanie hooked him up with. I don't think he ever got paid a dime for any of the work he did either. Stephanie feels responsible for the whole debacle, so she once again backs out of her ultimatum to kick Mark out of the house.

Meanwhile, Mark makes his family's already-serious debt situation even worse by sinking their money into yet more foolhardy get-rich-quick schemes. They buy a rental property they can't afford to maintain, and when that goes bust, Mark spends several thousand dollars of his wife's money to train for his insurance sales license. He spends three months in a training course, then he takes the licensing exam once and fails. He never tries to pass it again, let alone sell any insurance, though he does spend a couple of mania-fueled days passing out water bottles at local summer festivals to help promote a local insurance agent—again, for no pay.

After all these ventures fail, Mark spends a couple of years enrolled in endless "computer classes" at the local VA.

Mom and I discuss Mark's latest "career move" by phone one afternoon when I'm pregnant with my second child. "Mark can't drive me to the doctor today, Anna, because he's busy with all these computer classes. What should I do?"

"Can you take a cab? If you're short on money, I'll wire you some."

"I guess I can take a cab today," Mom sighs. "But Mark is booked in all these computer classes for months at a time, and I can't take a cab every single time. Can't you come down here and drive me?"

Now it's my turn to sigh. "Mom, you know that I can't leave my job and family in Chicago just to drive you to doctor appointments. Mark lives close to you, he doesn't have a job, he has nothing better to do than to drive you places. Why can't he do it?"

"Well, he says these classes he's taking at the VA are really important for him to be able to get a job."

"Mom, Mark has been *taking classes* for twenty years. He already has a college degree he's never used. He's never worked a day in his life. What makes you think he'll get a job now?"

"Well, he insists that this time it'll be different."

"Yeah, likely story."

More than a year passes, and Mark is still taking the same introductory-level computer classes at the VA, "studying" how to use the same word-processing programs he's already used for the past fifteen years. He never seeks employment because of course that was never his motivation in the first place. The VA career classes he can take for free are just an excuse for him to get out of his house.

Some months pass. I visit my mom and grandparents in Indiana. Memaw and Papaw Jones don't mince words when it comes to my brother. "Mark is the laziest thing I ever did see," Papaw says in his thick mountain accent. "Mark told me when he was a teenager that he'd never do manual labor, and boy, he kept that promise, all right." Memaw just sighs and nods her head in agreement.

While I'm visiting relatives in Indiana, I see Mark very briefly at a historical reenactment festival event that Dad and several other family members are attending. Mark doesn't speak to me, or to anyone else for that matter. He just sits in his chair motionless, his eyes glazed over, a blank expression on his face as he stares into space. Mom tells me later that he recently got a job serving subpoenas. "He gets paid for each subpoena he serves," she explains.

I have trouble understanding this, as usual. "I thought only deputy sheriffs serve subpoenas in Indiana," I say. "Mark's not a deputy sheriff."

Mom just sighs. "I don't know Anna, I don't ask him too many questions about it." And she leaves it at that.

But only a week or so later, when I'm back in Chicago, Dad comes to visit on Father's Day, and he has a very different story to tell. According to Dad, not only has Mark and Stephanie's financial outlook brightened enough for them to be able to afford to accompany Dad and his wife on a week-long vacation at a large historical reenactment jamboree in central Pennsylvania the following month, Mark also allegedly has not just one, but *two* jobs.

"He's still serving subpoenas," Dad confirms, not commenting on the fact that the job is pretty weird for a heavily medicated paranoid schizophrenic to have in the first place. According to Dad, Mark also just joined the staff of an Indiana congressman, working out of his Indianapolis office.

I do a double take. *"What?* Are you *sure?"*

"Yep."

*Are you fucking kidding me?*

I don't say this aloud. I blink several times, trying to regain composure. I cannot get my mind around this at all. "A congressman hired *Mark?* To *work* for him? Are you *sure?"*

"That's what he says."

I wonder then why on earth Dad would believe a tall tale like that given my brother's checkered past, but I know that Dad has always had a blind spot where Mark, his eldest son, is concerned. Still, my husband and I exchange bewildered looks. This makes no sense whatsoever. I think my brother Mark is about as likely to get hired by a congressman as he is to be named the next king of England.

I shrug off this news and retreat to the kitchen in search of some fresh iced tea. But Dad's wife Tracy follows me and takes me aside in the pantry. "I just found out Mark is going on this vacation with us on the way over here," she whispers, seething. "Your Dad has known for weeks and just got around to telling me. And do you know why Mark and Stephanie and the baby can suddenly afford it? The registration fee for the jamboree alone is almost five hundred dollars for the three of them, to say nothing of all the other expenses."

I admit that I really have no idea.

"One of your dad's business associates fronted Mark the money," his wife explains. "On your dad's recommendation, no less. Not to mention sold them some camping equipment on an IOU. I told your dad not to go down that road, but of course he won't listen to me. He never does when it comes to Mark."

I pat my stepmother lightly on the shoulder, not knowing what to say. Something tells me that in a month or two, that so-called business associate is going to be out a significant chunk of money, not to mention pretty upset with Dad.

But I have to find out more about Mark's supposed new job working for a member of Congress. Either Dad has fallen hook, line, and sinker for Mark's latest line of bullshit or the whole world as we know it has just come crashing down.

The reporter in me wants to just call the congressman's offices directly and ask if they employ my brother (I have plenty of experience dealing with congressional staffers in my work as a policy analyst and journalist, after all), but since this is a family issue I decide on a more discreet approach. So I call my mom instead.

"Mom, I need you to find out something for me," I tell her when I call her the next day.

"What?"

"Does Mark really work for a congressman?" I give her the politician's name and she recognizes it immediately from hearing it dozens of times on the evening news.

"Wow! Mark works for him?"

"That's what Dad told me yesterday."

"Really? Well that's great!" So this is news to Mom too.

"Mom, I need for you to find out if it's really true. Because I have a sneaking suspicion that it's not."

"Why would your dad lie about something like that?" Mom asks. "I mean, I can think of plenty of *other* things your dad would lie about, but—"

"Mom, I think maybe it was Mark who lied to Dad. Just look into it for me, okay? Mark talks to you more than anyone else. And report back to me right away. Otherwise I'm just going to call the congressman's office myself."

"All right hon. Just do me a favor and don't call anybody until after I talk to your brother first. I don't want you to embarrass yourself."

I cast my eyes skyward. I am well past embarrassment where my brother is concerned. "I promise I won't, Mom. But I want you to look into that whole subpoena-serving thing he's supposedly doing too. That seems pretty fishy in and of itself, given Mark's background."

"All right, I'm having lunch with Mark tomorrow. I'll see what I can find out."

Sure enough, Mom calls me back two days later with a full report. "Well, I talked to Mark about the congressman thing," she says. "Turns out all he did was *apply* for a job at the guy's office, but it didn't pan out. Something to do with all the work he does for the veterans."

"*What* work Mark does for veterans? I thought he quit doing that when he quit working for that crackpot lawyer who never paid him."

"No, he still does it. It's all on the computer. I don't know exactly what it is, but it's all on the computer."

"Uh huh. Are you sure he isn't just messing around playing World of Warcraft or something? Because you know how he likes to do that."

"I don't know, Anna. I don't ask Mark too many questions these days. Whenever I do it just gets me too depressed."

Gee, I wonder why.

"I did talk to him about the subpoena thing too. He's doing that for sure. And he does get paid for that. He gets paid for every subpoena he delivers successfully."

This still isn't adding up for me. "I always thought you had to be a deputy sheriff to serve subpoenas in Indiana," I say. "You know, with a gun, and law enforcement training and everything. Since most people who are getting subpoenaed don't want to be and tend to get pretty pissed off about it."

"Well, Anna, that used to be true, but I called around and found out that because of budget cuts, in our county they can't afford to pay sheriffs to do it anymore, so they're hiring people like Mark to do it. He's done one of them successfully so far. I asked him if it scared him to do it and he said no."

"*One*? So he has served exactly *one* subpoena successfully. In more than two months of supposedly doing this?"

"Far as I know, yeah."

The very notion of my grossly obese, heavily medicated brother Mark, who moves with all the agility and speed of a tree sloth, chasing people down to serve them with legal papers is nonsensical. Boy, the Indiana taxpayers are sure getting their money's worth when it comes to him. Then again, they're privatizing prisons and paying the private prison guards minimum wage in Indiana these days too, so what else can I possibly expect?

"You know Mom, people get shot and assaulted for serving subpoenas sometimes. Which is exactly why they used to have cops do it."

"I know, Anna. Like I said, I try not to think about what Mark does these days too much. It's just too much for my nerves. Last time I got so worked up about Mark I almost ended up in the hospital."

I thank Mom for the legwork and hang up.

Sometimes my family resembles an Alexander Payne movie.

I'm up late one night watching a reality-TV program on cable that takes place in the psych ward of New York City's Bellevue Hospital. I find it while flipping channels, and I'm immediately transfixed.

The show's narrator explains that it takes place in the lockdown unit at Bellevue, where many of the patients are lifelong schizophrenics. The patients share their current set of delusions with the camera. I watch a middle-aged man tell the camera that he is God and the only reason he's been readmitted to Bellevue for the umpteenth time is because the rest of the world does not recognize him as the Supreme, All-Powerful, and All-Knowing God. Another middle-aged man walks up, tells the camera he's been living in Bellevue on and off for seven years and he's met at least eight different Gods in that time, and walks off.

The camera wanders up and down the ward, and there are interviews with patients whose stories and symptoms I recognize instantly. A screaming young man who sits locked in an isolation cell as he raves about the unfairness of the world reminds me of my brother the failing college student who falsely accused a professor of sexually abusing him rather than deal with his own demons. The middle-aged man who thinks he is God is cut of the same cloth as the Mark who claimed the Catholic Church should fight a fascist religious war of his own design. A beautiful young woman who says the FBI is coming to Bellevue to kill her next week could be my teenage brother when he claimed World War III was imminent and UFOs were landing in our backyard.

I recognize these people and their symptoms because I've grown up alongside a brother who's had every single one.

My husband shuffles into the living room, pajamas rumpled from sleep. He looks from the flickering television screen to me, then back to the TV again. "Why are you watching this?"

"I have to," I say. "I know these people. I know them all."

# 7

# WHERE ARE THEY (AND WHERE AM I) NOW?*

Life doesn't stop at the end of a book. I wrote this book in fits and starts over a period of about seven years, with many revisions to reflect the ever-changing state of my family's mental health. Like any family, we've had our ups and downs. My own pattern is mostly ups; since my rock-bottom in 2002, I've done extraordinarily well, both personally and professionally. After working a series of staff writer jobs, I launched my own freelance-writing business in 2007 shortly after the birth of my son, and I remain successfully self-employed. I'm happily married with two great kids, and I'm mentally very stable and healthy. I haven't had a psychotic break or even mild depression since those dark days in 2002, though I did have a brief problem with stress-induced anxiety a few years ago that was directly related to the ongoing mental health problems people in my extended family continue to struggle with and the damaging impact those problems inevitably made on my own life. To deal with it, I saw a psychotherapist for about ten cognitive behavioral therapy sessions to help me brush up on my coping skills, and I came off that brief bump in the road stronger and healthier than ever. Even given all the work I've already done, though, these occasional "tune-ups" are essential to staying well, I've found.

How else do I stay well? It's a combination of things, really. The

---

*Thank you, Google.

main reason I've been able to avoid the repeating patterns of dysfunction that plague my mother and brother is because I've mostly removed myself from their entrenched way of life. I moved far away from the small town where they live—and away from the gossip, the prying eyes, the constant bullying and teasing that are so commonplace in my extended family's culture. Unlike many of my relatives, I don't drink excessively, overeat, smoke, or engage in compulsive shopping or video-game-playing, nor do I associate with people who do. That decision alone means I cannot fraternize with large swaths of my extended family—but that's not such a loss. They don't miss me, and the feeling is mutual.

I exercise regularly and eat a healthy diet—which might sound trite or even self-important, but multiple studies have shown that making healthy physical choices also boosts your mental health and can even directly combat mental illnesses ranging from depression to schizophrenia. [1]

But that's not all I do. Mental health is an ongoing process that requires constant work. Meditation and mindfulness have played a tremendous role in giving me the insight to change the self-destructive behavior patterns I developed growing up, along with giving me the assertiveness required to stand up to anyone who attempts to bully me back into my old patterns—whether it's enabling other peoples' dysfunction, accepting cruel treatment that I do not deserve, or surrendering to simple peer pressure.

I meditate in all sorts of ways—and not just by sitting on a cushion and chanting, though that's one of my favorites. A true Zen life allows you to find meditative benefit in almost any activity, whether it's cleaning the bathroom, taking a walk, or deciding which box of cereal to buy at the grocery store. By living in the present and studying its every glorious detail, past failures and future worries slip away, and the world just *is*. Dwelling in the present moment without judgment or fear is the key to springing the trap of negative emotions that can feed so many destructive behavior patterns, I've found.

If there's one thing that mindfulness has taught me, it's that I am not my parents. I am not my brother, and I am not doomed to a life of misery just because of my DNA. I have the ability to take control of my own behavior, as well as the consequences of that behavior. Furthermore, cognitive behavioral therapy has a strong mindfulness component that meditation only enhances.[2] My therapists over the years have always encouraged me to continue doing meditation while developing my mindfulness skills. Thanks to these skills, I've been able to avoid the need for antianxiety medications and antidepressants—though I also recognize that medication can be the right choice for some people.

Over a period of years, I've also trained myself not to get trapped by negative self-talk that both my mother and brother are masters at. Instead of saying, "I can't do x because . . ." and just giving up, I go out and do x anyway, without worrying about what others might think. Not only that, I pat myself on the back for my professional accomplishments instead of constantly second-guessing myself, as I often did when I worked in the corporate world. That take-charge confidence has served me well in self-employment as well as in my personal life.

I've also learned when and how to lean on others, like my husband and some of my friends, like Jacey and Sharon, who have also had their own struggles with mental illness. I reach out to those friends of mine who understand what these kinds of struggles entail, and we cheer one another on, swap war stories, and keep each other up to date on how we're learning to cope. On the flip side, I've also learned the hard way that there are some people you just can't trust when it comes to your mental health, and it's especially important not to overshare in today's social-media-driven world. There's still a lot of hostility and stigma out there, and anyone with a history of mental illness must accept that reality if they're going to succeed, either personally or professionally.

Most of all, I've grown more humble. I know that I'm not infallible, and I'm also not afraid to ask for help when I need it. And asking for help is the most important—and often, most difficult—step for anyone with mental illness to take.

Here's a summary of how the other major players in this book are doing.

*Mom* recently had another relapse of her mental illness and after a long downward spiral, found herself divorced, penniless, and suicidal. Her now ex-husband Bob had a psychotic break of his own that involved, among other things, him taking up with a convicted felon who, along with Bob, threatened to kill my mother. I was forced to drop everything, drive to Indiana, and remove Mom from Bob's house for her own safety; she then spent several months in a series of psychiatric institutions. Mom was later declared mentally incompetent by a court of law, and I was appointed her permanent legal guardian. The whole saga is another story for another book—likely my next one. She now lives in an Indiana assisted-living facility for elderly people with mental disorders, and as her guardian, I manage her affairs from afar with the help of local relatives.

*Dad* married his third wife, *Tracy*, in 1990, and they are together to this day. However, they lead a polyamorous lifestyle, with an open marriage that is no secret to anyone who knows them well. Dad also currently lives and works in another state from his wife and current set of children, traveling back to see them occasionally on weekends. I don't know if he has an outside girlfriend right now, but he usually does—and it's just something I've grown to accept. He even jokes about it sometimes. Despite all that's happened over the years, Dad and I get along quite well now and see each other frequently, though we never discuss anything even remotely related to mental illness or our family's checkered past. Dad lives in quiet, happy denial where that topic is concerned, and I don't begrudge him that if it's the choice that works for him. Our relationship is very much in the present, and nonjudgmental.

Dad's ex-wife *Martha* still lives in Indiana and runs a successful mail-order company; I have no direct contact with her, and haven't for over twenty years.

*Mark* is still married to *Stephanie*. He recently got a heavy adjustment to his antipsychotic meds that slurs his speech, with extreme weight gain as a side effect. We speak only a few times a year and seldom visit one another. Under the constant care and supervision of VA psychiatrists, Mark remains unemployed, though he has proven to be somewhat helpful when it comes to dealing with Mom's immediate needs—like chauffeuring her back and forth to doctor appointments, which I cannot do from my home in the Chicago suburbs.

*Dieter Franzl* became CEO of a large Austrian mobile telecommunications company. As CEO, he apparently enjoyed doing outrageous publicity stunts to advertise his company's services—including racing Formula One cars emblazoned with the company logo. When the recession hit in 2008, Dieter lost his CEO position when his employer got bought out, and he remained unemployed for a couple of years. He recently became a high-ranking executive with a German telecommunications company. As far as I know, he's still single.

*Todd Naismith* became a high-school history teacher, and he's now launching a political career of sorts. He also finally married his on-again/off-again girlfriend *Marcia* after almost fifteen years of dating. Marcia now works in arts administration. They live in the Northeast, and they even have a baby now.

*Dean* still lives in Chicago and works mostly as a freelance theater actor and Japanese language interpreter. Following our breakup, he spent several years living with his parents. I hear he's married to a professional Hawaiian hula dancer.

I currently live in the Chicago suburbs with my husband George and our two children. My career as a freelance writer and playwright has taken off in the past few years, with my plays receiving productions around the country and internationally. I make a good living as a journalist, and I've sold several novels under a pen name. A good life, all in all.

# EPILOGUE: THE STATE OF FAMILY MENTAL ILLNESS IN AMERICA

**M**ental illness is the single-greatest cause of disability and premature death in the world, according to the World Health Organization (WHO).[1] The *Global Burden of Disease* study copublished by the WHO and the Harvard School of Public Health in 2010 estimates that mental illness in all its forms, including suicide, will account for 15 percent of the overall socioeconomic disease burden in established market economies like the United States by the year 2020—more than the disease burden of all cancers *combined*.

This study also found that major depression ranks second only to ischemic heart disease in terms of overall disease burden to established market economies (*disease burden* is calculated in terms of lost years of healthy, productive life due to either premature death or prolonged disability). Statistically speaking, disability and premature death caused by major depression cost society just as much—if not more—than blindness and paraplegia combined. Schizophrenic psychosis produces economic disability equal to that of quadriplegia.

According to the WHO, major depression is the *single leading cause* of disability worldwide among all persons five years and older. (Major depression can also occur in conjunction with other mental illnesses, including borderline personality disorder.) Mental illness is particularly lethal among people in the prime of life; it is the cause of more than 40 percent of disability impairment and premature deaths among persons aged fifteen to forty-four, and it accounts for more than 90 percent of suicides.[2]

Mental illness makes an even more significant impact on the lives of women worldwide; major depression is the *single leading cause* of disability and premature death of women worldwide, in both established market economies and developing ones, according to the WHO study. Schizophrenia and bipolar disorder also consistently rank among the top ten disease-burden conditions affecting women in established market economies.

Despite this tremendous cost burden, and despite the fact that mental illness costs society far more than all forms of cancer combined, in 2005 the National Institutes of Health (NIH) spent *four times* more U.S. tax dollars on cancer research than on mental illness/mental health research ($4.5 billion versus $1.5 billion, respectively). This funding discrepancy—fully approved and mandated by Congress—is representative of the severe stigma mental illness still holds in our society.

In developing countries, persons with severe mental illnesses like schizophrenia, bipolar disorder, or advanced clinical depression are often isolated from mainstream society without any real treatment, locked in asylums that are little more than prisons, and sometimes even killed. This might seem barbaric to us in the developed world, but the fact is, if we evaluate the quality of our own mental healthcare system based on the disease burden statistics listed above, the United States and other countries with developed market economies are not much better at preventing, treating, and managing mental illness than developing countries that simply warehouse the afflicted in prisons or abandon them to the streets. One can argue that despite all the lauded advances in recognizing and treating mental illness in this country, we do the very same thing here. Indeed, substantial proportions of the long-term homeless and incarcerated in the United States are the chronic mentally ill.

One of the objectives I hoped to fulfill with this book was to show that mental illness is at heart a disease of families. Although the social stigma against mental illness in our society remains profound enough that parents, children, and extended families will deny and suppress family histories and family-based sources of mental illness as much as possible—and will seek out and blame external societal forces (such as poverty, racism, sexism, war, job stress, and bad luck, ad nauseum) whenever and wherever they can—mental illness and mental health both begin at home.

A 2005 study by the National Institute of Mental Health (NIMH) found that more than half of lifetime cases of mental illness begin by age fourteen and that despite the availability of effective treatments, there can be long delays—sometimes even decades—between the first onset of symptoms and the seeking/receipt of effective treatment. The study also found that this frequent delay in treatment also facilitates the development of multiple comorbid mental illnesses, including self-medicating substance abuse. In contrast to many other chronic ill-nesses—e.g., diabetes, heart disease, hypertension—that often develop later in life, mental illness strikes early in life and is primarily a disease of the young, with half of all lifetime cases striking by age fourteen and three-quarters by age twenty-four. This same NIMH study found that mental illness in general is far more common than previously thought. At any given time, 26 percent of the general population displays symp-toms sufficient for diagnosis of one or more mental disorders within the past twelve months—whether or not the affected have sought treat-ment (and more than 60 percent of the time, they haven't).[3]

With mental illness cases so widespread, and those cases more often than not striking children and young people before they even graduate from high school or college or move out of their parents' homes, to ignore the family component of mental illness to the extent that we have is dangerous at best, and catastrophic at worst.

Most published treatment guides currently available for addressing mental illness in the family assume that mental illness affects only *one* member of the family. All the published tools I've found (from private mental health organizations, universities, local and state mental health societies, and the federal government) are designed to advise the sup-posed "well" family members on how to "deal" with having an afflicted loved one in their midst. This treatment paradigm fails to address the fact that in many cases, mental illness impacts the whole family, wheth-er from the ripple effects of stress, stigma, and guilt because one or more family members is ill, or from the fact that mental illness itself tends to run in families.[4]

My own experience and mountains of clinical research statistics both show that mental illness does not occur in isolation, and to approach the incidence of mental illness in the family environment as if it were a single, unfortunate voice in the wilderness is an institutional mistake of gargantuan proportions. Throughout the course of my research, I have found *no* treatment guidelines, informational brochures, self-help books, or anything else that specifically addresses mental illness from a comprehensive, multigenerational family perspective other than the broadest epidemiological studies whose purpose is solely to determine if there is a statistically significant increase in risk for developing mental illness among the offspring of mentally ill parents (there is)[5] rather than to develop comprehensive treatment paradigms for addressing the mentally ill family as a whole. And while the Affordable Care Act will likely reduce the number of uninsured somewhat, in Republican-controlled states that have refused Medicaid expansion, you will continue to see a large proportion of the population without health insurance. Meanwhile, private insurers still remain resistant to providing robust mental health benefits that are comparable to the coverage physical ailments receive.

With the health insurance plans that do exist relying increasingly on the dispensation of psychoactive drugs at the expense of cognitive behavioral therapy for both individuals and families (a huge measure of the influence Big Pharma has on current American healthcare policy)— I doubt whether a shift toward family-based cognitive behavioral treatment in American mental health treatment paradigms will occur anytime soon. Indeed, Big Pharma *makes a killing on* psychoactive drugs, with sales of antipsychotics and antidepressants generating $16 billion and $11 billion respectively in Big Pharma revenues between 2001 and 2010 in the United States alone.[6] Keeping the mentally ill on expensive drugs that may or may not improve their condition in the short term (and provide little to no effect in terms of reversing the disease permanently) is very big business in this country.[7]

The fact that the American mental health system now relies almost exclusively on pharmacological therapy for treating major mental illnesses should be cause for alarm. While recent advances in drugs for treating depression, bipolar disorder, and schizophrenia are to be lauded, *drugs should not be exclusively relied upon for treating the mentally ill*. As I hope the anecdotes in my memoir have shown, there are still far too many opportunities for psychiatrists to improperly administer psychoactive drugs to patients who are vulnerable to addiction to these drugs or who could even use them to commit suicide. Even non-habit-forming antidepressants have been shown to increase the risk of suicide among child and adolescent depression patients, to the point that the U.S. Food and Drug Administration (FDA) recently placed its most severe "black box" warning on those drugs.

Further, though most practicing physicians will not admit to it, there is a substantial underground economy in which dispensing psychiatrists push the "latest and greatest" expensive, brand-name psychoactive drugs on their patients, regardless of whether those drugs make sense for treating those individuals. The motivations salespeople offer to doctors to engage in this unethical (and potentially lethal) practice can vary widely—from free pens and prescription pads and expensive meals and golf outings to all-out, tit-for-prescription-tat cash kickbacks. Though this practice of pharmaceutical companies "bribing" physicians to prescribe their products with free lunches, dinners, golf trips and pens is increasingly regarded as unethical, in most cases (except for direct cash kickbacks, which can be easily disguised on paper as legal "consulting fees"), it is perfectly legal.

Some states also still allow physicians to dispense drugs from their own private, wholly-owned pharmacies (as Dr. Nickelback did), which motivates unscrupulous physicians to generate profits directly from the drug markups. Powerful lobbyists for various pharmaceutical companies push both insurers and the government hard for policies that will benefit the companies' profits above all, and as a result, insurance reimbursements for expensive drugs rise while reimbursements for long-term cognitive behavioral therapy from psychiatrists, psychologists, clinical social workers, and other allied health practitioners is shrinking. Managed healthcare plans might pay for only five—or at most, ten—cognitive therapy sessions per year, almost never enough to bring about the level of personal insight and long-term behavioral changes necessary to alter destructive behavior patterns (and with it, brain chemistry) in the chronically mentally ill. Insurance coverage for other types of cognitive therapy from complementary medicine disciplines (e.g., art and music therapy, occupational therapy, yoga, meditation, and mind-body exercise classes) that have consistently been shown to be effective when combined with traditional Western treatment methods in the mental health systems of other countries—most notably, India—are almost unheard of in the United States. As a result, the long-term cognitive behavioral strategies often shown to be the most effective at controlling and managing severe mental illness over the long term are increasingly becoming luxuries only the rich can afford. The rest of us are relegated to popping pills in a mainstream drug culture so passé it is frequently satirized on television shows like *The Simpsons* and *South Park* and made the topic of ridicule on late-night TV talk shows and standup comedy routines.

Compounding the increased financial barriers to obtaining cognitive behavior therapy in addition to or as an alternative to drug-based therapy is the overall social stigma of mental illness, which remains profound and pervasive despite recent strides in our society toward breaking it down. For example, many American universities have reportedly recently adopted highly publicized policies to *expel* students who display depressive symptoms or suicidal tendencies.[8] While the university administrators adopting these ludicrous policies explain they are primarily for "liability" purposes, or a misguided attempt to keep mental illness from "spreading" in dormitories (like mumps or chicken pox) and to "protect" other students from engaging in so-called copycat behavior, in reality these policies act as an added incentive for depressed or otherwise mentally ill college students to hide their illnesses—often resulting in exacerbated symptoms, substance abuse, even successful suicide attempts—and as an added disincentive for them to seek help and treatment.

As universities develop prejudicial, Orwellian policies designed to oppress and harm the mentally ill, so does Corporate America. Most corporate employees are afraid to speak out or seek treatment for their mental illnesses, and they have good reason to keep silent. Firings of employees suffering from mental illness remain common, despite the fact that this practice is prohibited by the Americans with Disabilities Act. Those who do seek help or counseling, either from employer-based assistance programs or employee health insurance policies, often find that information about their illnesses, which by law is supposed to be kept confidential and separate from their personnel files, is instead used against them—either at annual raise time or as an all-out justification for termination.[9] Major corporations have also been slow to offer health insurance plans to their employees that cover conventional mental health treatments at parity with other types of medical care, even when state and local laws mandate it. Perhaps most sinister and Orwellian in nature, corporations are increasingly using unscientific "personality tests" in their hiring practices in an effort to "weed out" the supposed mentally ill from their applicant base—up to and including discrimination against persons who, according to these pseudoscientific tests, merely have the *potential* to become mentally ill.[10]

I can certainly attest to the stigmas that have victimized and oppressed me—past and present—in corporate, social, and institutional settings, both as a mental health consumer myself and as a relative of multiple mental health consumers. In addition to being ostracized in school and in social settings, I've been fired from jobs as a direct result of both more than once, and in no case was assistance or support offered by my employer, even when the employer had an "employee assistance program" as part of its fringe benefits package. I believe these supposed "employee assistance programs" too often are used improperly to weed out "problem" employees from the ranks rather than assist them.

It is tragic that such backward notions of mental illness and the mentally ill themselves continue to pervade our society, given that good treatment and support *is* available, and when that good treatment and support is properly administered, *recovery is possible*. I'm living proof of that.

Since I began writing this book, my husband George has opened up about mental illness in his own family—including the story of a cousin of his who makes a living driving a taxicab on the island of Macau. That cousin, a known family eccentric and a probable paranoid schizophrenic himself, once told George how every night, his wife removed her head from her body, set it on the night-table, combed her detached head of hair as if combing a wig on a dummy, then refastened her head to her body. He apparently told this story in total seriousness and seemed to believe in it as much as he believed in his own existence.

"I think maybe my cousin is messed up the way your brother is messed up," George says. "I was too embarrassed to talk about it before now, but your writing about your brother helped change that."

I hope that if nothing else, this memoir makes family mental illness less embarrassing for everyone. After all, misery loves company—and company makes us bosom friends.

# RECOMMENDED READING

If you found this book helpful in dealing with mental illness issues in your family or circle of friends, I highly recommend the following other titles, which should be easily found in your local bookstore or library.

Burroughs, Augusten. *Running with Scissors*. New York: St. Martin's Press, 2002.

Campbell, Bebe Moore. *72 Hour Hold*. New York: Alfred A. Knopf, 2005.

Early, Pete. *Crazy: A Father's Search through America's Mental Health Madness*. New York: GP Putnam's Sons, 2006.

Green, Hannah. *I Never Promised You a Rose Garden*. Henry Holt & Co., 1964.

Kaysen, Susannah. *Girl, Interrupted*. New York: Vintage, 1994.

Kreisman, Jerold J. MD, and Hal Straus. *I Hate You, Don't Leave Me: Understanding the Borderline Personality*. New York: HarperCollins, 1989.

Mason, Paul T., and Randi Kreger. *Stop Walking on Eggshells: Taking Your Life Back When Someone You Care About Has Borderline Personality Disorder*. Oakland, CA: New Harbinger Publications, 1998.

Secunda, Victoria. *When Madness Comes Home: Help and Hope for the Children, Siblings, and Partners of the Mentally Ill*. New York: Hyperion, 1997.

Styron, William. *Darkness Visible*. New York: Vintage, 1992.

Thompson, Tracy. *The Beast: A Journey through Depression*. New York: Plume, 1996.

Torrey, E. Fuller, MD. *Surviving Schizophrenia: A Manual for Families, Consumers, and Providers.* New York: HarperCollins, 1983.

Whitaker, Dieter. *Mad in America: Bad Science, Bad Medicine, and the Enduring Mistreatment of the Mentally Ill.* New York: Perseus, 2002.

Wurtzel, Elizabeth. *Prozac Nation.* New York: Riverhead, 1995.

# NOTES

## 1. HEARING VOICES

1. Mary Soliman et al., "Bipolar II Disorder in Adults: A Review of Management Options," *U.S. Pharmacist*, November 2011, www.medscape.com/viewarticle/754573.

2. Perry D. Hoffman, PhD, "Borderline Personality Disorder: A Most Misunderstood Illness," National Alliance for Mental Illness, www.nami.org/Template.cfm?Section=20075&Template=/ContentManagement/ContentDisplay.cfm&ContentID=44745.

3. Erik A. Fertuck, PhD, "Borderline Personality Disorder Is Real: Part I, Diagnostic Validity," *Psychology Today*, Science at the Border, April 27, 2009, www.psychologytoday.com/blog/science-the-border/200904/borderline-personality-disorder-is-real-part-i-diagnostic-validity.

4. American College of Pediatricians, "The Teenage Brain: Under Construction," May 2011, www.acpeds.org/the-college-speaks/position-statements/parenting-issues/the-teenage-brain-under-construction.

5. Jane E. Brody, "An Emotional Hair-Trigger, Often Misread," *New York Times*, June 15, 2009, www.nytimes.com/2009/06/16/health/16brod.html?_r=0.

6. Borderline Personality Disorder Resource Center, "What Is Borderline Personality Disorder? Co-occurring Disorders," New York-Presbyterian Hospital, http://bpdresourcecenter.org/co-occuringDisorders.html.

7. Deborah Daniels Carver, MD, "Clinical Aspects of Borderline Personality Disorder," *Medscape Psychiatry & Mental Health eJournal* 2 (1997), www.medscape.com/viewarticle/430852.

8. Oliver Freudenreich, MD, "Differential Diagnosis of Psychotic Symptoms: Medical 'Mimics,'" *Psychiatric Times*, December 30, 2012, www.

psychiatrictimes.com/forensic-psychiatry/differential-diagnosis-psychotic-symptoms-medical-%E2%80%9Cmimics%E2%80%9D-.

9. Janice Lloyd, "Many with Mental Illness Go Without Treatment, Survey Says," *USA Today*, January 19, 2012, http://usatoday30.usatoday.com/news/health/medical/health/medical/mentalhealth/story/2012-01-19/Many-with-mental-illness-go-without-treatment-survey-says/52653166/1.

10. Not his real name.

11. Todd Leopold, "The Creative Struggle of Brian Wilson," *CNN.com*, January 17, 2012, www.cnn.com/2012/01/13/living/brian-wilson-creativity/.

12. Lauren Paige Kennedy, "20 Questions for Carrie Fisher," *WebMD*, November 2010, www.webmd.com/mental-health/features/questions-for-carrie-fisher.

13. Nate Jenkins, "Dick Cavett Talks about His Depression," *Huffington Post*, June 20, 2008, www.huffingtonpost.com/2008/06/20/dick-cavett-talks-about-h_n_108332.html.

14. Not her real name.

## 2. VIENNA, AUSTRIA, OCTOBER 1999

1. Not his real name.
2. Name changed.
3. John Bateson, "The Suicide Magnet That Is the Golden Gate Bridge," *Los Angeles Times*, September 29, 2013, http://articles.latimes.com/2013/sep/29/opinion/la-oe-bateson-golden-gate-bridge-suicides-20130929.
4. Not his real name.
5. Not his real name.
6. Not her real name.
7. Richard A. Sherer, "Personality Disorder: 'Untreatable' Myth Is Challenged," *Psychiatric Times*, July 1, 2008, www.psychiatrictimes.com/articles/personality-disorder-%E2%80%9Cuntreatable%E2%80%9D-myth-challenged.

## 3. CHICAGO: OCTOBER 2001–APRIL 2002

1. Not her real name.
2. Not his real name.
3. Name changed.

4. Mattie Quinn, "No Easy Solution for Uptown's Mentally Ill Population," *Medill Reports*, January 13, 2013, http://news.medill.northwestern.edu/chicago/news.aspx?id=214141; Emmanuel Adeshina, "Uptown 'Ground Zero' for Chicago's Mental Health Crisis, Alderman Says," DNAinfo.com, December 28, 2012, www.dnainfo.com/chicago/20121228/uptown/uptown-ground-zero-for-chicagos-mental-health-crisis-alderman-says.

5. Not his real name.

6. Not her real name.

7. Not his real name.

## 4. 1993–2002: NINE YEARS TO ENLIGHTENMENT

1. Not his real name.

2. Daniel Thomasulo, PhD, "A General Theory of Love, Part 1," *Psych-Central*, World of Psychology, February 9, 2011, http://psychcentral.com/blog/archives/2011/02/09/a-general-theory-of-love-part-1/.

3. Janice Lloyd, "Many With Mental Illness Go Without Treatment, Survey Says," *USAToday*, January 19, 2012, http://usatoday30.usatoday.com/news/health/medical/health/medical/mentalhealth/story/2012-01-19/Many-with-mental-illness-go-without-treatment-survey-says/52653166/1.

4. Not her real name.

5. C. N. Alexander et al., "Transcendental Meditation, Mindfulness, and Longevity: An Experimental Study with the Elderly," *Journal of Personality and Social Psychology* 57 (1989): 950–64.

6. P. Carrington and H. S. Ephron, "Meditation and Psychoanalysis," *Journal of American Academy of Psychoanalysis* 3 (1975): 43–57; Padmasiri de Silva, *An Introduction to Buddhist Psychology*, 3rd ed. (Lanham, MD: Rowman & Littlefield, 2001).

## 5. MOM: A RELAPSE

1. Not his real name.

2. Not his real name.

3. Not his real name.

4. Name changed.

5. Name changed.

6. Not her real name.

## 6. MARK: THE LOST CAUSE

1. Not his real name.

2. Associated Press, "Newtown Shooting Police Files Released," *CBC News/World*, December 27, 2013, www.cbc.ca/news/world/newtown-shooting-police-files-released-1.2477011.

3. Sergio Paradiso, MD, et al., "Emotions in Unmedicated Patients with Schizophrenia during Evaluation with Positron Emission Tomography," *American Journal of Psychiatry* 160 (2003): 1775–83, http://ajp.psychiatryonline.org/article.aspx?articleid=176453.

4. National Institute of Mental Health, "What Is Schizophrenia?" www.nimh.nih.gov/health/publications/schizophrenia/index.shtml?utm_source=wordtwit&utm_medium=social&utm_campaign=wordtwit.

5. P. V. Gejman et al., "The Role of Genetics in the Etiology of Schizophrenia," *Psychiatric Clinics of North America* 33, no. 1 (2010): 35–66, www.ncbi.nlm.nih.gov/pmc/articles/PMC2826121/; Daniel R. Weinberger, "Biological Phenotypes and Genetic Research on Schizophrenia," *World Psychiatry* 1 (2002): 2–6, www.ncbi.nlm.nih.gov/pmc/articles/PMC1489838/.

6. Munchausen's syndrome is not to be confused with *Munchausen's by proxy*, in which the sufferer deliberately inflicts physical injury or feigns illness in a child or loved one under his or her care to receive attention and sympathy.

7. Not her real name.

8. John Price and Anthony Stevens, *Prophets, Cults and Madness* (London: Gerald Duckworth & Co., 2000); Steven Hassan, *Combatting Cult Mind Control* (Rochester, New York: Park Street Press, 1988); Linda A. Teplin et al., "Crime Victimization in Adults with Severe Mental Illness," *Archives of General Psychiatry* 62, no. 8 (2005): 911–21.

## 7. WHERE ARE THEY (AND WHERE AM I) NOW?*

1. Rick Nauert, PhD, "Healthy Food Can Improve Mental Health," *Psych Central*, July 10, 2008, http://psychcentral.com/news/2008/07/10/healthy-food-can-improve-mental-health/2587.html; Deborah Kotz and Angela Haupt, "7 Mind-Blowing Effects of Exercise," *US News & World Report*, http://health.usnews.com/health-news/diet-fitness/slideshows/7-mind-blowing-benefits-of-exercise.

2. James D. Herbert and Evan M. Forman, *Acceptance and Mindfulness in Cognitive Behavior Therapy: Understanding and Applying the New Therapies* (New York: John Wiley & Sons, 2011).

## EPILOGUE: THE STATE OF FAMILY MENTAL ILLNESS IN AMERICA

1. World Health Organization, Global Status Report on Non-Communicable Diseases 2010 ( Geneva: World Health Organization, 2011).

2. World Health Organization Global Burden of Disease Report 2002, www.who.int/healthinfo/global_burden_disease/en/index.html.

3. National Institute of Mental Health NCS-R Study 2005. Cited at "Major Depressive Disorder among Adults," www.nimh.nih.gov/statistics/1mdd_adult.shtml.

4. Tara Clark, "Mental Illness and Families," Jewish Family Services of Milwaukee, Robert & Mimi Habush Family Center, www.jfsmilw.org/news/articles/mental_illness_families.htm; Barry J. Milne et al., "Predictive Value of Family History on Severity of Illness: The Case for Depression, Anxiety, Alcohol Dependence, and Drug Dependence ," *Archives of General Psychiatry* 66, no. 7 (2009): 738–47.

5. Fritz Mattejat, PhD, and Helmut Remschmidt, PhD, "The Children of Mentally Ill Parents," *Deutsches Arzteblatt International* 105, no. 23 (2008): 413–18.

6. Brendan L. Smith, "Inappropriate Prescribing," *Monitor on Psychology* 43, no. 6 (2012), www.apa.org/monitor/2012/06/prescribing.aspx.

7. Harriett Fraad, "Profiting from Mental Ill-health," *Guardian*, March 15, 2011, www.theguardian.com/commentisfree/cifamerica/2011/mar/15/psychology-healthcare.

8. Sally Satel, "Expel Students Who Might Kill Themselves?" Center for the American University at the Manhattan Institute, December 21, 2009, www.mindingthecampus.com/originals/2009/12/expel_students_who_might_kill.html.

9. Dan Fastenberg, "Employers Can't Fire Workers with Bipolar Disorder, Court Rules," *AOL Jobs*, April 3, 2012, http://jobs.aol.com/articles/2012/04/03/employers-on-notice-you-cant-fire-workers-with-bipolar-disorder/; Nick Birkenhauer, "Terminated Employee with Bipolar Disorder Awarded $315,000 in ADA Case," *JDSupra Business Advisor*, March 3, 2012, www.jdsupra.com/post/documentViewer.aspx?fid=dff1b455-3ee5-4880-a2f2-11a95909b932.

10. Bennett Drake et al., "Against Types: Personality Tests Are Everywhere—From the Workplace to the Courtroom. But Critics Say the Tests Themselves Don't Pass the Test," *Boston Globe*, September 12, 2004, www.boston.com/news/globe/ideas/articles/2004/09/12/against_types/?page=full.

# ABOUT THE AUTHOR

**Anna Berry** is the pen name of a successful journalist, mental-health advocate, and author from the Midwest. *Unhinged* is her personal memoir of family mental illness, addiction, and recovery. In order to protect her own privacy as well as the privacy of persons described in this memoir, she wishes to remain anonymous. Visit her site and blog at annaberryauthor.wordpress.com.